LANDSCAPES OF FREEDOM

LANDSCAPES OF FREEDOM

★ ★ ★ ★ ★ ★ ★ ★ ★ ★ ★ ★ ★

Restoring the History of Emancipation
and Citizenship in Yorktown, Virginia,
1861–1940

REBECCA CAPOBIANCO TOY

THE UNIVERSITY OF
SOUTH CAROLINA PRESS

© 2025 University of South Carolina

Published by the University of South Carolina Press
Columbia, South Carolina 29208

uscpress.com

Printed in the United States of America

Library of Congress Cataloging-in-Publication Data
can be found at https://lccn.loc.gov/2025004385

ISBN: 978-1-64336-534-3 (hardcover)
ISBN: 978-1-64336-592-3 (paperback)
ISBN: 978-1-64336-582-4 (ebook)

Publication is made possible in part by the generous support of the
William E. Dufford Fund for Civil and Social Justice Publications.

CONTENTS

LIST OF ILLUSTRATIONS

★ ★ ★ ★ ★ ★ ★ ★

Introduction

In downtown Yorktown, Virginia—a place celebrated for the role it played in George Washington's campaign against British forces during the American Revolution—there is a monument. Without any additional explanation, its four sides list the names of individuals who served in the United States' various wars. An internet search reveals that the monument commemorates "York County Citizens who lost their lives in our Nation's conflicts."[1] It is not, however, a monument to people from York County who served exclusively in the United States military. The Civil War portion of the monument lists individuals from York County who served in the Confederate army, though the text of the monument does not make this distinction clear.[2] Instead, by failing to identify what military individuals served, the monument conflates service in the Confederate military with service in the US military. Such a slippage is not surprising, given how in the decades following the Civil War, white Americans embraced the idea that soldiers in both armies were "all Americans," and ignored the fact that the Confederate States of America had declared itself distinctly separate from the United States. The "War of Rebellion," as official federal records of the war called it, became the "War Between the States" as if the two armies had come to confront each other to do battle over the nature of the same American nation.

This conflation of historical fact, however, is not the monument's most egregious inaccuracy. While claiming to represent individuals who fought in all of the United States' wars, it fails to list the names of Black York County residents who served in the Civil War. It lists white soldiers who fought for the Confederacy, but not the Black soldiers who fought for the United States Army—the very army that saved the American nation from dissolution. It does not list men such as Seaborn Hodges, who was born in Yorktown, enlisted in

Figure 1. Two sides of the War Memorial Monument in downtown Yorktown, Virginia. Author photo, 2021.

the 36th United States Colored Troops (USCT) at Yorktown or Henry Harrison who was also born in Yorktown, worked as a farmer, and likewise served in the 36th USCT.[3] Even this mistake might be expected of a monument that dated from the first one hundred years following the Civil War. Historians have acknowledged that monuments crafted to commemorate the Confederacy served to construct a South where white supremacy and Jim Crow segregation reigned. But this monument dates from 2001—far too recent an addition to Yorktown's memorial landscape to explain such a clear and painful lapse.[4]

This monument embodies a problem that has plagued Yorktown since it became a mecca for the American nation—a place visitors go to commune with the founding days of the American republic. Those who made the first efforts to preserve Yorktown's landscape imagined it as a place with a distinct role to play in the founding of the nation. Yorktown became a carefully constructed myth that white Americans could experience through a memorial landscape that asserted that only white Americans performed a fundamental role in the establishment of the United States. The 2001 soldier monument echoes this same message: that white Americans are the true inheritors of the nation because they are the only ones who fought for it.

In the process of establishing this myth, the organizations who sought to reconstruct Yorktown's Revolutionary history ignored crucial aspects of its Civil War and post–Civil War history. While claiming to be preserving a historic landscape, these organizations chose to destroy the physical evidence of Yorktown's nineteenth-century history that was still present on the landscape when preservation efforts commenced in the early twentieth century. While less prominent today than they were one hundred years ago, markers of a dynamic history of emancipation and Black freedom remain on the landscape if one knows where and how to look. Still, what is left does not do justice to the vibrant past.

During the Civil War, refugees from slavery fled to Yorktown by the thousands, establishing a community not on the periphery but in the very heart of the war. Unlike dozens of other refugee communities that took shape across the war-torn South over the course of the conflict and then dispersed, the community at Yorktown endured. Black residents fought fiercely and creatively to retain the community they had established during the war and used that foundation in the postwar era to continue to build their lives within the American nation. They frequently came into conflict with the very people who history has painted as their saviors—the US Army, the Freedmen's Bureau, white

Northerners, and white Republicans. But the cause of most of those conflicts was a simple one: Black residents wanted to chart their own path for the future; they sought self-determination, and they wanted to be partners with, not subjects of, federal administrators. They wanted to be equal citizens, and they were unwilling to accept second-class status.

In the wake of the Civil War, Black residents built and maintained a vast landscape of freedom in York County. Not limited to a single neighborhood or hamlet, their networks of political power extended throughout and beyond the county limits.[5] They crafted organizations and championed leaders who could support their aspirations, and they maintained memorial practices that reinforced the reality that they were American citizens. Through these organizations and commemorations, they continued to make claims on the postwar nation, asserting time and again that as citizens they deserved to have a government responsive to their needs, not a government that restricted the terms of their independence.

Landscapes of Freedom seeks to begin the work of restoring this history to its rightful place in York County, and in US history more generally. Black Americans were not simply recipients of white benevolence during or after the Civil War. They were, rather, creative and powerful actors, forces to be reckoned with and acknowledged. If Yorktown is a place where American independence was born in 1781, it was equally a place where American independence was negotiated in the everyday struggles of Black Southerners who claimed freedom for themselves. A historian Steven Hahn has noted, in the wake of slavery's dissolution during the Civil War, Black Americans began to build "political relations, institutions and aspirations within their own communities." Yet how they accomplished this "remains one of the most remarkable, though yet relatively unexplored, chapters in American history."[6] By looking at one such community, *Landscapes of Freedom* adds to this chapter, examining how this community struggled for freedom and citizenship. It also explores why the federal government eventually displaced this community from the land they had claimed in the postwar period to make way for Colonial National Historical Park.

In exploring the intersection of wartime freedom, postwar politics, and contests over national identity through commemorative practices, *Landscapes of Freedom* draws on the work of historians Chandra Manning and Amy Murrell Taylor who have written significant studies on refugee communities as they existed in the war-torn South. Both books provide essential information about the experience of refugees from slavery during the war and the material and logistical pressures brought to bear on their efforts to achieve a measure of independence. Both Manning and Taylor stress that the contingencies of war, and often the sheer magnitude of need created by the conflict across all levels of society, made the experience of wartime freedom difficult and dangerous. These are crucial observations because too often the story of wartime emancipation ends with the moment an individual became free of bondage and celebrates this freedom without understanding the perils that lay ahead.

By necessity, both Manning and Taylor's works are wide ranging, taking stock of the refugee population across the entire South. In contrast, *Landscapes of Freedom* focuses on a single community. As Hahn has also noted, formerly enslaved people built new political communities "from many of the basic materials of everyday life," and, as a result, to understand the dynamics of this process one must investigate this work at the ground level.[7] A community-level investigation enables us to see the dynamics of community organization, leadership, and negotiation and further allows us to watch those dynamics evolve over time. The work of making freedom meaningful did not end when the Confederacy fell or when slavery was finally abolished. Likewise, Yorktown's story continued long after the guns fell silent and federal occupation ended.[8]

While *Landscapes of Freedom* relies on institutional source bases such as diaries of white missionaries, US soldiers' letters, and notes from federal agents, it seeks to elevate the voices of Black actors that are contained within these records. Within the thousands of pages white visitors wrote about their time in Yorktown, the words, actions, and desires of members of the Black community are also accessible. This study emphasizes those portions of the sources and seeks to center the narrative to which they testify. Although Black residents rarely had the opportunity to record their perspectives in a formal repository, and thus they are underrepresented in surviving sources, they were no less central to the process of transforming the postwar United States.

Scholar Heather Andrea Williams has observed that "African Americans move out of the background first when you look for them, and second when you read several sources together."[9] Her work specifically on Black educational efforts reveals that while white teachers and Freedmen's Bureau agents are often the center of postwar histories that detail the transition from slavery to freedom, formerly enslaved people were the first to push for access to education.[10] Moreover, before white missionaries arrived, Black Southerners utilized the resources they had available to begin teaching one another, understanding that "an educated Black population could bring about a seismic change in the American South."[11] *Landscapes of Freedom* utilizes a similar strategy of reading multiple sources together to better understand the central role Black community members took in defining the terms of their freedom.

Tracing the history of the Black community in York County after the Civil War, *Landscapes of Freedom* does not end in 1865 or 1877. Continuity in political strategies and leadership become visible by bridging the Civil War and post-Reconstruction periods. As writer and activist W. E. B. Du Bois pointed out, the Civil War destroyed the planter class, even though historians have often talked about a dominant social class as if it endured from the antebellum period into the postwar period.[12] Social relationships, as a result, had to be negotiated and renegotiated in the decades after the Civil War. There were opportunities for new political alliances, especially in Virginia where parties such as the Readjusters made strides toward creating interracial political coalitions in the latter decades of the nineteenth century. Moreover, as historian Jane Dailey has demonstrated, the postwar era was not an extended prelude to Jim Crow. The legal barriers to Black politics associated with the rise of Jim Crow were reactions to white southerners' "specific and concrete encounter[s] with black social, economic, and political power."[13] A study that focuses on Black Southerners' politics and shifting alliances also reveals how they refused to be pawns in national political struggles waged by white Republicans or in Virginia by Readjusters. Instead, Black residents in York County operated as independent political agents who expected their right to self-determination to result not only in voting rights, but in a right to vote for representatives selected from their own community.

In exploring the postwar political landscape, this study also takes public commemorations seriously as strategies for engaging in expressly political debates. By organizing and participating in commemorative ceremonies, Black residents were making claims on the nation, asserting their central place of belonging in the United States, and redefining what citizenship should look like. As historians Mitch Kachun and Kathleen Ann Clark have demonstrated, Black Americans utilized public ceremonies to reinforce collective identity and define a public culture that could support group cohesion.[14] They also used these public events to demonstrate that they were, in the words of Kachun, "worthy of full inclusion as citizens."[15] *Landscapes of Freedom* approaches these public ceremonies as texts that can be read to understand Black political aspirations in the postwar period.

As historian William Blair has explained, commemorations specifically of the Civil War were part of a broader restructuring of public space. If, as Du Bois pointed out, antebellum class relationships were disordered after the war, they had to be reorganized. Commemorations were part of this restructuring, declaring, as Blair has argued, "who had the right to march in the streets, have graves tended by federal authorities, or have ceremonies endorsed by the president." They were efforts to "define who citizens were and demonstrate how participants struggled for recognition and rights from the national state."[16] Thus, like newspapers and political debates, public ceremonies were another outlet to advocate for what the postwar nation should become.

Numerous historians have documented the rise of Civil War commemoration and the impact it had on how members of the nation remembered the seminal conflict. Historian David Blight detailed how by the semicentennial of the war, dominant national narratives depicted the war as "a tragedy that forged greater unity" and a struggle that saved an "essentially good" union while ignoring the unresolved legacy of emancipation.[17] That this narrative emerged supreme was not an accident. As historian Caroline Janney explained, the war generation understood that "the memorials people built, the ceremonies they made sacred, and the stories they told had immense power." They had the power to bind people together. Consequently, the stories individuals selected to remember and pass on through ceremonies "held enormous potential for staking claims of authority and power."[18] In some cases, as historian Adam Domby has more recently documented, this involved constructing entirely false memories in order to fabricate a seemingly solid white South that had not existed prior to the Civil War and to counter political inroads made by splinter parties who successfully assembled interracial coalitions.[19] Black Americans were no less aware of this potential, and engaged in a public dialog about the nature of the postwar nation through ceremonies that demonstrated an acute awareness of how politics were waged in the United States.

Terms

I am hesitant to make any definitive statements about language because it is constantly evolving. However, the nature of this study and of many that have come before it compels me to at least comment on the language choices I have made. While historians have continued to use "freedpeople" "freed person" and similar variations to refer to people who became free during and because of the Civil War, I do not. When sources use the term, I leave it in place, but in my own references to formerly enslaved people, I have tried to intentionally use different nouns. My reasons for this are twofold. First, it is a matter of precision. In many studies of wartime freedom and the immediate postwar period, "freedpeople" has come to refer to entire Black populations. Yet there were numerous free Black people who resided in the antebellum South, especially in places like Yorktown, and they were part of the Black communities that remade freedom and citizenship in the postwar era. I do not wish to erase them from the historical record by using a term that excludes them. Instead, I use phrases like "the Black community" or "Black residents" that I hope incorporate all the people engaged in the work of constructing freedom and citizenship. When referencing population statistics that include a distinction between "Black" and "mulatto," I include all people identified as either one in the Black community. I also think that by making "freed person" or "freedman" synonymous with Black people in the South, we as historians reify a racial rhetoric that has held sway for far too long in the United States and assumes that to be Black is to be enslaved. It should not be necessary to qualify "Black person" with "free," because the natural state of all human beings is free. It becomes a necessary qualifier when speaking of the antebellum South because to live free alongside the system of slavery as a Black person was an abnormality within a social structure that denied Black people's basic, fundamental, and equal humanity. But it should not be necessary, because all people are naturally free, and it is only when a system of oppression is exerted upon them that that freedom is restricted. I qualify Black people as free only to ensure clarity to their circumstances when the tendency may be to assume that they were enslaved.

The second reason is that the debate about "who freed enslaved people" tends to be wrapped up in any use of the term "freedpeople" or "freed person." Both terms suggest that it took actors beyond the enslaved community to make them free when, in fact, legal protections of freedom often followed individuals' own efforts to make themselves free. I agree with historians such as James Oakes who have argued that the question of "who freed enslaved people" is not a particularly useful question because it conflates emancipation and abolition.[20] Again, it is a matter of problematic semantics that have plagued US history and deny Black Americans' fundamental equality and citizenship. People became free the moment they released themselves from the forces of slavery that held them, whether the federal government or anyone else acknowledged that freedom. To be free and equal under the law is a different question than simply to be a person who is free. Moreover, as historians such as Hannah Rosen and Kate Masur have demonstrated, Black Southerners forced the federal government to acknowledge the citizenship they claimed and the parameters of citizenship they defined before lawmakers fully articulated those legal boundaries.[21] This was a process of negotiation and one in which Black Southerners often led the charge ahead of legal transformations.

Geographical Organization

In many ways, this study will always give an incomplete picture. One can only recover so much from the historical record, and as we know, the historical record is woefully incomplete and biased. An aspect of this study that has troubled me from its inception is selection of a geographic frame. Broadly speaking, this study focuses on York County and Yorktown. I have chosen this frame based on the organization of the Freedmen's Bureau—the bureau office at Yorktown had jurisdiction over this space. Additionally, during the Civil War, York County was unique from the land in the vicinity of Fort Monroe and was managed with less oversight, likely because of its geographic distance from the fort. Because I start the story with the Civil War, I try to maintain this organization throughout the rest of the study.

Of course this is an arbitrary choice. Not only have the boundaries of York County changed over time, but more importantly the boundaries of geographic space do not define Black communities. During slavery, we know, enslaved people formed networks that expanded well beyond the immediate spaces where they lived, and in so doing mapped alternative geographies onto the landscape. As freedom evolved, refugees from slavery charted new geographies, based in part on the Union army's movement and where they might find a margin of safety, but also based on the land they knew, the networks they already had, and the spaces they sought to claim.[22]

When the Union army came to Yorktown, refugees took up residence inside the fort, and likely outside of it too. Safety could better be defined as proximity to the US Army rather than necessarily a specific space within its lines. These lines, of course, were constantly in flux, and thus the physical spaces refugees occupied likely changed in a way that does not necessarily reflect the geographic reach of their social networks. Indeed, in records from the war period it is clear that residence in one Union army camp did not mean a person was unaware of what was happening in another. In the army's 1865 census of the

Black population of York County they noted residents who reported that they had family members elsewhere on the Virginia Peninsula, at places like Norfolk and Fort Monroe, demonstrating that their networks both of kinship and information expanded beyond the boundary lines the army had drawn. Freedmen's Bureau records also testify to residents of Yorktown's refugee community traveling into inconsistently occupied places like Gloucester, Virginia, to share resources with people beyond the limits of Yorktown and beyond the immediate control of the US Army.

While US General Isaac J. Wistar recorded that he established two specific communities upon his arrival at Yorktown, these merely represented neighborhoods the army laid out and helped build. Black residents lived in these places, but they also lived elsewhere, on the outskirts of these "towns," on the plantations where they already lived, and in the surrounding community and countryside. The population was always in flux, new refugees were constantly arriving, and it would have been nearly impossible to track exactly where, when, and why they moved.

Moreover, the history of the Black population of York County has often been told in reverse, starting from the point of dislocation, and explaining how a particular displaced neighborhood came to exist. This imposes boundaries defined by outside agencies, usually the agency doing the displacing such as the US Navy or the National Park Service. But it also stretches false boundaries back in time, imposing a seeming coherence on geographic space that did not exist until the federal government drew lines around a place for the purpose of obtaining it.[23]

What is abundantly clear is that the Black communities of York County, Williamsburg, Yorktown, James City County, and the surrounding areas were intertwined. Likely long before the Civil War, enslaved people assembled communities in the shadows, where the watchful eye of enslavers could not regulate their behavior. However, it would also be presumptive to insist that this community network simply transitioned into the era of freedom with the same geography it had before the war. The massive influx of refugees from other places, not to mention the physical devastation of war, would have drastically altered the prewar landscape of the Black community. Federal efforts after the war to remove Black residents from abandoned lands and "return" formerly enslaved people to the land from which they had fled would have further altered the landscape. Perhaps it made these communities all the more intertwined, as individuals met new people and moved to new places.

Regardless, it is certain that any boundary necessarily drawn for the purpose of historical study must be arbitrary. In acknowledging this, I hope to accomplish two things. First, I simply hope not to lead anyone astray. Communities are permeable, their boundaries are always in flux, and geographic boundaries are forever changing. Second, I hope to acknowledge that descendants might know their history differently or know places differently. In attempting to write a history that can tell us something about the larger experience of freedom after the war, I know I cannot fully do justice to the specifics of individuals' experiences. It is perhaps the aspect of microhistory that troubles me the most. I cannot trace everyone, I cannot talk to everyone, and there will be aspects of the story that do not get told.[24]

Where possible though, I have tried to locate people geographically, in specific spaces. I think this is important precisely because of the twentieth-century history of dislocation. It is an acute injustice that people who fought so long and so well to gain ownership of the land that in many cases they had earned long before freedom through their unpaid toil eventually lost that land. Moreover, it is important to pinpoint where that happened, whenever possible, because we know that land is a significant aspect of identity, and people deserve to know what land their ancestors fought for and who took it away. Moreover, in telling the history of dispossession, we cannot fully understand it unless we understand who perpetrated it and why. Thousands of Black Americans lost their land and homes in York County, Yorktown, Williamsburg, and the surrounding areas in the twentieth century, but the justifications for these takings were different. All of those justifications matter, though, because collectively they overwrite the history of Black Americans in this storied section of Virginia. As historians strive to better tell the history of slavery and its contribution to the making of the United States in places like Williamsburg and Yorktown, we must also tell the history of Black Americans after abolition in these same spaces. Their lives—in both their triumph and their tragedy—are just as centrally part of the making of the United States as the founders who occupied the Capitol in Williamsburg or the trenches at Yorktown.

Sources

By necessity, the source base for this study is eclectic. All history is dependent upon the source bases available, and this was no different. Moreover, in exploring a longer length of time, the source bases necessarily change as time passes. During the Civil War and immediately after, federal agencies heavily documented daily life in York County. With their departure and the shift back to civil authority, Black residents must be searched for and found in the mundane records that mark all counties, especially deed books.

This study is also an exercise in finding underrepresented people in the archive, people whose records never made their way to a repository. Still, just because they do not have designated collections at a university or state library does not mean that their voices and intentions do not survive. Quite the opposite. Tucked into the hundreds of thousands of pages of Freedmen's Bureau records are copies of petitions written by Black residents to their local bureau agent, their state representative, and Bureau Commissioner Oliver Otis Howard. Between the lines of deed book records and court records, the intentions of formerly enslaved people can be grasped. In the remarks of derogatory Democratic newspaper coverage or the comments of other white observers, the actions and influence of the Black community are still visible.

Understanding what these records can tell us about the lived experience of Black Southerners during this period requires, first, a lot of patience. It further requires a lot of scrolling through endless pages of microfilm and cross-referencing names in disparate sources to reconstruct a glimpse of a person's life, family, and neighborhood. Second, it requires peeling back, to the degree possible, the layers of prejudice and interpretation that colored the way white observers wrote about Black people. It is certainly limited, but it is no less significant for its patchwork character. Perhaps it is all the more important because it forces us to acknowledge that no matter how many sources we have and no matter how much we think we might understand a person from the pages of their letters or diaries, we can never fully recover the past or even an individual life. So many of the dynamics that make a person a person and a community a community we can never retrieve.

The following chapters proceed in a loosely chronological and thematic fashion. Starting with the war itself, chapter 1 explores the origin of the wartime refugee community at Yorktown in the wake of US General George McClellan's 1862 Peninsula Campaign. Bridging the end of the war and the immediate postwar years, the next three chapters detail Black residents' efforts to establish an independent community through the construction of educational opportunities, social organizations, and engaging in productive enterprises. Chapter 5 focuses on Black petitioners' who brought cases before the Freedmen's Bureau Court and explores how they utilized this forum to define and defend the rights they claimed as US citizens. The federal government conceived of these wartime refugee communities as transitory, but as their efforts to expand and support their community demonstrate, Black residents did not. In its twilight years, the Freedmen's Bureau worked diligently to try to disperse the Black population of York County and Black residents worked just as diligently to resist that effort. Chapter 5 explores how and why Black residents fought to retain the land they had claimed during the war while chapter 6 explores the extent to which they were successful in their efforts. By 1870, Black residents had drastically altered the landscape of York County and that new reality clashed with white visitors' expectations. Still, in the final decades of the nineteenth century, Black Southerners would become the keepers of both Yorktown's Revolutionary and Civil War history. Black residents were largely responsible for the care and maintenance of Yorktown's historic places from the Victory Monument and historic Custom House to the Yorktown National Cemetery. They also retained the memories of historic events that helped preservationists in the twentieth century identify specific sites such as the spot where Cornwallis surrendered to Washington. From this place of community strength, Black residents fought to retain the political power they had crafted during and after the Civil War. Chapter 7 investigates how the Black community sought to retain political autonomy at the end of the nineteenth century and into the twentieth, demanding full and equal participation in Republican politics. Finally, the conclusion details the creation of the National Historic Site at Yorktown and the rationale behind the National Park Service's decision to construct Yorktown as exclusively a Revolutionary War site. This decision led to a process of dispossessing Black landowners from what is now Yorktown National Battlefield.

Yet, the history of this resilient community is no less vital to the history of the United States than is what George Washington and his army accomplished in 1781. If national historical parks are places that we go to learn about the nature of the American nation and to consider what the past can contribute to our collective future, then they need to better represent the lived experience of all Americans.

Better and more inclusive history at these historic sites is an essential step towards building an improved understanding of our collective past for the American public. In the fall of 2022, I had the pleasure of meeting Mali Lucas-Green, who is a descendant of Moses and Mildred Green, two individuals once enslaved in Culpeper County, Virginia. In the summer of 1862, Moses fled to freedom over the Rappahannock River but soon returned to gather Mildred and their children and liberate them too. In the process of recrossing the Rappahannock —whose name means "rapidly rising waters"—two of their children were tragically lost. The Greens built a remarkable life in freedom, insisting that their children receive a quality education in Washington, DC, and producing family members who were integral to the evolution of the capital city.

Mali walked into our National Park Service visitor center in Fredericksburg, Virginia, one day and shared this story with a ranger, Maddie Hollis. Recognizing how remarkable the story was, Maddie shared it with me. At the time we were approaching the 160th anniversary of the Battle of Fredericksburg and decided to invite Mali to share her family's story as part of our formal public programming.

Moses and Mildred's story in and of itself is extraordinary, but it turned out that Mali had a lot more to teach us than just her family's incredible history. Mali explained that growing up she did not know Moses and Mildred's history. Instead, she went to school in Georgia where her teacher showed students films like *Gone with the Wind,* and Mali was left feeling like her place in the world was that of Mammy when in fact she wanted to be Scarlett. As a young person, Mali told us, she struggled with her identity and in particular her connection to her family. She described this period of her life as a moment of crisis and shared artwork she produced at the time that gave vivid life to the pain she experienced because of this dissonance.

For Mali, this shifted when she learned Moses and Mildred's story from an estranged family member, Oscar, who had kept that history alive. She learned that her ancestors were warriors—strong, brave, resilient people who changed the course of their family's story by the power of their own initiative. Knowing this, Mali told us and the audience, changed her.

Not only did learning the history change her, but Mali also explained to us that having her story welcomed at a National Military Park began a process of healing. As someone deeply invested in understanding her family's past, Mali has traveled to a variety of battlefield parks and other historic sites. She explained that she never felt welcomed in those spaces, and in fact she often felt like people saw her as a "rabble-rouser" and a threat. They did not think she belonged, and they made sure she knew that. But getting to tell her family's story as part of National Park Service programming, Mali explained, started to heal that wound.

I mention this not to applaud our efforts in this event. Mali deserves all of the credit here—it is her family's story and she shared it with immense courage and grace. But among the many things Mali taught us was the power of knowing your family's story and the power of knowing that your family's story belongs in a place associated with the history of the American nation. When Mali talked about what it felt like to learn a version of history where her ancestors belonged only to the category of side characters in someone else's saga, the harm and the pain were plainly evident. As an educator herself, Mali also explained how destructive it is to all children to not see themselves reflected in the history we tell. Excluding voices from the past does more than skew the historical record, it continues to cause harm in the present.

Acknowledging the stories that have been forgotten from national parks and other historic sites is about more than telling a fuller and more accurate story. It is also about embracing all people as valued members of our body politic and helping people in the present see that their voices have always mattered. Those who have historically had the least amount of formal power have still accomplished great things. In the case of those who lived through the US Civil War, those great things often included deciding to chart one's own path in freedom rather than waiting for the US Army or the federal government to do it. That was certainly the case in York County.

CHAPTER 1

★ ★ ★ ★ ★ ★ ★ ★

"They Appear like Freemen"

Establishing a Free Black Community in Wartime

In 1861, a refugee from slavery on the Virginia Peninsula told a Northern reporter, "Black people knows what they're about, these times."[1] With this, the interviewee pointed to an important aspect of wartime emancipation that often gets overlooked when historians debate the military and legal unfolding of emancipation. Black Southerners knew that the war created opportunities to push for their own freedom, and they navigated the wartime landscape with great insight as well as great risk. They calculated their decisions to the observations they made about the war's impact on their lives, the potential for securing freedom, and their determinations about which army would be successful. Wartime emancipation created a liminal legal status for refugees from slavery that was not resolved until Congress passed the Thirteenth, Fourteenth, and Fifteenth Amendments. Even where individuals managed to claim freedom, their rights and status as citizens remained undetermined over the course of the war. Yet in advance of federal policy determining Black people's legal status or outlining the boundaries of freedom, residents of Yorktown began constructing the conditions for freedom that laid the foundation for their postwar lives. It is certainly true, as Chandra Manning and Amy Murrell Taylor have powerfully demonstrated, that wartime freedom was fraught and often incomplete.[2] It is equally true that Black residents understood their task as more than one of survival.

At Yorktown, Black residents made deliberate wartime decisions about their futures that supported an ambition of independence and freedom defined not by the federal government, Union commanders, or benevolent workers, but by refugees themselves. Amid the war, Black residents engaged in independent enterprise, built homes, and appropriated resources to serve their needs as free individuals. While instability and the constant threat of troop movements troubled most refugee communities in the wartime South, Yorktown's relative stability during the war ensured that the Black community had the opportunity to establish a society that could endure after the war was over. A state of relative independence also characterized the work Yorktown's Black residents undertook during the war. While a few similarly secure communities existed elsewhere, notably at Fort Monroe, Virginia; Roanoke Island, North Carolina; and Port Royal, South Carolina, white administrators spent a great deal of time delineating what freedom should look like for refugees in these places.[3] The eyes of the US public turned to such places to forecast what emancipation might mean on a larger scale. By contrast, Union commanders at Yorktown seem to have attempted to regulate Black business to some degree while allowing Black residents in York County's most populous areas to direct their own labor. As a result, the community that emerged at Yorktown by 1865 was largely the making of Black refugees rather than the heavy hand of federal authorities. As historians Ira Berlin, Barbara J. Fields, Thavolia Glymph, Joseph P. Reidy, and Leslie S. Rowland noted, "Throughout the South, the character of the war helped determine who would be free, how they would become free, and what freedom would mean."[4] The character of the war at Yorktown was such that conditions allowed for a unique degree of self-determination on the part of Black refugees as well as the steady accumulation of property and construction of social systems that remained protected until the war's close. Black residents themselves would seek to define what freedom would mean.

This determination to take charge of their fate began with the decision to become direct agents of the US Army during the 1862 Peninsula Campaign. While Fort Monroe remained under federal control from the start of the war, and famously became the site of the Union army's first forays into military emancipation in 1861, Confederates controlled the surrounding Hampton Roads area and Yorktown until May of 1862. In his attempt to take the Confederate capital at Richmond, US General George McClellan laid siege to Yorktown in April of 1862, and the Confederate commander, General John Magruder, abandoned his fort there in May. Black residents of the peninsula provided detailed information to the Union army ahead of the campaign. In March of 1862, US spy Allen Pinkerton reported that "William H. Ringgold, an intelligent colored man," specified the exact Confederate units holding Yorktown, their numerical strength, and the position of their guns.[5] Ringgold had apparently left

Gloucester, directly across from Yorktown, in November of 1861, and continued to monitor Confederate defenses at Yorktown through the winter of 1861.[6] When the Union army arrived outside of Yorktown in May of 1862, refugees from slavery—described as "contrabands" in reports—continued to provide crucial information about the Confederate defenses.[7]

As historian Glenn David Brasher has argued, Black residents of the Virginia Peninsula played a key role at Yorktown as well as in the broader Peninsula Campaign. As soon as US forces arrived outside of Yorktown, refugees from slavery "streamed into Union lines" and offered their assistance in the Union war effort. In these early days, before Black men could formally enlist in the US Army, they extended their services to federal soldiers as body servants, laborers for the commissary department, and workers at the port on the York River.[8] As Ringgold's example demonstrates, they also provided critical military information that would be essential to the Union army's advance towards Richmond. Brasher concludes that the efforts of Black residents on the peninsula in abandoning slavery and providing what labor they could for the Union cause helped push federal policy toward a more expansive emancipation, culminating, after the campaign, with the Second Confiscation Act, a precursor to the Emancipation Proclamation.[9]

Though Yorktown's siege played a fairly small role in the overall campaign—Magruder anticlimactically abandoned the fort under the cover of night—it loomed large in the imagination of soldiers and the American public. As the site of the Revolutionary-era siege and George Washington's famous victory over British General Charles Cornwallis, control of Yorktown took on new meaning in the eyes of the war-torn nation. Soldiers frequently commented on this reality in letters home and sought out notable locations such as the cave in which Cornwallis took shelter during the eighteenth-century siege. For instance, a soldier from the Eighth Pennsylvania Regiment noted in a published letter in his local newspaper that his unit camped within "fifty yards of the old intrenchments that were thrown up in time of the Revolutionary war." Interested in the Revolutionary history surrounding them, the soldier and his comrades visited "the spot where Washington had his Headquarters in his time at Yorktown," shortly after occupying the city.[10] A New Hampshire soldier similarly recounted visiting "the identical house where Cornwallis signed his surrender," and the spot where "his doughy lordship delivered up his 'ancient blade,' not to Washington, but to the brave Lincoln, who you will recollect, was once placed in similar circumstances."[11] Such commentary on the Revolutionary history of the landscape indicates that Union soldiers were keenly aware of the historic nature of the city they were occupying.

Federal occupation of Yorktown, however, would prove to be just as significant to the ongoing struggle for freedom in 1862 as it had been in 1781. This occupation made Yorktown a haven for refugees from slavery and US soldiers protected that haven for the duration of the war. Within the Union army's sphere of influence, refugees from slavery distanced themselves from the bonds of enslavement and began to create a functional freedom long before the war's outcome, and constitutional abolition, became reality. Yorktown became the nucleus of a larger landscape of freedom in which formerly enslaved people began constructing freedom and citizenship in advance of federal policies ensuring their legal status.

Yorktown's Black settlement was not a model community like those at Port Royal, South Carolina; Roanoke Island, North Carolina; or Freedman's Village in Arlington, Virginia. Moreover, its distinct history often gets overlooked in favor of the history of the more famous fort downriver at Old Point Comfort. Yorktown was, first and foremost, a military post that the Union army took interest in holding for its strategic position and for its significance to American national imagery. Indeed, in determining whether or not to evacuate Yorktown after the failed campaign, Major General John Dix noted that federal high command decided to retain the city "to avoid the moral effect of abandoning a place recently captured and familiar to the whole Country through its historic associations."[12] Though the US Army's taking of Yorktown was less than spectacular, Dix and his fellow officers understood that its value lay in the area's Revolutionary legacy. Yet although Yorktown's military importance would fade in the light of more significant campaigns in the East, or perhaps because of it, it became a place in the war-torn southern landscape in which formerly enslaved people could begin structuring the freedom they knew the war could help create. The relative security of York County within federal lines and the US Army's consistent hold on the peninsula for the duration of the war ensured that shifting battle lines did not threaten Black residents' efforts in establishing social and political organizations, acquiring property, and reuniting their families as they did elsewhere in the occupied South.

Before Yorktown ever came into the hands of Union soldiers, Black residents on the Virginia Peninsula were already envisioning and working towards freedom. As Brasher has noted, as soon as the war broke out, enslaved people on the Virginia Peninsula understood that the war presented an opportunity for freedom.[13] When US troops first began arriving in the area because the federal government retained control of Fort Monroe, white residents fled inland towards Richmond. Many of the people they had enslaved, however, remained behind.[14] When Frank Baker, James Townsend, and Shepard Mallory arrived at Fort Monroe seeking shelter from slavery in 1861, they did so in a calculated effort to ascertain what the Union army's policies towards enslaved people were. The three men provided important information to US General Benjamin Butler about the state of Confederate defensive fortifications along the river. They also noted that other enslaved people would soon follow if these men received shelter at the fort.[15] Perhaps most importantly, but less frequently noted, Baker, Townsend, and Mallory had come to the fort to protect their families. The man who claimed ownership of them was attempting to "refugee" them to North Carolina, which would have separated them from their families who lived in Hampton, Virginia. For this reason, they sought the Union army's assistance in preventing their relocation and subsequent separation from family.[16] This now famous act was more than a desperate flight from slavery. It was a calculated claim to freedom that made clear one of freedom's most important elements in enslaved people's eyes: legitimate and acknowledged family ties.

Federal forces began massing at Fort Monroe in March of 1862 as General George McClellan prepared for his attack on Richmond. Confederates' use of enslaved labor to build extensive fortifications along the peninsula, Brasher has noted, resulted in a lengthy and ultimately failed campaign. Yet the frequent reports of this labor, and the advantage it provided to the Confederate forces, helped move Northern public opinion towards acceptance of "hard war" tactics including policies that directly impacted the home front. This conception of "hard war" would eventually come to embrace emancipation. But in the spring of 1862, this change in US policy was undetermined.

When the Union army finally made it to the outskirts of Yorktown, enslaved people, as elsewhere, fled to Federal lines, seeking shelter, and offering their labor. Both then and now outside observers read these efforts as evidence of enslaved people's "loyalty" to the Union cause and belief in the emancipatory future of the US armies.[17] While the latter helped guide enslaved people's decision-making, it is equally true that these efforts represent their ability to take advantage of the economic opportunities presented by the war. By offering their services as body servants, workers for the commissary department, or laborers loading ships on the York River, Black residents moved ably from enslaved to paid labor. Others took the opportunity presented by the large influx of soldiers to begin their own business enterprises, independent of army contracts, and sold newspapers from Fort Monroe to soldiers at Yorktown or sold goods to Union soldiers.[18] This was a concrete step towards establishing economic independence in freedom.

It is easy to overlook the significance of these economic activities considering the overwhelming realities of living in a war-torn landscape. As Taylor has demonstrated, an investment in independent labor could quickly be lost based on the whims of the Union army.[19] But the fact of its loss should not diminish the recognition of the effort refugees from slavery made in working immediately towards their futures in freedom. Robert Ruffin, a formerly enslaved man, remembered in 1871 that "during the war a man could make money faster." Ruffin had relocated to Yorktown in 1863 from the place of his enslavement outside of the city when he learned of the US Army's occupation. Taking over his father's store, Ruffin quickly became adept at turning an independent profit and grew the grocery business substantially.[20]

Upon taking Yorktown, US soldiers regularly noted interactions with refugees who remained behind within and around the fort. Following Confederate General Magruder's abandonment of Yorktown, a soldier in the Forty-Ninth New York explained that as they explored the fort, "contrabands who had just come inside our lines" pointed out Magruder's headquarters "that he left only the night before."[21] Another soldier from the Twenty-Second Massachusetts wrote home, describing a conversation in which he asked a refugee why the Confederate army had abandoned Yorktown with little resistance.[22] At least some of these refugees may have been enslaved laborers conscripted into Confederate service to build the fortifications that surrounded Yorktown, a practice common on the peninsula. In their advance towards Yorktown, a soldier from the First Connecticut wrote home, "Wherever I have been I find that slave women and children are numerous," but when asked where the men were they replied, "'Gone to Yorktown' . . . with significant looks."[23] General John B. Magruder, in command of Confederate forces on the peninsula, implemented an extensive impressment program to coerce the labor of free and enslaved Black men for the construction of defensive works along the peninsula. Yorktown's defenses were particularly formidable and required a large labor force. As the Confederate army moved up the peninsula towards Richmond, they took these laborers with them to help fortify their position over the course of the campaign.[24] Many of these forced laborers, however, remained behind when the chaos of Magruder's retreat from Yorktown created the opportunity for escape.

Union soldiers almost exclusively referred to the people they encountered in Yorktown as "contraband," a word that had come into popular use after the passage of the First Confiscation Act. Though the language of the act did not use the word, it suggested that because the Confederate army had forced enslaved laborers to assist in the war effort, they could be considered contraband of war. The term itself did not accurately describe the legal conditions of such laborers under the terms of the First Confiscation Act however, as Congress sought to distinguish between property and persons held in service. Still, that Union soldiers used this term to describe the people they encountered suggests that these individuals were enslaved laborers who the Confederate army had impressed and that they had remained behind in the town, taking the opportunity presented by Magruder's retreat under the cover of night to claim freedom for themselves.[25]

It bears noting here that Yorktown became somewhat infamous in histories of the Civil War for the numerous accounts of Black men assisting the Confederate army in their defense of the city. Accounts published widely in the North iterated stories like one recorded by a soldier from the First US Sharpshooters who stated, "In the afternoon I went over to the Rifle Pits, where Berdan's Sharp Shooters are stationed and had the pleasure of seeing a Rebel Soldier killed by one of them. He was a negro."[26] Another soldier from the Nineteenth Massachusetts described a different situation, noting, "The other day the sharp shooters had an excellent position, which commanded a couple of the enemy's guns; afraid to work the guns themselves, they set a number of negroes at work loading them." He elaborated on why he believed the white Confederate soldiers had done this, reasoning, "They probably thought we were such radical abolitionists that we could not shoot a negro."[27] This soldier's insights provide a useful point of departure for considering these accounts that have often been inaccurately used to suggest that the Confederate army enlisted Black soldiers. In this case, the US soldier observed Confederates abandoning their guns and putting Black laborers into the line of fire, ostensibly by force. These Confederate soldiers were not allowing Black men to fight alongside them, but rather forcing Black men to work in the line of fire so that white soldiers were in less danger.

It is telling that this soldier concluded his letter by describing "contrabands" informing Union soldiers after the siege was over that "it surprised [the

Confederates] considerably" that US soldiers willingly fired on Black men. Accounts abounded of conversations with "contrabands" indicating that even if some Black men had wielded guns against the Yankees during the siege, many had subsequently remained behind, choosing not to go with the Confederate army. Moreover, this line, though stated in passing, suggests that the person with whom the soldier was conversing had witnessed Confederate soldiers' efforts firsthand during the siege. Yet this person too remained behind, choosing to strive for freedom rather than support the Confederate army in any capacity.

Using the opportunities created by war to claim freedom had a long history on the peninsula prior to the Civil War, and more specifically, in Yorktown. During the American Revolution, Virginia's colonial governor, Lord Dunmore, offered freedom to enslaved people who would side with the British cause. At Yorktown, British General Charles Cornwallis used the labor of hundreds of Black people who had fled slavery to construct the earthworks to fortify the city. When the situation became dire, however, Cornwallis ordered these Black refugees out of the fort and into the waiting arms of the Continental Army, where General George Washington ordered them returned to their former enslavers.[28] This episode illustrates the long history of wartime freedom on the Virginia Peninsula, but also the ambiguous nature of wartime claims. Choosing to come into US lines in 1862 held no more guarantees than it had in the Revolution, and outcomes could be different depending on who refugees encountered upon arrival and the fate of the units whose protection they sought. Elsewhere in the occupied South, when the Union army lost ground, individuals who had sought protection within its lines often fell into Confederate hands.[29]

As the US Army proceeded up the Virginia Peninsula towards Richmond, soldiers continued to comment on the enslaved people who chose not to flee with white residents. On May 20, 1862, a soldier from the Thirty-third New York explained that as they passed "many beautiful plantations" they "came up and overtook scores of contrabands."[30] The decision to stay on a plantation was not an accident, nor was it simply a consequence of the chaos of war. Soldiers' accounts of meetings with formerly enslaved people made clear that like Shepherd, Townsend, and Mallory at Fort Monroe, they had made a concerted effort to stay, at times despite warnings of what might happen should they encounter Union soldiers.

A member of the Fifth Vermont explained that as the Union army progressed, Confederates had to "work to keep their slaves along with them." In many cases, fleeing owners could not combat the desire for freedom. The same soldier elaborated that some of the refugees "said that their masters told them that if they . . . were taken by the Yankees they would have their heads off, or torture them severely."[31] This was not an idle rumor, but a widespread belief. Dwight Chapin, of the Oneida Cavalry, noted that refugees "first ran at our approach," believing that the "ruthless invader" would do them physical harm.[32] Still, those who would be free chose to take their chances. Chapin further reported, "Efforts were made by the rebels to drive the negroes off . . . but they have an impression that their freedom is secured to them on our approach, and all efforts to get them away are futile." He challenged his readers, "Tell me, that they wouldn't prefer freedom."[33] As Chapin demonstrated, the choice to resist white enslavers' efforts to force enslaved people to flee along with them was also a choice to seek freedom with the US Army.

This first decision to extricate oneself from the bonds of slavery was a weighty one, and that decision defined how refugees from slavery chose to present themselves to the Union army. Reports from US soldiers around Yorktown do not describe people waiting to be rescued, but rather people taking advantage of the moment and approaching the Union army on their own terms. That Union soldiers frequently referred to their first encounters with Black residents of the peninsula as "contraband" signals the fact that they had already taken the steps away from slavery required under the terms of the First Confiscation Act. Indeed, the soldier from the Fifth Vermont observed that already "they appear like freemen, and they will be such under the confiscation act."[34] While the First Confiscation Act would confirm their status within Union lines, these refugees on the peninsula had already released themselves from the bonds that held them in slavery.

The timing of these refugees' flight is also important because soldiers' accounts identify more people than those who would have formally fallen under the terms of the First Confiscation Act. In May, as the US Army proceeded up the peninsula, the Second Confiscation Act, which would expand the terms of military emancipation, had not yet passed. Although Senator Lyman Trumball had introduced a "Bill to Confiscate the Property of Rebels and Free their Slaves" in December of 1861, "the emancipation bill" as it was commonly called at the time, did not become law until July 17, 1862.[35] This new law, known later as the Second Confiscation Act, officially broadened the scope of military emancipation to include enslaved people who ran into Union lines from rebellious owners, enslaved people deserted by owners who came under the control of the US government through military occupation, and enslaved people residing in areas previously occupied by rebel forces and afterwards occupied by US forces.[36] Thus, these refugees acted in advance of laws, seeking and claiming freedom for themselves. Moreover, as they routinely acquiesced to the repeated interviews undertaken by US soldiers, refugees from slavery created a narrative that would help sway public opinion in the North towards broader terms for military emancipation.[37]

Lieutenant Eugene Nash, of the Forty-fourth New York, remembered that "colored people for miles around flocked to Yorktown as soon as occupied by our troops." Restrictions of the First Confiscation Act, which technically only applied to Black men directly engaged in the war effort, did not limit their flight. Rather, "the old and young, male and female, came in, bringing all their earthly possessions." While Nash acknowledged that their possessions were limited, and that it became necessary for the Union army to provide food and shelter, he also noted "they were willing to work, and readily engaged in putting the town in a cleanly and wholesome condition." This moment, Nash observed, was "the dawn of a new life" for refugees.[38] Formerly enslaved people intended for that new life to begin immediately.

In the wake of the Peninsula Campaign, Black refugees' numbers would grow. Within less than a year of the Union army's occupation of Yorktown, *The Cavalier,* a newspaper established by resident Union soldiers, reported that there were more than 2,000 refugees from slavery inside Fort Yorktown.[39] By early 1864, *The Friend,* a Quaker newspaper, reporting on benevolent activities in the area, noted that "there are about thirty thousand" refugees from slavery "in the vicinity of Fortress Monroe, Point Comfort, and Yorktown."[40] These numbers would continue to grow over the course of the war.

Some scholars have asserted that refugees from slavery in and around Yorktown, including at Fort Monroe, were not actually free because the Emancipation Proclamation, which took effect seven months after Yorktown came under Union authority, exempted the Virginia Peninsula.[41] This assertion, however, contracts the history of emancipation and abolition on the peninsula by focusing exclusively on the parameters of the proclamation and forgets the importance of the First and Second Confiscation Acts to the long history of military emancipation. By the time Abraham Lincoln issued the Emancipation Proclamation, Congress and the president had already declared enslaved people who had taken shelter within Union lines at Fort Yorktown and Fort Monroe permanently free.[42] To Republican policymakers, there was a distinction between the full abolition of slavery, which they believed the Constitution disallowed, and emancipation of particular people, which they believed war powers put within their grasp. This distinction was important to individuals who did not have the opportunity to come into US lines on the Virginia Peninsula, but in the case of refugees who came under the purview of the occupying Union forces at Yorktown and Fort Monroe, the Second Confiscation Act had already permanently protected the freedom they had claimed. More importantly still, Black residents at Yorktown began acting as free people—seeking to establish homes, pursuing independent employment, and reuniting their families—before Congress officially determined their legal status.

Moreover, in the gap between emancipation and abolition was opportunity for negotiation. Military emancipation may have declared formerly enslaved people free, but without constitutional determinations their status within the nation remained unclear. Black residents of Yorktown built their own practical freedom within this liminal legal space, and laid claim to the foundations of citizenship even though citizenship was not yet guaranteed.

Refugees also pushed the boundaries of the Union army's influence and the quasi-legal space defined by military occupation. The edges of the Union army's control were permeable, and refugees took advantage of this reality by sharing the resources they acquired in freedom beyond US-occupied zones. Colonel William Davis, of the 104th Pennsylvania remembered that "the contraband system gave us considerable trouble" because "crowds" of Black residents would leave Yorktown and go to Gloucester on Sunday mornings where they held "communication with their friends outside" of the picket line. Gloucester, across the river from Yorktown, was not securely within US lines. Still, Davis observed, "Nearly every" Black person "came with a well-filled bag to pass over the line," and residents of the refugee community would pass clothing and government shoes to those outside.[43] Thus, Black residents of the Union stronghold expanded the network and landscape of freedom on their own terms, as Davis noted, sometimes despite the efforts of Union soldiers to stop them.

In some cases, the line between free and forced labor was also thin. As Amy Murrell Taylor has noted, this was true throughout the Union army and the situation remained similar at Yorktown.[44] Stephen Buckson of the Fourth Delaware reported that although Black residents "are all free . . . they are putting them in the service and making them do all the hard work cutting wood and building fortifications."[45] Thus, Buckson simultaneously acknowledged that Black residents were free in name, yet in some cases did not have full control over their labor. While the Union army intended, at least, to pay these forced laborers, in December of 1863 an agent of a Quaker association reported that "a number" of men employed by the government "state they had received no pay for five or six months."[46] This problem of delayed pay was common throughout the Union army.

With this new occupation of Yorktown, the balance of power would fluctuate on the peninsula for the duration of the war. Though the US Army held Yorktown, creating a somewhat stable place for refugees to congregate, the threat of Confederate attack always existed. Simultaneously, some Union soldiers were allies in name but not in practice. Federal policy required US soldiers to protect the freedom of people who came into their lines, but that did not mean white soldiers were prepared to support the forms of freedom that refugees sought. In their introductory issue the editors of *The Cavalier,* whose banner proclaimed, "THE UNION FOREVER AND FREEDOM TO ALL," were careful to clarify that they did not consider themselves abolitionists. "Let it be distinctly known," they explained, "that 'white folks' are meant" in the declaration on the masthead.[47]

However hesitantly Union occupiers may have approached their newfound role as liberators, Federal policy required that they protect the liberty of refugees from slavery, and their presence in Yorktown radiated a sphere of opportunity beyond the physical boundaries of the city. After a reconnaissance into Gloucester, Mathews, and King and Queen County from Yorktown, a major in the Fifth Pennsylvania Cavalry reported, "I released 7 negroes who had been imprisoned by the citizens, and notified the inhabitants that if they arrested negroes without cause, or assisted in taking citizens of the county who had deserted the Southern rebel army . . . or arrested Union men in any way, they would be themselves arrested and severely punished."[48] These missions into the surrounding countryside could present opportunities to grasp freedom for some, but, as this episode demonstrates, their reach was sporadic. In another instance, Union officials reported, "refugees and escaped prisoners, knowing of the pickets at all the upper fords and bridges, almost invariably come down parallel with Charles City road," in hopes of crossing the Chickahominy River to safety behind Union lines.[49] Whether Union soldiers saw themselves as agents of Black freedom or not, enslaved people frequently took the opportunities presented by US soldiers' presence whenever they engaged in operations beyond Yorktown.

By the spring of 1863, thousands of refugees from slavery had congregated inside Fort Yorktown. Brigadier General Isaac J. Wistar, a native of

Philadelphia, arrived in Yorktown in early summer of 1863 to take command of what would remain an important post for the duration of the war.[50] In his autobiography, Wistar recalled that conditions in the fort were appalling. Fort Yorktown encompassed "a couple hundred acres," including the city itself, and 12,000 refugees lived packed inside the small area with "dirty, idle, and neglected troops." Supported by government rations, the refugees, according to Wistar, were "lying about without order under any ragged shelter they could get, in every stage of filth, poverty, disease, and death."[51] Conditions were so poor and disorganized, Wistar reasoned, "a handful of resolute and well-fed men could have captured the place." To Wistar's eyes not only were conditions terrible, but the state of disarray weakened US forces' ability to hold the fort should Confederates threaten the peninsula.

As Wistar observed, conditions at Yorktown had rapidly become untenable. In the 1850 census, York County's total population of free and enslaved people numbered 4,461.[52] If the 12,000 refugees Wistar observed was an accurate count, then a population almost three times the size of the entire prewar county was packed into the city limits.[53] It is worth noting that York County also had a sizeable free Black population prior to the Civil War, though it is unlikely they were part of the number Wistar observed. Of a total population of free persons numbering 2,279 the 1850 census identified 454 as "black" or "mulatto."[54]

Setting his mind to right the situation, Wistar ordered everyone out of the fort and did not allow his men to camp inside its lines. Identifying a "large area of abandoned fields" directly outside of the Fort, Wistar surveyed and laid out two- and four-acre plots of land, "with street and building lines; and all the able-bodied negroes set to work building log cabins of prescribed form and dimensions."[55] Soldiers would come to call this newly established community "Slabtown" a name common to other such settlements that reflected the wood slabs with which occupants built their homes. At some point after the war, residents would begin calling the settlement Uniontown, but all official records prior to 1870 identified it at "Slabtown."

Though in his memoir Wistar referred to Slabtown's location as a "large area of abandoned fields," this land was in fact a single farm. Frederick W. Powers owned the farm as well as other large plots of land in York County. When the Confederate army had occupied Yorktown, they took possession of F. W. Powers's property—which he had only recently inherited from his father's estate—and Powers and his wife, Caroline, had moved to Richmond. Freedmen's

Bureau agents would later attest to the fact that Powers did not take "an active part in the rebellion."[56] However, his absence from the property and its proximity to the fort at Yorktown likely contributed to its selection by Wistar for a refugee settlement.[57]

Wistar assigned a sergeant and small force "of selected negroes" to police the community at Slabtown.[58] Wishing to correct what he portrayed later as a problem of idleness, Wistar had the provost marshal sell oystering permits to Slabtown's residents, and the army "obtained" seeds and tools for them.[59] Under Wistar's watchful eye, Slabtown became "large and populous . . . and was, to a considerable extent self-supporting."[60] According to Wistar, "the most capable residents were from time to time placed on abandoned and unoccupied farming-lands outside of town," further spreading the population to avoid disease and enable people to work for themselves.[61] Though Wistar portrayed himself as the originator of these plans, his predecessor, Major General Erasmus Keyes, had begun the process of moving refugees to outlying plantations prior to Wistar's arrival. Keyes reported in May of 1863 that "there are as many now on the plantations in this vicinity as can be employed to advantage."[62] In fact, by the end of the war the refugee population was spread over twenty to thirty different farms in York County. It is difficult to ascertain the exact number of farms as different people referred to them alternately by their pre-war owner's name, historic name, and sometimes the name of the property itself.

Elsewhere in the occupied South the Republican administration watched with interest as various Union commanders experimented with the imposition of "free" labor systems on Black refugee populations. For example, while in command in Louisiana at the end of 1862, Benjamin Butler settled formerly enslaved people on plantations organized on a wage labor system.[63] Wistar's actions at Yorktown do not appear to have been a similar experiment. Instead, he framed his decisions in terms of military necessity, believing that the organization of the refugee settlements would help increase the strength of Fort Yorktown by reducing overcrowding and disease. Indeed, unlike generals such as Butler, Wistar does not seem to have taken much interest in the disposition of refugees from slavery's labor, and instead depicted his actions as simply matters of regulation.

Perhaps he saw no need because during this period Black residents carried on successful business operations of a variety of forms, most notably oystering and fishing, on their own. Wistar remembered that the provost fund which consisted of "the proceeds of licenses and taxation . . . yielded several thousand dollars a month, largely derived from the sale of licenses for fishing, oystering, trading, and so forth."[64] According to Wistar, most of the white population had fled the area, so these tax revenues were almost certainly exclusively the result of Black residents' labor. In fact, the community had become so prosperous that Wistar noted it had "attracted from the enterprising people of New England, numerous cranks or self-styled missionaries . . . who infested Slabtown in ever-increasing numbers, and as a rule, were by no means averse to extracting a pecuniary profit from their pious labors."[65] One "crank's" extortion of Black residents became such a problem that Wistar expelled him from the military district.

In addition to Slabtown, Wistar established a second settlement, alternately called Newtown or Acretown. By population at least, Newtown rivaled and sometimes exceeded Slabtown in size. Located on farmland owned by Stafford G. Cooke, this community was also about two miles outside of Yorktown and a walkable distance from Slabtown. Unlike Powers, Cooke had remained local, spending the war across the river in Gloucester County after General Magruder forcibly removed him and his family from their home, which was between battle lines, prior to the siege of Yorktown. Like Powers, Cooke apparently took no part in the war.[66] It is unclear when exactly Wistar established this second neighborhood, but it appears it may have occurred in the winter of 1863 into 1864 because an correspondent for *The Friend* reported in December of 1863 that "surveys have been made . . . for the location of a new settlement, where one or more acres of land will be given to each family." At that time there was already a school and meeting house under construction for the settlement.[67]

Later census records of the refugee population of York County rarely mentioned from where people had escaped, though they did frequently note how many refugees did not "belong" to the county, meaning they had escaped from slavery elsewhere. Both Powers and Cooke had enslaved people prior to the war, however, and at least in the case of Cooke it seems certain that if he remained in Gloucester throughout the war, those he had enslaved were well within range of escaping into Federal lines. York County's 1850 census of enslaved people indicated that Powers enslaved eighteen people, ages one year to sixty, and Cooke enslaved eleven people, ages four to seventy.[68] Though the whereabouts of these particular people are unknown, it is clear that the populations of Slabtown and Newtown represented far more people than those who had originally been enslaved in those places.

To describe these two settlements as simply refugee encampments is to disguise how organized they were from the start. As Wistar mentioned, his troops helped lay out regular streets and plot two- to four-acre residential lots, which Union records would identify with numbers akin to house numbers. A census of the Black population of York County taken by the US Army in March of 1865 recorded almost four hundred numbered homes in Slabtown. Though Wistar remembered moving all of the refugees from the fort to Slabtown, likely if they all did move to this singular location initially, they did not stay long. The Union army rapidly claimed more farms in the surrounding area, spreading out the refugee population in an effort to provide the land necessary for them to labor sometimes independently and sometimes under the supervision of a farm superintendent.

Postwar records attempting to determine the fate of these settlements carefully specified that residents of Slabtown and Newtown had been "forcibly removed [from Fort Yorktown] by order of Brig Genl Wistar." As Wistar's memoir suggests, he understood this decision as one of necessity; the conditions inside the fort were terrible and could not support such a large population. Still, Wistar had assured Black residents that "they should not be molested so long as the U.S. forces were in possession of the District."[69] Since Union forces held the district for the duration of the war, these settlements experienced a relative stability not replicated in many other places in the wartime South.[70]

Slabtown and Newtown notably differed from other places refugees settled within York County and elsewhere on the peninsula because of the density of population. Union records identified all other locations as "farms," indicating that those who resided in these places had the opportunity to cultivate the land. These settlements likely resembled the "government farms" established near Fort Monroe. However, as Wistar's specifications of the lot sizes in Slabtown indicate, these locations did not provide land that could support farming. Residents in both places routinely kept hogs, chickens, and other livestock for their personal support along with keeping gardens. Such efforts could support the needs of the household while residents engaged in self-directed jobs outside of the home. Many of those residing in these neighborhoods worked as oystermen, carpenters, and other skilled laborers. Additionally, Wistar's descriptions of the lot sizes should not suggest that each family received an entire two- to four-acre lot. According to the 1865 census, there were cases of multiple families living at the same location, though the census does not indicate if that meant they resided in the same house, or simply on the same plot of land. Regardless, these two communities certainly rivaled Yorktown proper in their population sizes and more closely resembled towns than many other refugee settlements in the wartime South. Slabtown and Newtown's "metropolitan" nature further allowed for the creation of organizations that would help residents shape and pursue their own visions of freedom.[71]

Yorktown's strategic importance on the Virginia Peninsula, and the Union's subsequent desire to hold it through the duration of the war, provided residents a sense of stability and security that did not exist elsewhere in the wartime South. Following the upheavals of the Battle of Chancellorsville and anticipation of General Robert E. Lee's campaign north in 1863, *The Cavalier* noted, "While in other parts of our great country there is much excitement and many fears for the safety of persons and property . . . we the occupants of the renowned city of Yorktown and vicinity enjoy a full sense of perfect security."[72] It was not without effort, however, that the Union army made Yorktown a "place of safety." Confederate attacks threatened Union outposts as close as Williamsburg and Fort Magruder in 1863.[73] Throughout 1863 and 1864, Wistar sent expeditions out from Yorktown into the surrounding countryside. Guerilla outfits and otherwise ill-disposed white residents presented a problem for the security of which *The Cavalier* boasted, and in October of 1863 at least one unit of US Colored Troops led an effort to suppress "guerrillas and boat crews organized by the enemy" in neighboring Mathews County.[74] In his report of the excursion, General Wistar described these soldiers as "better than any old troops I ever saw . . . they seem to be well controlled and their discipline . . . has dispelled many of my prejudice."[75] Their service not only helped establish the security necessary to protect the refugee population at Yorktown but further helped raise the opinion of Black soldiers in the eyes of US commanders.

Like those who had assisted the Union army in its capture of Yorktown, Black residents of the peninsula continued to play an active role in military affairs in the area. For instance, in March of 1863, one man, identified as "that well-known person, 'an old and intelligent contraband,'" brought news of a Confederate advance against Union lines in Gloucester, across the river from Yorktown. He reported "marks of the bivouac of the departed chivalry [*sic*] within *one mile*" of Union pickets.[76] Many more Black men proved eager to join the fight in an official capacity. The following September *The Cavalier* reported that upon the opening of a recruiting office for a Massachusetts Black regiment in Yorktown, recruits came in "quite fast to the aid of Uncle Sam in these rebellious times."[77] By 1863 it was clear that with Union victory the final dissolution of slavery would have to come, though it was not yet clear how that dissolution would be accomplished.[78] This uncertainty, however, did not stop Black residents from joining the fight. Moreover, at Yorktown, Black residents persevered in building homes, pursuing independent employment, and accumulating property that would serve their needs in freedom despite the limitations and uncertainties imposed by war.

As far as Wistar and his subordinate white officers were concerned, their one complaint with the various Black recruits under their command was troops' propensity to accumulate more private property while patrolling the surrounding environs than commanders thought qualified as contraband of war. After a tour in Mathews' courthouse, Lieutenant Colonel George Rogers wrote to Wistar that he had ordered his troops to "take such private property as might be useful to contrabands, and to prevent any plundering by the men." Upon inspecting his camp, Rogers found "a motley collection of all kinds of fowl (dead and alive), fresh cured meats, and a promiscuous heap of all the smaller appliances of the culinary art, together with cloths, linens, ornaments of dress, and little objects of virtue."[79] The situation had gotten so out of hand, according to Rogers, that he had ordered his subordinates to shoot anyone who failed to follow the command not to plunder.

This discrepancy between what the troops believed they were entitled to as the occupying force, what was "useful to contrabands," and what qualified as plunder, suggests that these Black soldiers perhaps saw their activities as legitimate while their white officers did not. The appropriation of rebel property was commonplace. Indeed, both Confiscation Acts had acknowledged the wartime right to acquire property belonging to disloyal Americans. At Yorktown, as Wistar explained, the Union army confiscated property, including homes and farming implements, for the aid of the refugees. Rather than a lack of discipline, these reports indicate that white officers failed to understand the perspective of their soldiers, many of whom may have felt they were acquiring items that could be useful to their families back at camp.

These troops may have been acting in accordance with earlier notions of the legitimacy of claiming for themselves, their communities, and especially the Union army, possession of disloyal persons' property. Bringing assets such as farming equipment and horses along when a person chose to flee had multiple implications in the moment, all of them part of a larger matrix of appropriation that contributed to refugees' attempts to craft a meaningful freedom. When the war ended, a former Confederate wrote to Colonel Orlando Brown,

then in command at Richmond, that "in 1863 a Colored man then in my possession and held as my property took from my farm two oxen and cart and carried
them to Gloucester Point and delivered them to the United States forces."[80]
This was clearly not an act of personal appropriation, but a concerted effort to
contribute to the Union war effort and in doing so undermine Confederates'
ability to labor productively. By releasing himself from the bonds of slavery,
this man not only denied his former enslaver his labor, but further contributed
additional resources to the Union army. Apparently, this man performed some
service for the Union army, because in the aforementioned letter the former
Confederate complained that the oxen were "for some time . . . held by" the
Union army "and then turned over to the said colored man for some deficiency
of payment for services rendered by said man."[81] Working for the occupying
force was another form of labor available to Black residents of which they frequently availed themselves.

Similar instances of commandeering rebel property appear in records following the war, when former owners attempted to reclaim the property enslaved people had taken with them. In some cases, the person who originally
took the property had at some point later sold it, using this appropriation to
make money. In 1865, James Rhoads, the superintendent of schools for the
Friends Freedmen's Association wrote to US Captain A. S. Flagg that a man
named William Taylor purchased from "Mr C C Baker a white horse which is
now claimed by a man residing in Gloucester Co." The man claiming this horse,
Rhoads was careful to clarify, "has been an open enemy until the surrender of
Lee's forces." Advocating on Taylor's behalf, Rhoads stated, "It would be doing
an act of injustice . . . to take the horse away from Mr Taylor now" and he
requested that the captain issue an order "forbidding the secessionist further
troubling him."[82] In Rhoads's estimation, the horse belonged with William Taylor rather than a disloyal Confederate.

Cases such as these were so common that the Freedmen's Bureau agent in
Gloucester wrote to General S. C. Armstrong at Fort Monroe in May of 1866
asking how he should handle all situations with similar circumstances. Listing
other instances that had come before him, he described a Black man who took
doors "from a deserted house which had been gutted by our troops" and the
"larceny of part of a building by a freedwoman." Calling such episodes "larceny,"
however, belied their wartime context. "A large portion of Freed People find
themselves in the position of the above-named parties," the agent explained,
"they had not intentionally stolen but as was pretty generally practical during

the Rebellion they in common with many whites, appropriated to their own uses . . . articles which in the majority of cases were abandoned by their right-full [sic] owners." In most cases, these items were "of service in the construction of new habitations by destitute freedmen who were without the means of purchasing."[83] In other words, refugees from slavery understood the conditions of war allowed for the appropriation of private property, especially when that property belonged to those in rebellion against the United States. At Yorktown, as elsewhere, Union soldiers frequently confiscated farming implements and other resources that could be useful for supporting the refugee population. Refugees' use of those articles they had appropriated themselves to begin the process of constructing their lives is a testament to the ways in which formerly enslaved people acted as agents of freedom rather than recipients of it.

This bias in white soldiers' characterization of Black residents' behavior is one that exists throughout records from this period. Northerners like Isaac Wistar often arrived at refugee communities and made sweeping statements about Black people's "idleness" or general state of inactivity, giving the impression that they were waiting for someone else to begin the process of outlining what freedom would look like. Yet as these records show, those who would be free took it upon themselves to begin constructing freedom from the moment they left the confines of the place they had been enslaved. Taking horses, carts, and oxen helped a person prepare to engage in a productive enterprise. Moreover, that so many of those items changed hands by the time their former white owners attempted to reclaim them demonstrates that refugees engaged in an active trade economy even before the war ended. Records from immediately after the war demonstrate that despite the uncertainty of wartime freedom evident in federal policy, Black residents understood and expected that the freedom they were building would be permanent. Moreover, they would ensure that their community at Yorktown would, unlike many other wartime refugee settlements, endure long after the Union army ended its occupation.

CHAPTER 2

★ ★ ★ ★ ★ ★ ★ ★

"How Much We Can Do Ourselves"

Creating Institutions to Sustain a Community

In the opening pages of her memoir, Sarah Cadbury, a white Pennsylvania teacher who spent time teaching in Yorktown after the Civil War, included a sketch entitled "Slabtown, Virginia." Cadbury identified the four most prominent buildings in the image as "storehouse," "Mission House," "School house," and "Church." Behind the four main structures which are grouped together, a fort is visible in the distance, likely the entrance to Fort Yorktown. Scattered throughout the image are people engaged in various tasks, suggesting that the business of the place often occurred outside of these main structures.[1]

The image, and Cadbury's memoir, attributes these buildings to the Philadelphia "Friends' Freedmen Association" which labored in York County beginning in late 1863. In many ways, the image encapsulates how surviving records depict institutions such as churches and schools in refugee communities because the buildings appear in the image as orderly institutions delivered into the South by the Quaker Friends. They stand outside of the fort, but they remain partners in the work of remaking the South in the image of the North.

What the image cannot say, and what white teachers often failed to note in their many reports celebrating their accomplishments across the South, is who built these structures—Black residents in Yorktown. Here, as elsewhere, formerly enslaved people were more than recipients of white benevolence. They were active partners in creating and sustaining the institutions they believed would be most valuable in their efforts to remake freedom in their image. They also organized educational efforts that were implemented within those structures. Not only did they lend their labor to construct schoolhouses, but they also built churches and new congregations. In doing so, Black residents

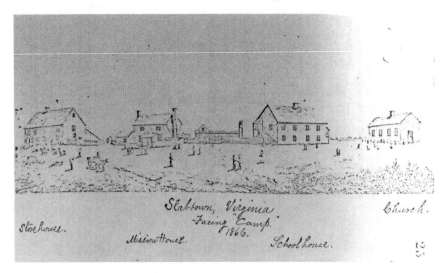

Figure 2. Sarah Cadbury sketch of Slabtown, Virginia.
Sarah Cadbury, *Letters from Slabtown*, 1866.

of Yorktown began the work of establishing a community in freedom and the institutions through which they would organize and strategize to pursue and protect their rights long before the Civil War ended or the federal government ensured perpetual freedom. Moreover, their work during the war enabled the community and its institutions to endure after the federal government left Yorktown.

One of the primary ways Black residents in York County began constructing their freedom was by taking advantage of educational opportunities. Typically, in histories of education in refugee camps, efforts appear to have depended on the activities of benevolent organizations from the North.[2] Many records that survive from these initiatives are letters written by Northerners to gain financial support from other Northerners, or by women like Sarah Cadbury writing home about their experience as teachers in the South. This tends to concentrate the narrative of the period on the white workers who taught in schools, while focusing less on the thousands of Black refugees who took advantage of these opportunities.[3] A closer reading of these documents yields important information about the perspective, goals, and initiatives of refugees and their role in creating and organizing their lives in freedom. Far from passive recipients of white teachers' instruction, Black residents in Yorktown worked to create an educational system and utilized education as a key foundation for the independent lives they hoped to build in freedom.

In thinking about Black refugees entering schools during the Civil War, it is easy to take this now common practice for granted. But to enter a school, and indeed to access educational opportunities on a wide scale, was a revolutionary act. Given that southern states did not have free public schools prior to the Civil War, there was no precedent for public schooling as a fundamental right of citizens, Black or white. In the antebellum South, teaching enslaved people to read was illegal. Consequently, there was no foundation for this type of education and most white Southerners were hostile to the idea of Black people receiving an education.[4] Thus, by seeking educational opportunities, Black residents of Yorktown joined with other Black Southerners in mapping claims to a new civil right while preparing themselves for other types of political activism.[5]

Amy Murrell Taylor encourages those studying refugee communities to remember that people who moved into these places "experienced their emancipation in slow motion." Freedom within camps was unmapped and unprotected, but still refugees "worked to make these places their own, to make them begin to conform to their visions of freedom."[6] Seeking literacy enabled Black residents to "prepare themselves for a life in freedom, by accessing the political information necessary to vote, or by reading the labor contracts on which the free labor system depended."[7] As Heather Andrea Williams has also emphasized, access to education was "on a short list of priorities" for Black residents "that included land ownership, fair contracts, suffrage, and equal treatment in legal proceedings."[8] They ordered their efforts and labor accordingly.

Moreover, upon closer investigation at Yorktown it becomes apparent that the first teachers in the refugee settlements of the area were in fact people of color. The nature of the historical record is such that the activities of white workers are the most visible in the archive, because they wrote the letters, kept the records, raised money through newspaper ads, and corresponded with federal agents.[9] These workers were integral to the development of an educational system at Yorktown, but they were partners in an effort instigated by Black refugees to gain access to education and by consequence tools such as reading and writing that would help them construct their lives after the war.

Yorktown was not unique in this reality but rather reflects larger trends that occurred across the wartime South. As Heather Andrea Williams has demonstrated, Black refugees initiated calls for educational opportunities and functioning schools. Within the vast written record produced by white teachers, these Black leaders often get overlooked. In some cases, they are mentioned, unnamed, in passing, and in other cases they are not mentioned at all. Yet it is still apparent that white Northern teachers answered a call that Black Southerners had already articulated for a system of publicly accessible schools, and even after white benevolent organizations arrived, Black residents remained partners in their educational activities rather than passive recipients of Northern ideas.[10]

Indeed, Black residents of Yorktown and the broader Virginia Peninsula petitioned benevolent organizations such as the American Missionary Association (AMA) for the materials they needed to launch an educational system. Alexander Lockwood, of the AMA, received word from Yorktown requesting books and mentioned that there were a "large number of contrabands anxious to learn to read." Later, Lockwood visited Yorktown and found Peter Cook, a Black teacher, utilizing the books the AMA had sent.[11] Lockwood and his fellow AMA leaders received similar requests in Virginia from Black residents at Newport News, Williamsburg, Downey Farm, and Camp Hamilton.[12] Likewise, Black residents petitioned government officials in addition to AMA agents. Lockwood noted that in July of 1862 Black residents of Norfolk wrote to the superintendent of contrabands at Fort Monroe expressing "a desire for school privileges for the colored people there."[13]

While a variety of benevolent organizations labored at Fort Monroe, Yorktown and York County fell under the exclusive purview of the Friends' Association of Philadelphia and Its Vicinity, for the Relief of Colored Freedmen. According to Freedmen's Bureau records, the Philadelphia Friends established a school at Slabtown by January 1863.[14] In October of 1863, *The Friend* published a report of the "Women's Aid Association of Friends for the Relief of Coloured Refugees" asking for donations to build a schoolhouse at Yorktown. An "earnest desire of the people for education" had precipitated this need.[15] However, in December of that same year, *The Friend's Review* published a report explaining that at Fort York and Gloucester "there is a small school kept by a coloured man held out of doors."[16] It seems likely that in reporting that the school at Slabtown had been established by the Friends in January of 1863, the Freedmen's Bureau agent after the war had assumed that the school did not start until the Friends' arrival. However, a school was already in operation by the time the Friends began raising money to build a schoolhouse. The teacher at this school, an unnamed Black man, received rations from the government and one dollar per month.[17] Rachel Dennis, a white teacher who would remain at Yorktown for the duration of the war, arrived in December of 1863.[18]

York County was not unique in this. Elsewhere in the South there were similar instances of Black teachers initiating schools that were later incorporated into formal systems coordinated by white benevolent workers. At Corinth, Mississippi, the American Missionary Association sent teachers and school supplies, but by the time of their arrival Black residents had already constructed a schoolhouse and sought instruction from "Union soldiers and from any among their number who could read."[19] Similarly, refugees established a school on Roanoke Island, North Carolina, prior to the arrival of any white benevolent groups.[20] As Heather Andrea Williams has pointed out, where the historical record tends to label many of these schools as "Friends Schools" or "American Missionary Association Schools," they could also have been called "freedpeople's schools." While missionary groups contributed both personnel and resources to the effort, Black residents of refugee communities across the South conceived of the schools, donated their church spaces to house the schools, built schools outright, provided fuel, and in many cases paid tuition to compensate teachers.[21]

Perhaps most famously, Mary Peake, a free Black woman, established a secret school in her church, First Baptist in Hampton, prior to the outbreak of war. This church burned with the city in the early years of the war, but Peake continued her efforts in Brown Cottage, located next to the Chesapeake Female Seminary in Hampton.[22] Peake remained an integral leader in the educational movement around Fort Monroe during and after the war.[23]

Black refugees' efforts were so widespread that in 1863 the American Freedmen's Inquiry Commission concluded that "sufficient evidence is before the Commission that colored refugees in general place a high value both on education for their children and on religious instruction for themselves." The commission came to this conclusion because "in various places 'one of the first acts of the [Black refugees] when they found themselves free was to establish schools at their own expense.'"[24] Similarly, John W. Alvord, the general superintendent of schools for the Freedmen's Bureau later reported to Oliver Otis Howard, "Throughout the entire South an effort is being made by the colored people to educate themselves. In the absence of other teaching they are determined to be self-taught. . . . They often say we want to show how much we can do ourselves, if you will only give us a chance."[25] Not only had Black refugees launched schools, but they also made their desire for education known to the US Army, and the federal administration through reports such as these.

In doing so, as Heather Andrea Williams has noted, they pushed "beyond the boundaries that sought to define and delimit their existence."[26] Again, though the federal government had yet to even guarantee their freedom, Black refugees worked to define what freedom should mean. In their eyes, meaningful freedom required access to literacy and education. Their desire for education and their efforts to provide educational opportunities for themselves moved white observers to meet the call and direct their efforts accordingly. Moreover, by the end of the war, in states, such as Virginia, South Carolina, and Louisiana, which came under Union control early and where Black refugees consequently had more time to coordinate their efforts, Black teachers outnumbered white teachers.[27]

This pattern of Friends teachers taking over from Black teachers repeated itself in religious instruction in churches. Nancy Battey, a white teacher working with the Friends in Yorktown, wrote in December of 1864, "Last Sabbath we entered the Sabbath School for the first time, the school has been conducted by two colored men, until now."[28] The white Friends teachers replaced the Black teachers and Battey explained, "Now we take it into our hands and they assist us."[29] Given the timing of Battey's letter, it appears that in 1864 at least, while white Friends teachers took over the formal schools, Black teachers continued instruction in the Sabbath Schools. By the end of 1864, the Friends felt it necessary to take over the Sabbath Schools as well. Though they did not specify their motivations for doing so, it is likely that they had increased the number of personnel they had available to extend themselves this far and they felt they needed to control education within the Sabbath Schools.

As the 1863 call for donations indicated, the desire for education presented a great need at Yorktown, where willing scholars sought whatever opportunities might be available. In mid-1864 A. N. Schofield reported that one of her students, "a man with one leg, about 50 years of age," had made so much progress reading that he "has now undertaken to teach a class in his own cabin." Schofield provided this teacher with primers and cards and had even arranged "to give him compensation at the end of the month." Already he reported fifteen scholars at his cabin school.[30]

This unnamed teacher was not the only Black person who continued to teach in Yorktown after the arrival of Northern workers. A June 1864 report indicated that "a coloured man named Peter Cook" taught students at Yorktown, indicating that Cook continued to teach after the arrival of white teachers. The desire for education was clearly greater than what the teachers could provide.

Cook taught alongside a Union officer and at least six other Friends were already engaged at Yorktown. *The Friend* reported that another two women were headed to Yorktown to join them. A schoolhouse at Newtown had already been completed, as well as one at a farm called Darlington where a large population of refugees from slavery would settle for the duration of the war.[31] The Friends hoped to build another at Williamsburg and "two other points on the peninsula." Black women "under the care of our teacher" also taught sewing and knitting at Yorktown and the thirty or so students who attended their classes were learning "rapidly."[32] By the end of 1864, the Friends had built several schools to accommodate refugees' desire for education in Yorktown and a store.[33] In most cases these schools met the needs of young scholars while night schools operated for adults who engaged in outside work during the day but wanted to attend school at night.[34]

As the war wound to a close in 1865, Black residents of York County, along with the Friends, had built a large educational network centered at Slabtown and radiating beyond Yorktown proper. The Friends' educational report for July 1865 described this network as "spread over a district of ten or twelve miles in length up the York river, and extending at one point across to the James river."[35] Like many others, the report did not mention that, Black residents of the area had initiated many of these educational activities and their efforts were subsequently augmented by the Friends' economic and political resources.

Always ready to acknowledge their own efforts, *The Friends' Review* celebrated their work at Yorktown as having been the "most permanent in elevating the freedman from his condition, on first emerging from slavery, to a higher position, socially, intellectually, and morally."[36] Records such as these reveal the way that many of those who produced the documentation of the early days of wartime freedom assumed that people who had been enslaved were almost certainly unprepared for what lay ahead. This same report further trumpeted the Friends' efforts not only to provide education in the form of training to read and write, something that was often denied to enslaved people, but additionally the "home life of the Freed-people has been inspected, and lessons of domestic economy and good management inculcated."[37] These assumptions about what formerly enslaved people did not know colored the way that white writers framed their observations of newly free people. Consequently, many records reproduce an image of Black residents wholly without the skills needed to survive in freedom, let alone make freedom meaningful. Yet a deconstruction of these same records allows for a more nuanced understanding of the lives that newly free people were making for themselves and reveals that in many ways they not only knew where they wanted to go but understood how to take advantage of the opportunities at hand to get there. That they utilized resources such as the Friends' schools demonstrates first a straightforward need for access to physical resources and second a deep desire to equip themselves for the lives they wanted to lead.

Another report explained to the Freedmen's Bureau agent at Yorktown that the Friends "endeavor not only to teach the children letters, but manners, industry, morality, and religion; and to do all we can to induce the older people to be clearly industrious, chaste, and law-abiding."[38] These goals suggest that the Friends' intention was not simply to provide the means necessary for newly free people to engage in a free-labor economy, because to do so would have required them to acquire farming tools, building materials, and similar physical goods. Instead, the Friends understood their role as training formerly enslaved people how to be citizens now that they had achieved freedom, and the Friends had a particular idea of what those citizens should look like. Included in the Friends' understanding of citizenship were specific forms of domestic organization. For instance, the superintendent of education reported "through the influence of our teachers upwards of 400 couples have been legally married, without expense to them, during the last eighteen months."[39] This framing intimated that it was only through the influence of white teachers that newly free people sought legal acknowledgment of their marital relationships.

Yet Black residents of the area sought legal marriage as soon as they had access to it, and when possible before the Friends arrived. In March of 1863, *The Cavalier* reported on one such marriage and indicated that others were ongoing. The marriage in question deserved particular attention as far as the soldiers who produced *The Cavalier* were concerned because Levi Washington, the groom, was a "patriotic person" and "private servant to Col. R. M. West, Chief of Artillery." Washington and his bride, Harriet Gardner, were married at Fort Yorktown in a ceremony attended by "a number of distinguished army officers."[40] Clearly this marriage was not simply a matter of making a relationship legal, as the Friends' conception of their efforts suggested to their readers. Instead, the marriage between Washington and Gardner was a celebration with widespread attendance.[41]

In a somewhat startling fashion, the Friends went so far as to assume that formerly enslaved people needed to be taught how to farm, something many enslaved people had been engaged in all their lives.[42] A May report from

Yorktown celebrated the procurement of the "services of George Blackburn, a young Friend . . . to take charge of our building and farming operations."[43] To the watchful eye of Northern benevolent workers, formerly enslaved people needed to be taught how to function outside of slavery. Yet newly free people left slavery ready to equip themselves for their lives in freedom, and did so with determined enthusiasm, carefully managing white people's expectations along the way. A closer look at the historical record, and evidence such as the numerous examples of Black residents starting schools in the York County area, suggests that the Friends' emphasis on needing to teach Black residents how to do tasks such a farm represents a skewing of reality rather than a representation of it.

In partnership with Black residents, the Friends achieved remarkable success in the construction of an education and economic network in York County by the close of the war. This involved not just providing teachers, but raising money to build schools, stores, and church buildings. The demand for education was so great that five schools operated with 415 students at Slabtown, another three schools at Newtown, and additional schools at Darlington's Farm, Bellefield Farm, Tinsley Farm, Warren Farm, and another in Williamsburg were also open. Already the Friends planned to build another school, this time at the Baker Wynne Farm, and followed a model of instruction established down the peninsula at the government school in Hampton. Though Slabtown and Newtown remained the largest settlements near Yorktown, the other farms in the area had large populations, with student enrollment numbering from fifty to more than one hundred scholars on each farm.[44] More schools would open in the coming months.

York County's educational system largely mirrored systems that developed throughout the wartime South. Missionaries at Roanoke Island coordinated day schools for children while adults who could not come during the day attended night school.[45] This day school and night school system was commonplace.[46] Roanoke Island's schools were also located throughout the community, though the island itself encompassed a much smaller geographic region than York County. Teachers focused on "the traditional three 'Rs'—reading, writing, and arithmetic."[47] As at Yorktown, white teachers on Roanoke Island attempted to proscribe lessons of "morality . . . thrift, industriousness, punctuality, and sobriety."[48] Teachers conceptualized formerly enslaved people as not yet ready for freedom, carrying with them either racist assumptions about the abilities of Black people or a belief that the institution of slavery had deprived individuals of the capacity to function in a free-labor society. Yet newly free people consistently demonstrated that they knew what they wanted freedom to look like and were capable of strategically implementing that vision.

Even in statistics on school attendance, the motivations and aspirations of formerly enslaved people start to become visible. Choosing to send one's children to school rather than keep them at home during the day to help, especially on the outlying settlements where people were primarily engaged in farming, indicated what parents wanted their children's futures to look like. An 1865 census of the Black population of York County reflected this prioritization, noting in the "occupation" column that most children who were considered old enough to labor were instead "at school."[49]

Although most adults worked during the day, reflecting economic realities, teachers reported that their night schools were filled with adults who arrived after a long day of labor. In some cases, people traveled long distances after working all day to attend school because not every farm settlement established by 1865 had a school. Margaret Thorpe, a teacher at the Fort Magruder school near Williamsburg remembered that two young men attended her evening classes after working all day as oystermen. These men "seldom took time to eat any supper before starting for their long walk to school." They would eat along the way if they could but Thorpe "never heard either one complain of fatigue or hunger."[50] Another elderly man came every night and Sunday, no matter the weather conditions, "carrying his Bible." Determined as he was to learn to read the Bible for himself, he "walked over five miles every time he came." When he mastered reading, Thorpe recalled, "it almost made one cry to see his joy."[51] Here again individual motivations begin to come discernable. This unnamed man sought the ability to access his Bible, and by extension religious understanding, on his own terms and without an intercessor.[52]

Others faced greater impediments than distance and hunger in their efforts to gain an education. Thorpe remembered that one man, together with his daughter and granddaughter, made the three-mile trek to school every night. However, "after the Ku Klux came into our neighborhood, this old man always came armed with sword and gun." This determined student revealed the value he ascribed to learning to read, commenting, "'Isn't this a most blessed privilege?'"[53] Students frequently expressed this belief that access to education was a privilege. Thorpe recalled that she had little trouble even with young students' behavior because "they looked upon it all as a 'great privilege.'"[54] Even children knew that engaging in educational opportunities was a task to take seriously.

In her telling of the story of the armed student after the war, Thorpe comically rendered the image of an elderly man carrying an old sword and gun, which she thought must date from the Revolution. She described the man carefully storing the weapons each class period as if it were a bizarre impracticality. Yet the threat to Black education and the need to protect oneself from hostile white neighbors was very real, as her reference to the Ku Klux Klan indicated. Thorpe herself experienced danger traveling between schools, recounting a time when some local white men attempted to knock her off her horse as she traveled through Williamsburg.[55] Thorpe's student's desire to protect himself and his family especially on a long and likely secluded journey to the school, was not only reasonable, but a further expression of how much value this man, his daughter, and his granddaughter placed on their education.

Moreover, in April of 1865, the Friends' instruction committee reported that one of the schools in Newtown had burned down, after residents had only recently completed its construction. Though *The Friend's Review* did not identify the cause of the fire, when another school, this time on the "land of Mr Bartlett" burned in May of 1866, the Freedmen's Bureau had no trouble attributing the destruction to disgruntled local white residents.[56] Writing to the district office at Fort Monroe, the bureau agent explained, "the villanous [*sic*] work was no doubt performed by returned rebels as Mr Douglas in charge of the school informs me that threats were frequently made by them." Not only this, but Douglas had reported hearing "six rounds of ammunition discharged which he understands the incendiaries fired in honor of their victory."[57] Clearly, white residents' hostility towards Black freedom and advancement was painfully real. Still, students expressed their desire for an education with their feet, their willingness to confront violent threats, and with their words.

The Freedmen's Bureau had leased the property on Barlett's farm for a school for a period of five years and had only just completed construction of the school building itself in April. Though the lease was for five years, according to F. J. Massey, the head bureau agent for York County, this school was "intended to be permanent." When the lease on Bartlett's property expired, the lumber from the school, if moved, was to be used "for the benefit of freedmen."[58] In burning the school, the incendiaries had deprived Black residents both of their school building and access to the materials that the bureau had earmarked for their future use.

Destruction of Black schools through fire was endemic across the South during this period, as was violence directed against teachers who labored in the schools, demonstrating that the white community understood the leveling impact education could have on their stratified society. Elsewhere on the Virginia Peninsula, incendiaries burned a Black school at Norfolk and disgruntled white residents made assassination attempts against Charles B. Wilder, the "Superintendent of Negro Affairs" at Fort Monroe, and against missionary workers.[59] In Columbus, Mississippi, teachers began receiving violent threats as soon as US soldiers withdrew from the area. Evincing their desire not only for education, but their willingness to protect the boundaries of their freedom, Black residents of Columbus pledged to arm themselves and defend the school as well as the Quaker teachers who worked there. They were successful in their efforts for a time, but in January of 1867 that school, too, burned.[60]

Apart from Rachel Dennis, teaching at Slabtown, Friends teachers rarely stayed in Virginia for a duration longer than a few months at a time. Black students endured a near constant change in teachers over the course of the Friends' tenure at Yorktown, and never knew if a teacher they had come to know would be coming back. In November of 1866, *The Friend's Review* published letters written by Black scholars requesting that their teachers return and expressing their desire to have more time for instruction. One student explained, "I hope to see you before long. The [winter] is coming on now very fast. . . . Oh! How I would like to go to school from now till Christmas." This particular person further expressed their desire to be able to read Scripture on their own, requesting that the teachers return with a Bible and "I will pay you for it when you com[e] down."[61] These seemingly simple requests, published in white newspapers to show how sincere the scholars were, represent another attempt to establish the terms of education by petitioning teachers to return earlier than scheduled and making requests on what types of books they should bring with them.

Another student letter stated, "William Fields remembers his respe[cts] to you . . . wishing that you may come to Yorktown . . . most of your [scholars] want you to come back. I do too worst of all." Fields' letter indicated that in the absence of Friends teachers, local people had continued work building and expanding their educational facilities themselves. Fields wrote, "I wish you could see the school-houses and the church . . . all looks very well, and very nice, far better now [than] it was before."[62] Scholars contributed to the school project in any way they could. Margaret Thorpe remembered one of her students, a man "making his way up in the world in spite of a large family of little children," as "anxious and hopeful to do all he can to help support the schools."[63] Through their petitions and support, Black residents acted as partners in educational efforts and sought to sustain the institutions they valued.

When the white teachers returned to Yorktown in December, Jacob H. Vining, the superintendent of schools, reported "the people seem overjoyed at our return." They expressed their joy by showing up to school in large numbers, immediately filling the four large schools already running plus two more schools that were still awaiting their teachers' arrival.[64] Vining attributed the overflow of students at all of their schools to the increased expenditure on the part of the Friends in building "large and commodious buildings," and the "change in public sentiment here, from opposition to the support of their education."[65] Yet the building of schools and even the acceptance of Black education were responses to initiative taken and demands made by newly free people who sought out educational opportunities at every turn.

Sarah Cadbury, another white teacher who taught in Slabtown in 1866, reported back to her family on the reasons some of the children gave for wanting to come to school, revealing how newly free people understood education as contributing to the freedom they were constructing for themselves. Cadbury described students responding to the question "Why should you learn?" One girl replied, "To learn to count money," and another "So we can read our Bible and love God." A boy puzzled the teacher with his response, "So we may know when people lie to us." When questioned further he explained, "We can read the papers and see if what they tell us is true. They told us the Yankees had horns, and if we had read the papers we would have found it was not so before."[66] Though Cadbury repeated this story with amusement, the students' answers evidence the concrete ties they saw between education and freedom. A desire to count money, and to be able to navigate the world fully informed, rather than at the mercy of others, would help newly free people establish themselves independently from white people's oversight.

These students' answers reflected what all Black scholars during this period knew to be true. Where white benevolent workers saw individuals who needed to be lifted out of slavery, newly free people understood their educational efforts as preparation for the freedom they were already living and struggling to shape. "Acquiring literacy in conjunction with freedom," as Heather Andrea Williams has argued, "had the potential to open access to democratic political activity, and that in turn held the promise of enabling African Americans to participate in shaping the civil society" that would emerge from the war.[67]

Though in September of 1866, Yorktown Freedmen's Bureau agent F. J.

Massey reported that schools had been established "at every point where they are desirable" in his subdistrict, demand for education continued to grow.[68] By March of 1867, Jacob Vining wrote to the Friends, "Our schools . . . have been crowded. The teachers under my supervision are all overworking." Not only were teachers overworking to meet the desire for education, but the Friends at Yorktown had "scholars enough for another large school and shall have to turn them away unless another teacher is provided."[69] Demand for reading materials was also high, outstripping what the Friends could supply. "Books are eagerly sought for," Vining explained, "read and listened to by those who cannot read." Enthusiastic to read what they could, Vining observed "large groups [of Black residents] collected for this purpose."[70] Community members congregated to share the limited supply of books and read to one another.

By 1868, the Freedmen's Bureau was working to make these schools independent of the resources provided by the federal government and the Friends.[71] In the fall of 1868, Samuel Chapman Armstrong, superintendent for the Freedmen's Bureau of the Ninth District in Virginia, wrote from Hampton to the new agent at Yorktown, Henry K. Ayres, "There will be no free schools at Yorktown this or next year." If the Friends sent a teacher, which he doubted would happen, they would expect that the Black residents pay the teacher's salary. Tuition would cost forty cents a month for one child, and seventy-five cents per month for two children. Families with three children would pay one dollar, and an additional ten cents per child. He concluded this news by stating, "Please . . . do all in your power to persuade [Black residents] to do their part in the maintenance of schools in their midst."[72] Again, Armstrong's words suggested that Black residents would need to be convinced to "do their part." But bureau reports indicate that they were already paying five cents a week—twenty cents a month—in tuition in the spring of 1868.[73]

Presumably, the local residents did not need much persuading to pay the increased tuition as Armstrong had commanded, because by November he wrote Ayres informing him that soon three Black teachers would arrive, one to take over the school at Fort Magruder in Williamsburg. At least one of the other two men would work in Williamsburg as well, and the other would teach in Yorktown if the need arose. Given his statements regarding whether or not another teacher would be needed in Yorktown, it appears that the educational situation in Yorktown was already under control because he was not certain Yorktown required another teacher.[74] At least one local white woman, Miss L. M. Shield, had also offered to open a school for Black students in Yorktown, suggesting that the demand for education remained high even after it was no longer subsidized by the Friends.[75]

Prioritizing and accessing education was one element of a larger effort on the part of Black Southerners to organize institutions that would support their claims to freedom and their access to rights of citizenship. As soon as the war ended, Black Southerners began meeting in public forums "in statewide conventions modeled after the antebellum ones that African Americans had held in northern states since 1817."[76] The roots of these organizations, like the roots of their schools, lay in the efforts Black residents had made during the war to form institutions that could support their political claims.[77]

Though white teachers' letters and records frequently reflected a perspective colored with paternalistic impulses, they still reveal forms of organizing and political expression among newly free people beyond the desire for education. In 1864, Nancy Battey described Lincoln's reelection to her brother, writing, "When we heard that Lincoln was reelected we let the children in school give three cheers for him."[78] Though Battey framed this celebration as "letting" the children cheer Lincoln, it is clear they felt his victory was their political victory too. Battey elaborated, "most of them understand that he is their liberator, and never has a president retired from the chair carrying as many blessing with him as Lincoln."[79] Though they could not yet vote for him, Black students openly expressed their support for a candidate who they felt aligned with their interests.

Margaret Thorpe remembered that the local Black community regularly engaged in public spectacles signaling their readiness to defend and discuss their rights. "One crowd would frequently march under the direction of a young man who had been a soldier," she remembered, and the teachers would stand outside the school to watch. Teaching at Fort Magruder, Thorpe and her fellow teachers resided in what had once been the headquarters of the fort. That she and her associates could simply stand outside the school to watch this event indicates that this regular drill session occurred in the central space of the Fort Magruder settlement. In so doing, the marchers claimed the physical space of the military fort that had once belonged to the Confederate army and used it to signal their willingness to defend their rights and ability to mobilize in force.

As historian Julie Saville has noted, such military-style rituals were common in refugee communities beyond York County. By adapting military ceremonies to their own needs, Black residents could "make their presence as organized bodies visible."[80] Thorpe's passing mention to these events belies the important role they played in organizing Black communities across large swaths of land. Marches and parades were the most visible manifestation of Black organizations that allowed Black residents to "establish a basis for more collective decision-making in rural areas."[81] Such military-style organizations established hierarchies of authority as well as communication networks that undermined the localism of plantation life. Those in command positions often helped disseminate news and communicated on behalf of the organizations with military and civil agencies.[82] Though Thorpe did not comment on—and likely was not privy to—the social networks that supported these parades, fragmented references from white observers suggest that the rituals Thorpe observed were part of a larger organization such as those Saville has identified in South Carolina.

Thorpe remembered other routine events in which the Black community would gather to both celebrate and map out their freedom. Formerly enslaved people congregated to sing hymns and exhort the crowd. One man, who Thorpe identified as Jim, praised God for his faithfulness in bringing them out of slavery, but focused on asking God to continue to help newly free people build a faithful life in freedom. Jim prayed, "Oh Lord drop a livin coal from de burnin altar 'moungst de dry bones, make de sinner start, and de wicked tremble for Christ's sake.'"[83] Quoting an old Testament story in which the dead in the Valley of the Dry Bones were brought back to life, Jim was asking his God to bring a revival among the people. "In Zion, O Lord," Jim went on, "shake out Yer tablecloth and caiter crumbs 'moung de hungry, wipe de weepin eyes and bind up de bleedin feet . . . We beg you turn de sinners to repentance before de settin' sun shall shut dem from de light." This was more than a prayer of celebration, but further an articulation of the kind of lives Jim hoped God would help his people build in freedom. Jim concluded, "O Lord You know our weakness, You has brought us out of de house of bondage, and made us free people, make us praise Your name for eber and eber."[84] In his acknowledgement of what he believed God had done for his people, Jim revealed that he understood his God as an active agent in political and social affairs. His words of request were more than a simple exhortation of the crowd. They were an expression of a belief that God had worked and had still more work to do, and an effort to participate in that work.

Religious expressions such as these, as historian Matthew Harper has argued, carried political weight for Black Americans in the emancipation period. Black Southerners' Biblical worldview helped them imagine a new social order, and they interpreted the coming of freedom as evidence of God's plan not just for their liberation, but for their future.[85] To Black Christians, emancipation was a Biblical prophecy fulfilled, and their understanding of emancipation as such motivated their movement out of white-controlled churches and guided their early political organizing.[86] Moreover, invoking emancipation as a promise fulfilled reaffirmed their belief in a more glorious future that was still to come, a future they fully anticipated constructing for themselves.[87]

Congress's passage of the Civil Rights Act in April of 1866, the first federal recognition of Black people as citizens of the United States entitled to all the rights that might entail, was further cause for major celebration. F. J. Massey, acknowledged the anticipated festivities in a circular on April 24 that read, "Owing to the large number of 'Freedmen' who will no doubt assemble this day to celebrate the passage of the 'Civil Rights' bill; and general order and quietness being of the first importance in order that all may enjoy the festivities of the day It is hereby ordered that the sale of spirituous or malt liquors to 'Freedmen' be discontinued for this day under penalty of immediate confiscation."[88] Massey's decision to take concrete steps to ensure "order and quietness" may have been a result of fear of violence between an overly enthusiastic Black population and the newly returned white residents. The local white community had met similar celebrations by Black people of achievements and victories with violence. In fact, in April of 1866, down the peninsula at Norfolk, white neighbors attacked a Black parade organized to celebrate the Civil Rights Act resulting in what has become known as the Norfolk Race Riot.[89]

Looking back on her days in Slabtown, Sarah Cadbury identified the reasons why the Black community felt the Civil Rights Act was worth celebrating. She added a footnote to her letter describing the event stating, "Early 1866 Congress enacted a measure to fortify the rights of the Negroes, known as the Civil-Rights Bill."[90] The celebration of "a measure to fortify" rights warranted days of planning ahead of time. On April 19 Cadbury wrote home, "There is to be a celebration in 'Shiloh' church next 3rd day afternoon & they asked permission of the teachers as it will suspend night school for that night."[91] That Cadbury specified that the community would hold their celebration at Shiloh is important, because Shiloh was a church formed and governed by the Black population. Based on Cadbury's descriptions, Shiloh was originally located in Newtown, while a different church operated in Slabtown inside the building the Friends had funded near the school and Friends' residence.[92] Thus, though Cadbury framed the event as requiring the Friends' permission, likely the celebrants wanted to ensure that those who chose to participate in the event would not be missing out on attending night school classes.

The letters of Friends' teachers leave evidence of at least two Black churches in Yorktown. Reverend Thomas Napper led Shiloh. A second church, which was not named, operated in the church building owned by the Friends located by the schoolhouse in Slabtown and was pastored by a Black man named John Carey.[93] These two men led what were clearly distinct entities, but nonetheless they frequently worked together. Friends' letters reference joint meetings in which both Napper and Carey spoke.[94]

Residents invited the teachers to attend their April celebration at Shiloh, and Cadbury described the event in detail in a letter home the following day. When Cadbury and her fellow teachers arrived at the church, "only a few" people were already there because "most of the men were to march from Slabtown across." This procession was "quite a show" according to Cadbury, as participants marched "two & two a large banner carried first & a smaller flag." As they filed into the church it became so crowded that Cadbury described it as "a sea of heads" and noted that "the windows were filled outside." "They draped the banner over the pulpit & a light youth sat & held the flag," Cadbury explained, "gently waving it as the cheers went up, which were many & hearty." Once settled, the crowd allowed Massey to give a "patriotic speech," and after Massey left, a long line of speakers followed. Thomas Napper served as chairman of the event and allowed each speaker five minutes.[95] "The general tenor" Cadbury concluded, "was thanks to God for causing the passing of the bill." While indicating how their understanding of political progress was integrally tied to the workings of a higher spiritual power, subsequent speeches also noted "what they must do now to show themselves true men & citizens."[96]

Multiple veterans of the United States Colored Troops spoke, emphasizing their service and their contribution to the Union cause. "One man said when in the army & about to go to battle, he was called on to 'come forward come forward' & he did go forward, & left his hand on the field," Cadbury reiterated, "Peace came & he was told he might step back out of the way for his betters but he thought he was entitled to come forward in the ranks now as then."[97] His service, and his physical sacrifice of losing a hand, were proof not just of his capacity to participate in the Union cause, but of his ability to continue to help shape the nation that would emerge from the war. Black Southerners, this veteran assured the crowd, did not have to defer to others in the cause of reconstructing the war-torn nation. Rather, as he had had on the battlefield, they would help lead.

Following the soldier speeches, a Dr. Daniel Norton gave a "capital written speech." Cadbury identified Norton as the "judge advocate," likely a nod to his service as a lawyer who frequently represented Black residents in the Freedmen's Bureau Court.[98] Formerly enslaved in Williamsburg, Norton had escaped prior to the Civil War and returned to York County during the conflict.[99] Norton had been invited specifically to give his address and was "bitterly severe on Andrew Johnson, & his affected manner gave full force to his address."[100] According to Norton, Johnson was dead—having died a political death, presumably, when Congress overruled his veto of the Civil Rights Act.

To conclude the event, "one of the elders knelt in prayer, & the mtg broke with the singing of a hymn 'The year of jubilee has come.'"[101] Though they broke the meeting up in time for night scholars to attend classes, Cadbury noted, only one scholar had arrived by the time she and her fellow teachers returned to Slabtown. Instead of holding classes, the teachers left to observe the ongoing festivities around town.[102]

That this event happened at Shiloh, a church presumably independent of the Friends' oversight, is an important reminder that though churches in the era of refugee settlements often get attributed to white benevolent workers' efforts, Black people organized their own. Here too, Friends' teachers often assumed that newly free people were in the process of gaining a Christian understanding, rather than acknowledge that formerly enslaved people had a religious worldview that was already formed and deeply connected to their politics.[103] Still, in the observations of the Friends' teachers, important realities about these churches and their successes in defining freedom become visible.

Shiloh was not the only church founded and led by Black ministers on the Virginia Peninsula during the emancipation period. For example, Alexander Dunlap founded a Black Baptist church in Williamsburg while Peter Sheppard led the Bethel African American Methodist Episcopal Church in Hampton.[104] Elsewhere in occupied Virginia, American Missionary Association workers observed that refugees "seem to prefer their own colored ministers to us." Another AMA missionary noted that refugees were "inclined to 'prefer a colored teacher'" in their church services.[105]

It seems likely that Black residents preferred the independence they experienced in Black-led churches to the paternalism evident in white-led congregations. Even Carey's church experienced a distinct level of oversight from the Friends, most notably in the fact that the white teachers kept the key to the church building and the congregants had to return the key after their services were over. Unwilling to spend extra amounts of oil to light the church, and generally disapproving of the services that tended to go long into the night, Friends teachers required the services to end by a certain time. Sarah Cadbury recalled one meeting that went longer than the teachers approved: "The sounds and unsettlement continuing after ten Mary went over and made them leave and give her the key."[106]

This comment about "unsettlement" was a constant refrain in teachers' observations of Black services, as the teachers did not approve of the level of excitement often involved in Black residents' religious practice. Describing the "unsettlement" at this particular event, Cadbury explained that she and her fellow teachers had left the service long before ten. "Carey does not get up such excitements," she complained, "& I think it is a remnant of heathenism such yelling religion."[107] This "yelling religion" of which she disapproved referenced the sermon performed by Thomas Napper, who had apparently filled in for Carey. Again, this tension was not unique to York County but was replicated in other settlements in the wartime South. Amy Murrell Taylor notes that many white Northerners "found themselves impressed by the vigor of Black preachers but skeptical that they had the knowledge and discipline to be sanctioned by their organizations."[108] If white missionaries would not sanction Black preachers to speak in their churches, Black residents would establish their own and hold separate services. [109]

Yet Cadbury and her fellow teachers frequently sought Napper's services out, at times traveling to Shiloh specifically to hear him preach. Upon arriving at the service, Cadbury reported, "We found a room full, the service about done, and one woman whirling around, held by a man, in a 'power.'" Though they disapproved of such behavior, Cadbury also noted that the teachers listened in to a conversation Napper was having with some girls outside of the church. Though she described its delivery as "homely," Cadbury confessed Napper's teachings were composed of "good sound doctrine."[110] In this, Napper had clearly surprised Cadbury as she found that despite her distaste for his animated style, she had to acknowledge he knew his Bible and Christian teachings.

Other white teachers complained similarly of Black church services that involved too much activity as far as the benevolent workers were concerned. "The excitable people protract their evening meetings far into the night," Lucy

Chase wrote from Norfolk, Virginia, in 1864. She continued, "Their spiritual gratifications are emotional, rather than rational, and they rock, and sing, and wail, and howl."[111] Yet this attempt to dismiss newly free people's understanding of their faith as emotional rather than rational ignored the many ways in which these churches and their leaders exhibited a deep understanding of the Bible, as Cadbury's reference to "sound doctrine" indicates. Despite her reservations about their style of worship, Cadbury frequently expressed wonder at how well the Black preachers knew the Bible, and as the comments of teachers with regard to students' desire to learn to read the Bible for themselves indicate, refugees were constantly working towards deepening their faith.

Cadbury confessed to her family that though the Black ministers' style of speech was often different from what she was used to, "they have such lots of scripture at their tongues & bring in constantly most apropros quotations from all parts of the Bible." Far from simply emotional appeals, these pastors drew on a vast knowledge of Scripture and a deep understanding of how it related to and applied to the topics at hand. Carey even "indulge[d] in poetry," according to Cadbury, and she frequently reflected on services as good despite their differences.[112] Margaret Thorpe likewise noted an appreciation for Carey's sermons, commenting, "His sermons are original, earnest, and quaintly expressed."[113]

What white teachers described as remnants of "heathenism," can also be interpreted as evidence of community participation in church services that often served not only to strengthen people's faith through teaching, but to imagine what the future of freedom held for people who had finally left slavery behind. It was in many ways a deeply democratic space in which members of the community were welcomed to fully participate rather than simply observe.[114] Upon visiting the other teachers at Newtown, Cadbury described finding the teachers standing outside of the church observing the closing of a morning meeting. They found "a crowd of men & women jumping up & down . . . one man singing something & the rest joining in a chorus women screaming." Not subject to the oversight of the teachers and thus able to continue their services as long as they wanted, these congregants finally ended their meeting laughing "& some women lit pipes," further surprising their white observers.[115]

Black congregants participated in the church services in a variety of ways, dancing and singing, as Cadbury mentioned, but also offering their own thoughts when welcomed to speak from the pulpit.[116] In a joint service, after both Carey and Napper had spoken, a man identified as "brother Cook" got up to speak and "became eloquent and renewed the promise that tho their sins be black as scarlet & c." In response to his message, some women in the audience began what Cadbury described as a "dirge."[117] Yet what Cadbury initially described as a "dirge" also appears to have been a direct verbal response of affirmation to Cook's words. Another woman made her opinion clear, standing and declaring, "that's so" and "yes, He does."[118] In the absence of Carey or Napper, Sarah Cadbury noted that instead the church service featured "2 lengthy discourses from deacons."[119] In another instance, Cadbury noted that Napper performed an evening service with Peter Dorsey, a leading member of the church community.[120]

Whatever their methods, the churches had a discernable impact on the community even the white teachers had to acknowledge. In mid-1866, Sarah Cadbury noted, "There is a great religious revival here now," and her young students could be found praying after class. Outside of the classroom Cadbury noticed women in the community gathered "in a praying state of mind."[121] Formerly enslaved people across the South prioritized "the ability to order their own lives, removed from white direction" and the church was a central institution in this effort.[122]

Regardless of whether white neighbors approved of their habits, Black churches in Yorktown were undeniably centers of political power where congregants expressed and constructed their hopes for the future. They were also spaces where the Black community organized to ensure their visions of freedom were acknowledged and respected by white authorities. Sarah Cadbury described a service at the church in Slabtown in which a "young preacher from Acretown" spoke, followed by a "deacon of 'Shiloh,'" and then a young Black man. This last speaker "depicted how their condition was changed," and emphasized that the Black community no longer answered to white "master" and "mistress."[123] Finally, Daniel Norton spoke. Cadbury described Norton as "a light colored man of Slabtown who was elected by them to be in the Freedman Bureau Court and plead for them," a nod towards Norton's position of leadership in the community, and the trust his neighbors had placed in him to represent them. Norton spoke that night because though elected by the people, General Armstrong had told them they must pick a white person instead of Norton to represent them. "Speaking like a lawyer," Cadbury recalled, Norton declared that as the duly elected representative, he was in office regardless of Armstrong's desires and the congregation intended to "stand at his back."[124] Norton's mention of being "duly elected" was another reference indicating sophisticated political organization of the Black community in Yorktown. Bureau agents had instructed Black residents to pick a representative to fill the position on the court and they had used their own voting structure to do so.[125]

Bureau agents too recognized that the churches were the heart of the community and that when they needed access to the people they had to go through the church. Related to a matter of soldiers' bounties, General S. C. Armstrong instructed his agent at Yorktown, "bring this matter before the people through their churches," knowing that this was the best way to distribute information.[126] Sarah Cadbury recalled that Armstrong and Massey both used church services as opportunities to address the people.[127]

In some cases, Black residents chose to take their disputes to the church before resorting to the Freedmen's Bureau Court. In one such case, Richard Hamilton sought reimbursement of money Robert Francis owed him. Apparently, Francis and Hamilton had such frequent business interactions that they could not agree on how much money Francis might owe. They determined to take the matter before the church and settled upon an amount, but Francis did not have the money available to pay. Hamilton then took his case before the bureau court, who ruled in favor of the same amount that had already been decided upon, presumably in deliberation with the church.[128]

Another incident indicated the reasons why Black residents distrusted the idea of a white person representing them on the bureau court, and their willingness to arm themselves to protect their interests if necessary. On May 20, 1866, a heated conversation occurred between Robert Lewis, a Black man, and W. B. Jones, a white man, that resulted in Lewis striking Jones. According to Lewis, the conversation involved the "comparative merits of the two races" and he believed Jones was about to strike him when Lewis acted in defense and knocked Jones down. When brought before the court, Jones would not repeat the content of the conversation, and a witness claimed he saw Lewis strike Jones first. That there was more to the situation than the white justice, Robert H. Power, repeated to Lieutenant Massey in his account of the day's events seems likely because Power admitted that a friend of Jones, John F. Chapman, came into the court during the proceedings intoxicated and attempted to attack Lewis. The court determined that if Lewis could give security in the amount of $500, he would not be sent to jail, but Lewis unsurprisingly could not provide the securities. For his outburst, the court only fined Chapman "a small amount."[129]

When the court proceedings adjourned, Power explained, they found "a number of Freedmen in the street immediately in front of the door who appeared to be much excited." This group intended, Power observed, to ensure that Lewis "should not be carried away."[130] Unable to contact Massey, Power went to the "soldiers encampment," found the highest ranking officer, and informed him that he believed the group was about to cause a "disturbance" and requested that he send soldiers to the courthouse to retain Lewis.[131]

Before Massey could return and get to the bottom of the day's events, Robert Lewis escaped with the help of other Black residents. In a subsequent report on May 23, Massey explained to General Armstrong that Robert Lewis pretended he was sick and was taken to a doctor's office. While the doctor prepared medicine, Lewis jumped "through the window and ran for dear life." The guard, doctor, "and others" immediately pursued Lewis but "not less than two hundred 'Freedmen' sprang up as it were by magic fully armed [and] prepared to keep him at any cost." Massey's use of the phrase "sprang up as it were by magic" suggests that this was a coordinated effort. Such coordination would have been made possible by community organizations such as churches where residents could plan group resistance ahead of time.

Lewis, Massey reported, was "still at liberty." To his credit, Massey acknowledged that the situation was difficult, and that white citizens' hostility toward the bureau and newly free people contribute to the problem. White "Civil Authorities" had, according to Massey, "telegraphed Richmond for a regiment of Virginia Militia and state they will have the prisoner if it takes every white man in the County." For their part, Black residents "swear he will never be taken and are fully prepared for anything which may occur."[132] Still, Black residents were not arming themselves against the bureau but against their hostile white neighbors. Massey concluded his summation of events by assuring Armstrong that he had the ability to quell any disturbance that might arise, and that Black residents had already assured him that they would support his decision. It seems evident that in arming themselves, Black residents were not trying to start problems, but rather defend themselves against unjust and violent treatment at the hands of others. They were willing to work with the bureau when the bureau was willing to defend their interests.

Historian Robert F. Engs has noted that in the immediate aftermath of the war, as hostile white residents returned to the Virginia Peninsula, Black residents not only met white violence with violence of their own, but also "began to manifest an aggressive spirit of racial pride."[133] A "Black mob" publicly whipped three white men who "caused a disturbance in the Freedman's Store" in Hampton. In another instance, white Union soldiers staged a raid on another community called Slabtown, located in Hampton, and in response Black residents hung them up by their thumbs.[134] Engs observed that in York County, where the population discrepancy was largest between Black and white residents, Black residents were convinced that "Union victory put them on par with or a level above whites who had been rebels."[135] If local white residents would not respect that equality, Black residents would defend it by force. As the incident in York County indicates, sometimes this meant circumventing the desires even of US officials to ensure that Black residents could protect one another.

Clearly, Black residents had good reason to feel the need to arm themselves as well as mistrust the ability of white judicial authorities to render fair judgments in cases involving Black people. Moreover, the seemingly drastic response from the white community to go so far as to request militia units gestures toward a power dynamic at work that Black residents were prepared to take advantage of: The Black population in York County vastly outnumbered the white population.

When they felt Massey and his agents were not representing their best interests, Black residents did not hesitate to go above him. Again, these instances reflect a mentality among newly free people that they were partners with the bureau and as citizens had every right to negotiate with the government agency. By going above Massey, they sought to correct perceived wrongs and help the bureau in its mandated work to ensure that Black Southerners' rights were protected. Croxton Loomis, a Black resident of York County, took such action in August of 1866, addressing himself to "Genl S C Armstrong the Chief Ruler over the Peninsula of James" to contest a ruling against him by the bureau court. Loomis had stood trial in front of the court because, he claimed, one of Massey's "colored men" had charged him "of shooting a government ox." Loomis felt that the court had not proven his guilt, and that they had unfairly imposed a fine of twenty dollars.[136] The people Loomis identified as Massey's "colored men" were Aaron Jackson and Silas Smith, both employed as teamsters for the bureau. Jackson claimed to have seen Loomis carrying a gun while following an ox, and shortly thereafter he heard a gunshot and found the ox dead. Smith testified similarly, though he said he could not identify the man he saw following the ox.[137] It is worth noting that Massey organized the bureau court without Daniel Norton or another Black representative, and Loomis stood trial before Massey; Robert H. Powers, the presiding justice of York County; and Edward C. Darlington, associate justice of York County. According to Loomis, the testimony of Jackson and Smith failed "to prove any charge against me," but he likewise could not provide his own witnesses. Still, he was unwilling to pay the fine and wanted Armstrong to give him advice on how to proceed.[138] Records do not indicate what became of Loomis's trial, but Armstrong did forward the letter to Massey to inquire about the case.[139]

In another instance, Armstrong ordered Massey to investigate a petition that had come to him from residents of Garretts Farm, under Massey's jurisdiction. According to the petitions, Levy and Ana Foster complained "of being struck by one Duncan who lives on Garretts farm and of receiving no redress from you." Armstrong requested that Massey provide the facts of the case for his review.[140] Again, records do not indicate what the outcome of this petition was, but the fact that it exists testifies to an important reality. Black residents knew it was the bureau's responsibility to defend their rights, and when they felt those rights were not being properly protected, they pushed the issue and sought redress. Already in 1866 Black residents conceived of themselves as citizens and demanded that with citizenship came government protection of their rights.

Too often, studies of the refugee communities that emerged during the Civil War assume that when the war passed, so did these communities. It is true that in many instances, the physical reminders of those communities disappeared from the war-torn landscape. Yet the institutions that Black refugees created during this tumultuous period endured and would become the back bones of the free society Black Southerners built. As historian Cassandra Newby-Alexander has explained, it was during the "chaos of this crucial [military] occupation" and immediate postwar period that the Virginia Peninsula "witnessed the emergence of a Black leadership" who "fought for their autonomy through the founding of political and later quasi-religious institutions."[141] Men like Daniel Norton, Peter Cook, and Thomas Napper, and churches like Shiloh, would play integral roles in coordinating the Black community's efforts to construct a meaningful freedom in York County. Moreover, the institutions and political strategies the entire community developed during and immediately after the war enabled Black residents to maintain their claim on the postwar landscape.

CHAPTER 3

★ ★ ★ ★ ★ ★ ★ ★

"We Can Take Care of Ourselves Now"

Establishing Independent Labor and Industry

In May of 1866, Lieutenant F. J. Massey, the Freedmen's Bureau agent in charge of York County, wrote to his superior officer of a conversation he had had with a formerly enslaved man. "When asked if the new freedpeople would be able to provide for themselves," Massey reported the man had replied, "'We used to support ourselves and our masters, too, when we were slaves, and I reckon we can take care of ourselves now.'"[1] In this assertion, the interviewee highlighted the reality that white observers often missed: Formerly enslaved people had always been the backbone of the Southern economy. They emerged from slavery with the skills necessary to support themselves and knew that they were capable of doing so. Key to their success in these efforts would be the ability to direct the course of their own labor, rather than have their labor controlled by another external force. Black residents of York County had to navigate this tension between white benevolent workers' vision of managed Black freedom, and their own aspirations for independence.

A copy of an undated letter from members of the Black oystering community addressed to Major General John M. Schofield survives in Freedmen's Bureau records as a testimony to the way that the community understood their right to labor and access to independent industry. Schofield was the military governor of Virginia from 1867 until March 1868, when he became Secretary of War under President Andrew Johnson. Though the letter is undated, it likely originates from Schofield's time as governor of Virginia. The petitioners, Cary Redcross, Samuel Scott, John Rich, Charles Redcross, and James Christian represented the interests of oystermen in the York County area.[2] "In behalf of themselves and others who live by catching Oysters," they explained to Schofield that "the existing law of Virginia forbidding the catching of oysters in the months of June July and August bears grievously upon your petitioners." Recently, they explained, oystering had been "laborious and uncertain . . . [furnishing] the scantiest livelihood." The past winter and spring the weather had been "unusually inclement" and as a result oyster catching was significantly less productive during those seasons. Oystermen's labor during this period had "barely sufficed to buy their daily bread," and these men wanted to ensure they could provide for their families.[3] Anticipating the response from white authorities, the petitioners further explained, "it is in vain we are told to seek employment on the land, we have neither land, team, nor implements to crop for ourselves and we cannot get employment without going to a distance and leaving our families destitute." Additionally, they had invested their capital in boats and tongs and "our skill is to oyster, and our business is on the water." In this last assertion, the petitioners identified the inherent conflict at work in Yorktown. White authorities, eager to prove the merits of free-labor farming, sought to manage Black people's labor and encouraged them to farm for wages. Black residents, however, sought independent employment and wanted to protect their access to their chosen industry on the water.

These men felt the restriction on seasonal oystering was not the only problem. They further noted that "the state of Virginia charges each of us five dollars for a license to oyster, besides the usual State and County taxes." This was a heavier tax than "any other class of men who live by their daily labor is required to pay." They demonstrated their expertise in their field, going on to explain to Schofield that the justification for the seasonal restriction of oystering was based on a false premise. Those who had supported the restriction claimed that oystering in the summer months was "injurious to the beds," but, the petitioners explained, "the highest scientific authority, as well as common sense, pronounce the idea fallacious. Working in those months neither increases nor diminishes the number of oysters," and they went on to explain why this was the case. Those who had forced this legislation through, the petitioners insisted, "have other employment during the summer" and their "interests lie in an opposite direction from ours."[4] Allowing these laws to remain in effect would deprive these oystermen of their livelihood and with it their independence.

Cary Redcross and his fellow oystermen concluded their letter by appealing to their rights as citizens as well as to the same logic by which the Freedmen's Bureau had been operating for the previous two years. "We therefore humbly pray," they wrote, "that an order . . . be issued providing that all citizens of Virginia who have paid for a license to oyster, shall be permitted to catch oysters at any season of the year." If Schofield met their request, they assured him, "We can support our families." But if he did not do so, they would end up in the very position the bureau had claimed it wanted to avoid. "If driven from our lawful calling," they warned, "necessity will compel some to beg and many to steal, who would otherwise live by honest labor."[5] Their reference to "all citizens of Virginia" was a direct reminder that Black oystermen were now part of both the business and political community and that their rights must be protected the same as any other citizen's.

The petitioners' suggestion that without a change in policy many independent oystermen would become dependent on charity or resort to theft was not simply an appeal to Schofield's sense of justice. It was also strategic. In the latter years of the Civil War, and those that immediately followed the war, concerns about Black dependence were rampant among white workers in refugee communities. White observers filled their letters and reports with descriptions of refugees as helpless, needing assistance, and incapable of laboring for themselves. "Should we not consider the danger and suffering attendant upon the passage from slavery to freedom," *The Friend* intoned in July of 1864, urging its readers to contribute "funds to enable us to continue the work so favorably commenced."[6] Many white workers believed that having just emerged from slavery, Black people would not know how to be industrious members of society, and they directed their efforts towards addressing this concern. Thus, Cary Redcross and his fellow oystermen positioned their case so that their white audience, General Schofield, would be more inclined to be receptive if he was not already receptive to their basic appeal to mutual citizenship. This was a particularly insightful strategy because Schofield was not known for being sympathetic to the cause of Black citizenship or political equality.

As historian Julie Saville has argued, white Northerners who engaged in the work of Reconstruction believed they were "planting . . . a new social order." This social order rested on free wage labor modeled after their experiences in the North. Their work was part of an ongoing conversation that had commenced long before slavery began to crumble about the merits of free labor and what composed a functional economy.[7]

Moreover, the Northern missionaries who descended upon the war-torn South were not new to benevolent endeavors, but rather participants in a longer history of reform work that had been remaking the American North since the Revolution and especially since the Industrial Revolution. Institutions in the North such as penitentiaries, asylums, and halfway houses were not just sites of individual uplift, but spaces in which religious and quasi-religious workers sought to define the values and characteristics of the emerging American nation.[8] They sought to instill specific values and ideas in their charges that they believed would create a stable, functional society. In this vision, a stable, functional society was marked by manageable class relations and compliant workers. Benevolent workers in the South, sent from many of the same organizations who had sponsored these institutions in the North, should be understood in this context. Just as they had confronted a population in the North unwilling to unconditionally accept their prescribed values, in the South they encountered the same resistance. In the complaints of Northern missionaries who believed they observed sloth, filth, laziness, and a propensity to shirk work in the newly free population they were charged to assist, historians should look back and see an ongoing negotiation. That missionaries did not understand their circumstances as such is evidence of their unwillingness to recognize resistance as negotiation. Moreover, reformers were unwilling to accept labor systems that did not conform to their specific visions or laborers who did not support the interests of property owners.

Saville notes that in the South Carolina Sea Islands, formerly enslaved people "introduced patterns of land use and production that were rooted in a conception of freedom older than the historically peculiar form held out to them by Northern emancipators." Before white Northerners arrived, Black residents had instituted a system of farming that is difficult to fully recover given that available descriptions of it come from those same Northerners who described the arrangement as "disorderly," "barbaric" and otherwise labeled noncompliant Black refugees as impediments to the "bourgeois agrarian society" white administrators hoped to achieve.[9] Wartime plantation managers, Saville explains, "identified duty, industry, foresight, and energy with labor that produced the regional staple for a world market." Formerly enslaved people, however, often chose to engage in "nonwage alternatives" that allowed them to "produce what they could use directly." Thus, individuals chose to cultivate crops that could sustain their existence rather than work for wages and produce staple crops for a global market. White observers in turn chose to label these actions as "privilege, laziness, ignorance, and ease."[10] Though the arrangements white supervisors sought to establish differed in some respects, such as promising compensation in cash or in kind, they always envisioned "centralized management

by which workers could be obligated to perform a full range of general chores
. . . as features of a wage relationship." Newly free people, on the other hand,
"expected to organize agricultural production directly."[11] As Saville points out,
the bias of the historical record and the loaded terms with which white benevolent workers evaluated Black residents' efforts to direct their own labor makes
it difficult to recover exactly how formerly enslaved people organized their industry. But by re-examining these records, and emphasizing surviving sources
like the oystermen's petition, the process by which Black residents negotiated
their circumstances and sought to define their lives in freedom becomes visible
again.

Though each settlement's situation differed in their particulars, the same
fundamental problem of white Northerners' proscribed vision of "free-labor,"
defined as wage labor rather than independent subsistence, persisted throughout the postwar South.[12] In their letters, reports, and newspaper articles, white
benevolent workers reiterated a commitment to a free-labor society that required managed and directed labor for Black refugees. It was not so much a
freedom of labor they wanted to institute, but a freedom to labor for wages
under the watchful eye of white supervisors. When Black residents' expectations and desires conflicted with or impeded the progress of this vision, as Saville points out, their actions enter the written record in negative terms.[13]

At Yorktown, as elsewhere, the Friends arrived concerned about "making"
refugees become "self-supporting." While they recognized that the situation
at Yorktown presented something of a humanitarian crisis—a massive influx
of people to such a small, inhospitable place would always produce want and
suffering—the Friends were constantly anxious that their charity would lead
people to choose not to labor. As Chandra Manning and Amy Murrell Taylor
have artfully demonstrated, this was an unavoidable dilemma produced by the
necessities of war. Most of the refugee communities that resembled Yorktown
in their longevity—Roanoke Island, Port Royal, Fort Monroe, and others along
the Carolina coasts—came into existence early in the war because of their strategic military location. They existed at the entrance to navigable waterways
that the US Army prized for tactical reasons. Yet the very same geographic
realities that made these places valuable military installations simultaneously
made it difficult to protect and provide for the tens of thousands of people who
sought refuge behind Union lines. Coastal forts like Fort Monroe, as Manning
highlights, would never produce fresh water. The sandy soil and hurricane-
prone landscape of Roanoke Island would never support the agricultural needs

of a large population.[14] In York County, soil long ago depleted by tobacco farming would not regenerate to again support single-crop production.

Still, as the letter from the York County oystermen testifies, these coastal areas did offer alternate forms of industry. In the antebellum era, free Black residents on the peninsula worked in water-related industries as well as in skilled crafts such as carpentry, woodcutting, and teamstering.[15] Even large plantation owners utilized some of their enslaved labor force in harvesting the rich waters of the various rivers in the area.[16]

Prior to the outbreak of the Civil War, the region contained both large plantations and small farms, but as historian Edna Green Medford has noted, it also "possessed a sufficient quantity of nonagricultural industries" that had allowed for the diversification of the economy.[17] Hampton, Yorktown, and Newport News all served as trade centers, though to an outside observer, especially one from Northern cities such as Philadelphia, they would have appeared to be little more than villages.[18] Their respective counties were also home to "more varied manufacturing establishments," because of the small towns located therein.[19] In the eighteenth century, Yorktown had functioned as the main port of entry for enslaved Africans transported to Virginia, and enslaved residents of the city labored to keep the port functioning.[20] Tobacco farming's depletion of the soil had resulted in a need to diversify the economy so that farms produced wheat, corn, and oats in addition to tobacco.[21] Enslaved people hired out by their enslavers primarily worked on these farms, but they also worked on the docks, as carpenters and blacksmiths, and in sawmills.[22] Medford further notes that even small farmers engaged in these industries when they needed additional income.[23] A diversified personal economy was an established norm in York County by the outbreak of the Civil War.

Additionally, by 1860, the majority of people who did not farm worked in water-related industries, including fishing, oystering, and boat transportation. After agriculture and water-industries, the most common occupation on the peninsula was in the lumber industry.[24] Black residents' efforts to capitalize on these opportunities during and after the war are often lost in accounts of these communities written from the perspective of white workers. Histories such as those of Roanoke Island and Port Royal are almost exclusively focused on the worlds white Republicans wanted to build—worlds defined by Northerners who believed their efforts in the wartime South could lend credence to their argument that free labor was superior to enslaved labor. While concerned about the humanitarian needs of the Black refugees who inhabited these coastal communities, benevolent workers were also constantly concerned about making newly free people productive and measured their success by output and volume. In this framing, willingness to labor for someone else's profit defined productivity rather than a desire to labor enough to sustain a family's economic independence.

A closer look at the conditions at Yorktown, however, reveals that white reformers' ideas of success clashed with those of the Black residents whose labor they wanted to manage. Where white benevolent workers saw failure because of small outputs or resistant Black laborers, a second glance reveals Black Southerners charting a path to independence. That independence required only subsistence was not something white Northerners intent on proving the productive capacity of free labor could appreciate. To their eyes it looked like shirking work and aspiring to less than what was possible. Yet at Yorktown, as elsewhere, Black residents resisted white Northerners' efforts to direct their labor and to define the parameters of their labor and their opportunities. In some cases, such as with York County's oystermen, the very same geography that impeded white missionaries' farming efforts provided the means for Black residents' independent labor and entrance into larger trade networks.

As early as 1863, Black refugees at Yorktown were hard at work fishing and oystering amid the war's chaos. Isaac Wistar, the US commander who ordered the establishment of Slabtown and Newtown, remembered that when he arrived in Yorktown "permits to take oysters from the private beds within our jurisdiction were sold to negroes for cash, for which there was no public or known accounting whatsoever."[25] To address this perceived problem, Wistar had the provost marshal begin selling oystering permits.[26] Wistar and the Union army were not encouraging the creation of a new trade opportunity, but rather seeking to regulate one that was already well established.

Cary Redcross and his fellow petitioners also testified to this longevity of the trade in their petition. In mentioning the "capital" the oystermen had invested in their efforts, they reminded Schofield that they had made intentional choices about where to direct their resources and labor. In Cary and Charles Redcross's cases, and likely others whom they represented in their petition, this was especially true because they had worked as oystermen before the war. They had invested in their future, and their need now was a result of external forces that sought to limit their productivity, not a lack of effort on their own part.

Even those individuals who had not been free before the war were likely seeking to employ skills they had developed in slavery. Oystering and fishing with seines was a long-established practice in the region, and in the decades following the war, observers noted that "as a rule, the tongers in this section of Virginia are" people of color.[27] That so many of the people employed in this particular industry were Black in the postwar era suggests that they were also the people who had been primarily engaged in it prior to the war, and thus possessed the skill sets required. Oystermen could harvest oysters from small boats in shallow water by using tongs—large pincers that could scrape the bottom and pull up the catch—allowing for people of varying economic standing to enter the trade.[28] Those who could not immediately buy tools for themselves at times borrowed equipment from others. During this period, nature alone created limitations on when oystermen could work.[29] Thus, tongers especially worked for themselves, from their own boats, under terms of a license that allowed them to harvest in public waters, as the petitioners noted.[30]

In addition to independence, oystering also promised substantial financial reward. Going rates for oysters were high enough that oystermen could provide for their families while still saving money for the offseason as long as weather conditions cooperated.[31] Moreover, in the postwar period oystermen usually achieved a higher standard of living than farm laborers or independent farmers.[32] Women and children could join in the trade, sometimes working as oyster shuckers, though for less pay than men. This did not offer the same kind of independence as tonging, but shuckers could make a reasonable wage.[33]

Thus, the men who took their cause before General Schofield had a lot to lose if prevented from engaging in their chosen trade. Other Black oystermen resisted the new tax by refusing to pay it, which brought them before the bureau court in October of 1866. Fred C. Newman, the white inspector of oyster tax, brought ten men before the court under charges that they were catching oysters in his district, had not paid the oyster tax, and most importantly, were refusing to pay it. Unfortunately, the bureau court did not record the details of each case. Court records acknowledge that Newman's case against Jackson Tolliver, a Black oysterman, involved the tax and Tolliver's refusal to pay it. But rather than record each subsequent man's testimony, the clerk simply noted "same as case of Jackson Tolliver." That these men came before the court at the same time, however, suggests that they may have coordinated their efforts to refuse to pay the tax, and Newman had encountered their collective resistance.[34]

Still, the white Northerners who labored in these places put their faith in a free-labor society and attempted to make these places, and the people

Figure 3. Caricature of Black oysterman tonging. From *Puck* magazine, 1903. Library of Congress.

who inhabited them, "self-supporting." This term, too, is misleading. When the Friends employed the term "self-supporting" they did not mean that individual households should produce for their own subsistence. They meant, more specifically, that collective Black labor produced a profit for the community that could cover the expenses of the assets the benevolent groups distributed. Resources such as farming implements were not donations but rather investments in a future financial return. As early as February 1864, before the Friends had even established their first school in Yorktown, they reported back to their Northern brethren that they could ensure refugees would become self-supporting if they helped furnish them "with some agricultural implements, and seeds, roots, &c., for planting."[35] *The Friend* reiterated this assertion with evidence from John C. Tatum, a Friend who had recently arrived in Yorktown. Tatum had assured them that "one of the best modes of helping the freedmen, will be the furnishing of some aid in their work on the ground allotted to them."[36] This aid, however, was more than material because the Friends wanted also to supervise and direct cultivation.

It is easy to mistake the Friends' emphasis on "self-supporting" farming for independent farming, because the term "self-supporting" lends itself to that conclusion. Often, however, independent farming is not what the Friends had in mind. Rather, when they employed the term "self-supporting" they meant they wanted to establish financially viable supervised farming operations where Black people's labor paid for their basic needs. Operations on the Virginia Peninsula, directed from Fort Monroe, frequently took the form of "government farms," which were sustained by Black labor under the supervision of a white overseer.[37]

Charles Wilder, the General Superintendent of Negro Affairs in the Department of Virginia and North Carolina, described the system implemented on the peninsula in December of 1864. Wilder explained that instead of issuing refugees rations, government authorities had "encouraged" refugees to work by providing them "with such subsistence as they need, and it was charged against their share of the crop." In other words, US officials did not provide food for survival for free but rather took an equivalent amount of the crop after the harvest to cover the cost of what refugees had needed. Through this system, Wilder claimed, formerly enslaved people had gained "a self reliant knowledge that they can take care of themselves" and were thus prepared for freedom. This work of "preparing" formerly enslaved people for freedom depended "upon the influences brought to bear upon" them.[38] Again, in this statement Wilder assumed that for Black freedom to be a success certain outside "influences" had to guide their efforts.

First authorized by General John Dix, the commander of the Department of Virginia, in spring of 1863, this system Wilder celebrated involved relocating refugees who had sought refuge in the various cities of the peninsula onto outlying abandoned plantations. Many refugees had traveled from rural areas of Virginia, and white authorities believed they were not prepared for urban life and were better suited for agricultural labor.[39] Consequently, they justified removal from cities like Hampton, Newport News, and Yorktown, on the grounds that rural farm life was better for formerly enslaved people. Most individuals sent to government farms worked in field gangs under the supervision of a government-appointed overseer. As was the case in South Carolina, this newly implemented system displaced Black residents who had already established independent farms on abandoned lands outside of the various refugee settlements.[40]

By the time Wilder wrote his report in 1864, federal authorities had established at least eighty-five farms in James City, York, and Warwick Counties. As they did outside of Fort Monroe, a large portion of individuals employed on these farms worked in the gang system under the supervision of an overseer.[41] Government authorities took half the profits of the farming operations, while laborers were supposed to receive a share of what was left determined by the amount of labor they had performed.[42] Many, however, received rations instead of pay.[43] Though, as the Friends suggested, Black laborers were provided with the tools they needed to produce corn and other grains, the cost of those implements were also deducted from the profits of the operations.[44] By compensating individuals' labor with material goods rather than pay, government agents limited their ability to direct their resources as they saw fit. Thus, formerly enslaved people could not, for example, choose to budget their pay to invest in another industry or buy their own land.

By the end of the war, the Assistant Superintendent of Negro Affairs stationed at Yorktown, reported that he had twenty-three farms under his control in York County.[45] His letter suggested that conditions differed slightly at Yorktown because he had "received no instruction in regard to the management of these people, and have been guided by my own judgment." This involved, apparently, leasing 3,603 acres "almost exclusively to colored persons."[46] Though these leasing agreements may have given Black residents more control over their labor, the Friends in Yorktown had a similar system of benevolence that sought to compensate the Friends for the goods they "gave" to newly free people. For example, at Newtown, Black residents paid for more than three-fourths of the clothing items sent to the community.[47]

In May of 1864, the Friends reported from Yorktown that they had successfully established a knitting school and that yarn was in great demand. They anticipated stocking their store with more yarn in the future. Yet even in the celebration of their knitting training, their reports suggest that other women were actively seeking independent employment through knitting. In closing their report, the correspondent to *The Friend's Review* noted, "I have many applications for young women to knit and put it in the store, but I think it better to reserve that work for old women who cannot do anything else."[48] This pointed to an important distinction in the work the Friends had undertaken to teach Black women to knit. First, the Friends were having their knitting students produce clothing that could then be sold in the Friends' store in Yorktown. Second, some women who already knew how to knit wanted to sell their products in the store, but the Friends were distinguishing between women they believed could do other labor—young women—and those who could only labor by knitting —old women. This system, like government farms, ensured that the Friends could manage Black labor and profit from it, rather than have Black knitters do so directly. By stipulating who could sell their products in the store, the Friends made determinations about who was "fit" to do something else, such as farm for wages. This was, again, a managed labor system. Though white reformers called it a "free" labor system, they sought to deprive Black residents of the choice of how to allocate their labor.

Apparently, there was some level of distrust on the part of Black women towards this program, though Friends reports only gestured towards it. In a separate report from May, a Friends teacher noted that two sewing schools were operating in Slabtown, but they initially had trouble attracting students. "They regarded it like working for nothing," the teacher noted of Black residents, and applications for attendance did not increase until the school began "distribution of the reticules."[49] The correspondent did not elaborate on the concern that participants felt they were "working for nothing" by attending sewing school, but based on other reports it seems possible that students did not want to produce articles for sale at the store rather than for their own benefit. They wanted—and by withholding their labor demanded—direct compensation. An 1865 report also indicated that the Friends had "procured some coarse sewing to be done for one of the clothing houses of this city," further suggesting that the Friends were not just teaching people to sew, but were actually using "students'" labor to produce articles for distribution by the Friends.[50] Likely the Friends understood this as creating a self-sufficient community, but as the passing reference to "working for nothing" suggests, formerly enslaved people wished to labor for themselves.

In July of 1865, the Friends reported that their efforts to ensure Black residents supported themselves through labor was successful. *The Friends' Review* commented, "a number of hoes and other farming implements, and a quantity of seeds, were furnished to those thus employed, and the cost of these has been since returned to us from the proceeds of their labor." Again, this comment gestured towards the reality that though the Friends framed many of their efforts as donations of supplies to assist in Black residents' labor, they were equally invested in ensuring that Black residents bore the cost of their entry into independent work. Those living in Slabtown and Newtown, *The Friends*

Review continued, who did not cultivate the soil, "gain a livelihood by oystering and fishing; and shoemakers, carpenters, and wheelwrights, ply their respective trades." Again, the Friends framed these developments as the result of their own efforts to "encourage" Black residents into various trades. But oystering was already a well-established enterprise for Black residents of York County, not a consequence of benevolent encouragement. In 1850, York County's free Black population exceeded 2,000 people, and of the nearly one hundred free Black households, almost half claimed a head of household engaged in fishing or oystering.[51] Nancy Battey, a white teacher, acknowledged the prevalence of oystering in a letter home, explaining in December of 1864 that "we hope to commence evening school next week" but they did not expect large crowds because "many of the men go oystering and do not get home until later."[52]

While the Friends sought to design a managed labor system in which Black residents worked at approved trades, and farmed on land overseen by a white supervisor, bureau court records demonstrate that Black residents engaged in a variety of independent forms of labor and industry. As bureau court records regarding partnerships with boats and oyster tongs suggest, oystering supported additional industries in the buying, selling, construction, and repair of equipment. Local residents Anthony Roberts sued Henry Billups, Henry Redcross, and John Roberts before the bureau court for default of payment after he sold a canoe to the defendants for "sixty dollars for which they gave their note" but they had not paid.[53] Modern connotations of the word "canoe" obscure the nature of this case, as it is easy to assume the men were concerned about a small, relatively insignificant vessel. However, oystermen utilized boats called canoes that were larger than the typical two-to-three-person boat propelled by oars. Moreover, these canoes were in regular use by oystermen throughout the peninsula.[54] Evidence suggests these industries included both the Black and white communities in Yorktown, as James N. Topping, identified in court records as white, sued William Randall for nonpayment for labor claiming he "was employed by William Randal . . . to repair his canoe."[55] Similarly, Charles Collins, also identified as white in court records, sued James Dabney for nonpayment for labor, stating he "worked for defendant repairing skiff for which labor . . . is due."[56] Of note in both these cases is the fact that Black boat owners had employed the labor of white repairmen.

Partnerships would have been an expedient way to share labor as well as resources and ensure that Black residents could work independent of white supervision with less upfront investment costs. Pooling their money to buy

RAKING IN SHALLOW WATER—Drawn by Alfred Kappes.

WORKING THE BEDS OFF ANNAPOLIS—Drawn by M. J. Burns.
OYSTERING ON THE CHESAPEAKE—[See Page 22.]

Figure 4. *Oystering on the Chesapeake* in *Harper's Weekly,*
January 11, 1890. Library of Congress.

Figure 5. *Oyster Canoes Unloading at a Packing House* in "Oystering in Hampton Roads," by J. E. Davis, *Southern Workman*, March 1903.

equipment meant they did not have to rely on Friends or other benevolent workers to provide them with their means of production. These partnerships took many forms, as bureau court records attest. George W. Greenwood purchased two pigs and "loaned them out on shares" to Frank Hobdy to raise. Greenwood and Hobdy agreed that Greenwood would pay Hobdy half the price of the pigs after he sold them. Their partnership came before the court when one of the pigs died and Hobdy killed the other and sold it without paying Greenwood part of the proceeds. Hobdy, for his part, claimed he did not need to pay Greenwood because Greenwood had not purchased the feed for the pigs as their initial agreement had stipulated. Greenwood apparently acknowledged this because the court concluded the case stating that he was "willing to take the price he paid for the pigs" and Hobdy agreed to those terms.[57]

Samuel Williams and Abraham Spencer came before the court when their partnership for growing corn broke down. Samuel Williams stated that he and Spencer had "agreed to cultivate a crop of corn on equals shares" but now that the corn was ready Spencer wished "to deprive him of his just rights." Spencer claimed that he had already gathered part of the corn but was willing to divide it.[58] The court appointed a receiver to help divide the crop and ensure both men's investments were honored.

Residents also purchased horses together, likely so that they could mutually benefit from a horse's labor in farming or hauling and share the burden of the monetary investment required. William Washington and Horace Goodwin bought a horse in partnership for eighty dollars. Goodwin testified that he had "hired land and worked it having the use of the horse for the purpose." Washington had paid the larger sum in the transaction, providing fifty dollars of the purchase price while Goodwin paid thirty. According to Goodwin, Washington was to "work at his trade" while Goodwin farmed with the horse and split the proceeds of the corn he produced. However, Washington had apparently grown dissatisfied with the agreement and wanted the horse sold at public auction, which the court agreed to do.[59] Selling the item in question at public auction was frequently the bureau court's solution to partnership issues like Goodwin and Washington's. The judges passed a similar verdict in the case of Armstead Jones, Watt Washington, and Caesar Brooks when the three men came before the court with a dispute over a horse they had bought in partnership from a government sale.[60]

Farming, like oystering, generated additional industries such as hauling and trading in the produce. Richard Hamilton sued William Charnic after selling Charnic corn and boarding him because Charnic had not fully paid him.[61] Abraham McKinney appears to have been a trader or hauler of some kind, as Matthew Taylor brought him to court for default of payment when Taylor sold McKinney three hundred cabbages and paid him to carry them to Jamestown Landing. Based on the various testimonies of witnesses, it appears that McKinney was a middleman for a transaction between Taylor, who raised the cabbage, and "a man named Brown" who lived in Richmond.[62] Similarly, Thomas Jefferson sued Thomas Jones for default of payment after Jefferson worked for Jones "hauling" and had not yet gotten paid.[63] Though the details of this situation are lost, what is abundantly clear is that these men chose to engage directly in the farming economy—trading and negotiating the sale and transport of their produce rather than farming for wages and losing control of their crop.

Bureau court records represent only the fraction of partnership and business transactions that resulted in conflict, but they begin to suggest the diversity of industries Black residents engaged in during and immediately after the war. Though, as many petitioners indicated, white authorities wanted Black residents to seek paid employment in farming, individuals found alternative methods to support themselves. Moreover, that so many individuals brought cases related to their business interests before the court suggests that they fully expected the federal government to support and protect their independent enterprises. Despite the fact that federal officials often tried to pressure Black residents into other forms of labor, Black residents understood that as citizens they had a right to direct their labor and expected the federal government to protect their interests.

In one instance, Griffin Beckett sued Samuel Wooten, a white man, after Beckett "put his colt to the mare of defendant" and Wooten had not yet paid him for his stallion's services.[64] Beckett likewise sued Maxwell Crowfield for the same, though in this case Crowfield testified that his mare later died. Given that Crowfield did not reap the benefit of the pregnancy, he did not think he should have to pay Beckett. William H. Bayley, identified as white in the court records, stated that he kept accounts for Beckett and that it was customary to pay whether breeding services produced a pregnancy or not.[65] Daniel Norton, who bureau court records indicate was actively employed as a lawyer, also performed medical services for the community. Norton's medical practice appeared in court records when he sued Harrison Williams, asserting that Williams had "called on him for medical attendance for his wife" and owed him twenty-five dollars.[66]

Women's labor issues also came before the court. Mary Francis Lockley sued Charles Coyler, a white man, claiming that she had worked for another white man, John Cox, and he was indebted to her when he died. Coyler "took charge of the effects of said Cox and refused to pay her for her labor."[67] Mary Jane Graves sued Samuel Croxton for default of payment for labor, though again the court records did not specify the type of labor Graves performed.[68] Martha Lane, however, specified in her suit against Edmund Garlick that he had "nursed a man named Bird for five weeks before he died." Garlick became the administrator of Bird's estate and "sold the property at auction paying every one but her." The court decided in Lane's favor.[69]

Women's business transactions also often came before the court in the form of claims to payment for their children's labor. Louisa Kidd sued Peter Gillette after her son worked for Gillette for ten weeks and Gillette refused to pay for his work.[70] Likewise, Nancy Allen sued William Morris after her son worked for Morris for three months and had not paid him. In this case, Morris claimed that the boy had not fulfilled the three-month contract and had only worked for a month and a half. During that time, Morris said, he paid Allen's son in clothing "amounting to over twenty dollars." The court dismissed Allen's claim.[71] Adelaide Brisbee sued Daniel Jackson, for whom her daughter had worked almost five months without receiving payment. As in other cases, Jackson claimed he had fulfilled part of his payment by providing Brisbee's daughter with clothing, but acknowledged he owed her wages as well.[72] Hiring out children appears to have been common, as fathers likewise appeared in court to claim payment for their children's labor. For example, William Allen sued John Banks claiming that "he hired his boy to John Banks" and Banks owed him twenty-seven dollars.[73]

As Julie Saville notes, the labor of additional members of a family contributed to the construction of economically independent households.[74] The composition of households in York County in the postwar period allowed for such independence. Over two-thirds of the Black households that emerged after the war were composed of a mother, father, and children. Moreover, around 15 percent of Black households contained adult children over the age of twenty-one whose labor could contribute to the family economy.[75]

Forestry, sawmills, and woodcutting also served as important alternative avenues of employment for residents of the peninsula, especially in York County. Edna Greene Medford notes that the counties of the lower peninsula "abounded in unimproved lands covered with oak, pine, maple, hickory, walnut, and poplar." Sawmills dotted the landscape, and many Black workers labored in them processing ship timber and railroad ties for larger industries. They also produced cord wood for local markets and wood pulp for Northern markets.[76] Farmers could supplement their income with woodcutting and sell the timber from their own lots, and those who did not own land could work cutting the wood from other people's property.[77] However, postwar records also indicate that this budding timber industry attracted Northern investors and speculators to the area.

By 1867 Black residents' industriousness had impressed even Freedmen's Bureau agents. Lieutenant Massey reported in June, "This [county] is entirely tilled by the colored man and the industry and thrift he has manifest during this year has been the subject of remark both by his friends and enemies." Still, however, Massey believed that the large Black community was a problem. He continued, "There are still . . . too large a number of Freedmen remaining in this Co. so long as they remain here in large masses suffering and immorality must ensue."[78] In particular, a "clique" as Massey described them, existed and was working against the bureau's efforts to disperse the Black community.[79]

This group of people Massey identified as a problematic "clique" was composed of individuals who encouraged Black residents to resist the bureau's efforts to exclusively direct the course of their postwar lives. In other refugee communities, such as Freedman's Village at Arlington, Black residents expressed a similar dissatisfaction with the government's efforts. Historian Micki McElya observes that residents of the village just outside of the nation's capital stated that their condition was worse than slavery, and they would prefer to be independent of the supervision of overseers.[80] Residents of Freedman's Village "argued that the military was thwarting both their own aspirations to patriarchal independence and their desires to claim land and build a home free from white authority and surveillance."[81] Black inhabitants of Freedman's Village wanted to be free and felt that federal efforts to police their lives and labor prevented them from truly gaining the independence to which they aspired.

Despite efforts to control and direct Black people's freedom, residents of the Virginia Peninsula carved out independence for themselves in the immediate postwar period. John Townsend Trowbridge visited the area in the months following the end of the war and observed that the peninsula was "the thriftiest portion of Virginia I had seen." "Every house," Trowbridge noted, "had its wood-pile, poultry and pigs, and little garden devoted to corn and vegetables. Many a one had its stable and cow, and horse and cart."[82] The "little village" of Hampton "was surrounded by freedmen's farms, occupying the abandoned plantations of recent rebels."[83] Despite reports that the soil was poor, "the crops looked well."[84] "The business of the place," Trowbridge remarked, was sustained primarily by Black residents who were becoming wealthy, despite paying heavy taxes to the government. Unlike benevolent workers who frequently complained of idleness, Trowbridge asserted, "I made an extensive tour of these farms, anxious to see with my own eyes what the [formerly enslaved people] were doing for themselves. I found no idleness anywhere. Happiness and industry were the universal rule."[85] Trowbridge appreciated the independence these families had carved out for themselves.

An owner of a local sawmill, Trowbridge noted, was having trouble finding laborers for his mill because "the height of freedmen's ambition was to have little homes of their own and to work for themselves."[86] They were succeeding in this goal. One individual Trowbridge visited "had a little lot of half an acre . . . upon which he had built his own house and shop and shed." This person worked as a blacksmith and had a family who he "was supporting without any aid from the government."[87] However, this man had encountered a problem that would plague Black residents of the peninsula in the coming months: He did not own the land upon which he had built his home. "He was doing very well," Trowbridge explained, "until the owner of the soil appeared, with the President's pardon, and orders to have his property restored to him." The owner in question told the man he could rent the land for twenty-four dollars a year, more than twice what the land was worth, according to Trowbridge.[88]

Trowbridge explained that this problem was endemic in the area. Having settled land under the direction of the government during the war, these industrious Black residents were presented with a conundrum when the war ended. Former white residents, still legal owners of the land, were returning to the area and their terms for allowing newly free people to remain were irregular at best, and as was the case for the blacksmith, often unreasonable. Investigating the situation further, Trowbridge noted another instance in which a white landowner offered to rent parcels to Black families for eight dollars an acre, provided that the houses they had built would revert to his possession at the end of a year. According to Trowbridge, the land in question was only worth sixteen dollars an acre, indicating that this man wanted to charge fully half of the land's value for only a year's rent.[89]

Thus, having achieved a substantial level of economic independence during and immediately after the war, Black residents were presented with a new dilemma. With the return of confiscated lands to their prewar owners, current Black occupants were at risk not only of losing their homes, but further of losing the economic investment they had made in those homes and the land they worked. In the ensuing months and years, they would leverage the community ties, institutions, and "cliques" they had built during the war to combat this new threat to the lives they were building in freedom.

CHAPTER 4

★ ★ ★ ★ ★ ★ ★ ★

"They Were Now Citizens"

Defining Civil Rights in the Freedmen's Bureau Court

In May of 1865, General Oliver Otis Howard, head of the Freedmen's Bureau, issued a circular calling for assistant commissioners located throughout the Southern states to establish courts, which would have jurisdiction over cases in which Black individuals were involved.[1] These courts, known today as "Freedmen's Bureau Courts" were part of a larger effort on the part of the bureau to establish some level of judicial equity for Black Southerners. Historians such as James Oakes have asserted that these courts were restricted from the start because as soon as Southern states allowed Black testimony in courts, cases would revert to civil authorities. Within a year of many courts' establishment, they had already ceased to function.[2] Still, bureau courts became important sites of negotiation, places where Black Southerners could bring their cause before federally appointed authorities and where their white neighbors would have to answer for their actions.[3] Moreover, as historian Donald Nieman has noted, bureau courts were a means to resolve disputes among Black people concerning ownership of property, marital relations, and debts.[4]

Yet bureau courts were more than an instrument for adjudicating everyday disputes over property or debt. They were by their very nature sites of federal power, and because the US government had specifically established courts to replace civil authorities, they were corrective institutions. They were the beginning of a new, federally authorized social and political order. Or, at least, they had the capacity to be so. As Steven Hahn argues, the South of 1865 was a liminal political space. The foundation of social and political relations—slavery and the Confederacy—had "almost simultaneously been destroyed, but no new social or political system had either quickly emerged or been imposed to replace them."[5] Southerners, Black and white, in the wake of the war lacked secure standing in political society, and consequently, Hahn further argues, day-to-day life became politicized. Everyday acts such as negotiating labor disputes or bringing problems before federal authorities bore on the "general struggle over socially meaningful power."[6] 1865 was a year of possibility, and Black Southerners approached it as such. In bringing their cases before bureau courts Black residents were doing more than solving everyday disputes. They were claiming and charting the parameters of freedom and placing responsibility on the federal government for protecting and affirming those parameters.

Hahn's description of the 1865 South as a liminal space is an important one. Looking backward, the line from the end of open warfare to the Thirteenth, Fourteenth, and Fifteenth Amendments might appear straight, but it was not. Black Southerners were pursuing a revolutionary new system of government, not simply an extension of customary civil rights to another group of people. As Hahn further notes, the negotiation of this new system happened largely at the local level by means of personal confrontations and community conflicts.[7]

In the records of Yorktown's Freedmen's Bureau Court this negotiation is visible in stark relief. Though their petitions and the words with which they crafted their testimonies are filtered through the lens of a federal agent paraphrasing court cases and classifying issues into formal charges, the intentions of Yorktown's Black residents can still be discerned. Additionally, in their descriptions of their situations and the details of their cases, the work Black residents had already begun becomes clear again. They had not waited until 1865 to initiate their efforts to craft meaningful and productive lives as free people. In Yorktown, by 1865, many Black residents had already made significant strides towards constructing the foundations of freedom they found most valuable— reuniting their families, building a home, engaging in an independent trade, and investing in the tools of their trade, among others. As historian Hannah Rosen notes, Black Southerners "embraced the years after emancipation as a time of enormous possibility" and sought to realize those possibilities by bringing their cases before federal authorities and expecting state recognition of the rights necessary to support the freedom they were making.[8]

From the start, Yorktown's Black inhabitants' expectations of the bureau court reflected their larger political goals. Before the court could begin proceedings, the community protested its structure and demanded that the bureau allow them to seat a representative of their choosing. For Yorktown's Black population, this meant an established and trusted leader within their community: Daniel Norton. Bureau policy, however, proscribed men like Norton from serving on bureau courts. Although the regulations stipulated that while Black community members could elect a representative, that representative had to be white.[9] When the Freedmen's Bureau refused to seat Daniel Norton, the Black community organized to resist this incursion into their rights and met the bureau's refusal with staunch resistance and savvy political organizing. Their efforts to seat Norton, the representative of their choice, foreshadowed how the community would use the court as a platform from which to project and protect their vision of freedom.

Norton and his two brothers, Robert and Frederick, had been enslaved by a man in Williamsburg prior to the Civil War and grew up on a farm in Gloucester County, Virginia. Prior to the outbreak of war, Daniel and Robert escaped from slavery and went north, where Daniel studied medicine and became a doctor.[10] It appears that at least for a little while, Daniel Norton may have been living in Philadelphia, Pennsylvania, with his wife Edmonie, before returning to Yorktown in early 1866.[11] As Friends teachers' references to Norton's public speeches demonstrate, Daniel Norton quickly became a leader in the community. Ordered to organize a group of three men for the bureau court, Massey had sought the community's input on their election of a representative. When they elected Norton, Massey rejected their choice.[12]

Massey attempted to call a follow-up meeting to have the community select a new individual. Black residents refused to attend the meeting. In a report on the matter in May of 1866, Massey noted, "they were united on this man." Since "no attention was paid to the call" to elect a representative, Massey apparently addressed the Black community at a different meeting, presumably one they had organized for something else. Massey attempted to convince them to elect someone other than Norton, preferably a white man. Shortly after this meeting, according to Massey, Norton began holding meetings all over the county "endeavoring to prevent any other man from being chosen." Norton also circulated a petition asking that he be allowed to sit on the bureau court as the duly elected representative.

In describing these events, Massey portrayed Norton as a troublemaker set on coercing the Black community away from making a decision he believed was in their best interest—the selection of a white representative. Such a depiction was not uncommon. Throughout the postwar South, white middle-class observers met Black leadership with suspicion at best, and sometimes outright hostility. Black leaders who had the audacity to unite their community on goals at odds with white authorities' intentions frequently appear in the written record framed as troublemakers.[13] Yet Norton's actions reflect a strong understanding of political maneuvering, and his efforts to keep the community united reveal that he recognized that in solidarity they retained their negotiating power.[14] By circulating a formal petition, Norton and his followers challenged the assertion that only white men could carry the political responsibility of sitting on a court.

When Massey again addressed the community to convince them to change their course, they "declared they were independent of the Bureau, they were now citizens and could take of themselves." Not only were they independent citizens, but when the meeting ended Massey observed, they gave "loud cheers for 'Norton'" and fired "volley after volley of firearms . . . thus displaying that they were ready for any emergency." Such organized and armed displays of political will were also common across the postwar South.[15] Yorktown's residents thus employed two different methods to render their politics visible to white observers—in sequence they utilized their right to petition, and then displayed their dedication to their stated objectives by drilling in public. To Massey's eyes, this was something of a disaster and he could not understand why Black residents would not cooperate with the bureau's wishes. The need for the bureau court was great because Massey was sure that Black residents would not get justice in civil courts.[16]

Still determined to get to the bottom of what he considered unrest, Massey investigated further and found that there was a "secret organization among [the Black community] under the control of 'Norton' and other colored men from the north." At a meeting of this organization—which presumably was only secret in so far as white residents were not made aware of their activities—"a resolution was offered . . . to effect that any 'Freedmen' who at the election would not vote for 'Norton' was to be shot." Some Black residents had apparently admitted to Massey that they "dare not vote for any other person for fear of personal violance [sic]."[17] Filtered through Massey's eyes as these accounts are, it is difficult to know the extent to which threats of violence were made by members of Norton's organization. However, enforcing political cooperation and unity through violence was also a common tactic Black Southerners employed in the postwar period. Often associated with the advent of Black voting, the use of force and coercion to shape collective behavior reflected an awareness that the only way to carry an election was through overwhelming voter support.[18] Such was likely the case at Yorktown, where Norton and his associates understood that the only way to influence federal authority was through significant support from the Black community.

Bureau records often identified Norton as the source of the problem, as if he endeavored only to gain personal power at the expense of the Black population. Given that the alternate representative whom the bureau wanted for the court was a white man, demanding that residents remain united on Norton was about more than just the man himself. It was also about keeping a representative of the community in a position of power rather than making the community dependent upon the benevolence of a white benefactor. Moreover, Norton would remain in leadership in York County long after the bureau left, and both he and his brothers Robert and Frederick would serve York County in official-political positions. Thus, it seems unlikely that Massey's depiction of Norton tells the full story, and more likely that unable to conceive of Black residents as fully capable citizens, Massey dismissed their political organizing as the result of a few individuals inciting a mob.[19]

Again, a full appreciation of this decision to resist the bureau on the matter of representation requires recognition of just how uncertain the political situation was in 1865 and 1866. In the immediate aftermath of the war, as Steven Hahn points out, there was little evidence that the "spirit of *Dred Scott* would not prevail" and Black Southerners would not be consigned to the same second-class status that free Black Americans had occupied throughout the United States prior to the war.[20] By insisting that a Black representative sit on the court, Yorktown residents rejected the possibility of occupying this second-class position in which their basic rights to property and family might be upheld, but their political and civil equality restricted.

Massey never allowed Norton to sit on the court, but that did not stop Black residents from coming before the court to advocate for their interests. Bureau court records provide an incomplete image of many of the conflicts that brought petitioners before the court, but still they are one of the few places where several Black community members become visible again in the archive. Even when only a name and a charge is listed, court records identify people in the community whose lives are otherwise obscured. Moreover, though they rarely provided a full transcript of a trial, court records testify to other aspects of individuals' lives such as their occupations, family relationships, and efforts to gain independence. Within the records of the court, residents' aspirations, accomplishments, and interests become apparent, and collectively they give shape and depth to the lives Black residents of Yorktown were building in freedom.

Friends' teachers and bureau agents believed that they needed to prepare formerly enslaved people for freedom and shape their expectations for what lives in freedom should entail. Yet bureau court records make clear that Black residents disagreed with this philosophy and were prepared to advocate for freedom on their own terms. To bring one's case before the court was not to ask for a particular right or privilege of citizenship, but to claim that right and ask the government to acknowledge and defend it. When circumstances did not allow residents to bring a specific problem before the court, usually because some of the interested parties did not reside nearby, they still took their concerns to Lieutenant Massey and expected him to address them.

Black residents in Yorktown already knew what they wanted freedom to look like, and they began constructing that freedom as soon as the opportunity presented itself during the war. Most of the bureau court activities in Yorktown occurred in 1866 and 1867, starting less than a year after the war ended. In individual cases, the contours of the lives Black residents had begun to build become evident, and accomplishments that are erased elsewhere become visible again. Moreover, in many other locations, refugee communities were transient—whether because ever-shifting lines of battle uprooted them, or because the federal government abandoned settlement plans. In those cases, what newly free people accomplished in the war years and immediately after was erased from the historical record just as they were erased from the physical landscape. But at Yorktown they remained, and the lives that Black residents built during this period would remain the foundation of their freedom long after those tasked with teaching them to be free left Yorktown.

One of the primary concerns Black residents took before the Freedmen's Bureau Court involved cases of assault or threatened bodily harm. Though these cases occurred between litigants of varying backgrounds—between Black men and white men, husbands and wives, and between Black men—they collectively testify to a desire to maintain bodily autonomy and one's claim to personal safety. By bringing these issues before the court, litigants claimed the right to operate in a world where violence against one's person was unacceptable and demanded that the federal government protect that right.

For example, in 1867 Beverly Graves a Black man, took Thomas Gay, a white man, to court for assault. According to the Freedmen's Bureau census, in 1865 Graves was twenty-one and living at Newtown.[21] Graves contended that while both men worked at Mr. Gallagher's Mill, Gay accused him of drinking his milk. When Graves denied this claim, Gay "told me not to talk back." Graves walked away from Gay's remark, and as he was leaving Gay "struck me and knocked me against the wall of the engine room." S. C. Browning, a witness, testified that he observed the altercation and confirmed that Gay had hit Graves and followed him out of the mill. Gay acknowledged that he had indeed struck Graves, and that he did so because Graves refused to leave the mill when Gay ordered him out but rather "remained arguing." Gay further asserted that he had missed other items from the mill, and that he had laid the milk as a trap to catch Graves in the act of stealing.[22]

In taking Gay to court, Graves not only sought protection from bodily harm, but further rejected the unequal power dynamics at work between a white man and Black man at Gallagher's Mill. Graves's initial choice to reject Gay's accusation and refuse to vacate his job at the mill indicated a desire to claim the right to work and not be dismissed without cause. In charging Gay, Graves further rejected the social hierarchy that allowed a white man to abuse a Black man without repercussions and made a claim on the federal government, through the bureau, to protect his bodily safety. Deciding in Graves's favor, the bureau court fined Thomas Gay two dollars.[23]

Similarly, Miles Sewell testified before the court that Louis Charles, a white man, had assaulted and threatened to shoot him outside of "Mr Gallaghers store."[24] While exiting the store, Sewell explained, Charles kicked him. Sewell responded that Charles should look out, at which point Charles "attempted to draw his revolver and threatened to shoot him." Another white man, Richard Bryan, then "drew his revolver and also threatened to shoot him." Frank Dixon, a Black man who was with Sewell in the store, testified that he witnessed Charles kick Sewell. Charles became agitated when Sewell told him he "had better let him alone," at which point a third white man, Whittaker Lee, "asked Miles what he meant" and then "threatened to shoot Miles [Sewell]."[25] The particulars of this case make it difficult to glean exactly how the situation escalated so quickly, but the problem stemmed from Charles's violent reaction to Sewell's standing up for himself and objecting to Charles kicking him. This act of self-assertion appears to have led Charles and possibly other white men to draw guns and threaten to shoot Sewell. By bringing this matter before the court, Sewell not only demanded protection against physical violence but also claimed the right to engage in everyday activities such as shopping in a store without being subjected to white residents' demand for deference.

A third case involved a comparable incident in which a Black man protested a white man's violence against him in business proceedings. Benjamin Smith brought Frank B. Mark before the court under charges of assault, testifying that Mark had "beat him badly" after objecting to the price Smith had asked for oysters. In Mark's version of the story, Smith brought oysters aboard Mark's ship, the *Chrystal Palace,* and they disagreed on the price. In the course of what was apparently a convoluted business dealing, Smith's oysters were confused with someone else's, and Mark offered Smith less than what Smith felt his catch was worth. According to Mark, "Smith . . . became very saucy and finally called him a liar" at which point Mark "struck him and ordered him from his vessel." Mark admitted that he followed Smith from the boat, taking his gun and threatening to shoot him.[26] Again, the particulars of the case are murky, and it is unclear what exactly transpired that led Mark to assault Smith. But both men acknowledged that Mark had repeatedly hit Smith, and it was this act of violence that Smith insisted was a violation of his rights as a free man and citizen by bringing Mark before the court.

All three cases involved not just white men committing assaults against Black men, but white men engaging in such actions after behavior they felt did not exhibit sufficient deference to their status as white men. Each plaintiff —Beverly Graves, Miles Sewell, and Benjamin Smith—rejected a social order in which white men had the ability to demand deference through violence without repercussions. Graves's and Smith's cases also evidence a desire to be approached on equal terms in the workplace. And finally, by bringing the cases before the court, an extension of federal authority in the South, all three men laid claim to their rights as citizens to bodily autonomy and protection.

Black women also petitioned the court to defend their right to bodily autonomy and freedom from violence. Betty Larramore brought Frank Hobdy, a Black man, to court for assault after he repeatedly knocked her down for walking across his property. According to Larramore, she routinely passed on a walk bordering Hobdy's garden "to visit my neighbors." In this instance, as she was walking this same way, Hobdy "ordered me back and on my refusing to go, he struck me with his hand and knocked me down." When she got up, "he knocked me down again." Lucy Peterson, a neighbor, testified that she witnessed Hobdy run and attack Larramore, and further threaten to kill her, but did not know what had provoked his outburst. For his part, Hobdy explained that he had planted seeds and informed Larramore of this on the morning the altercation occurred. Upon seeing Larramore crossing where he had planted the seeds, Hobdy "told her she must not go that way, took hold of her and turned her round, when she fell down." Deciding in favor of Larramore, the court fined Hobdy two dollars in damages.[27]

In other instances, wives took their husbands to court for assault, claiming their right to their bodies within the bounds of marriage. Martha Turner brought her husband, Elijah, before the bureau court after he "became very angry with her without cause and beat her and struck her with the side of an axe." Elijah claimed that "she was disobedient," confirmed that he had struck her "and had done so before." He further asserted that he would beat her again. The court ruled in favor of Martha and sentenced Elijah to confinement at hard labor for a period of thirty days.[28]

Freedmen's Bureau Court records provide an imperfect accounting for cases such as these because they did not record a full transcript of the trials. Rather, agents summarized the testimony of witnesses and did not record the questions that prompted the responses. In the Turners' case, this leaves room for speculation about an important aspect of Martha's choice to bring her husband to court. In recording Elijah's testimony, the clerk wrote, "States that she was disobedient and that he did strike her and had done so before did not intend to hurt her would beat her again." This string of assertions suggests that the clerk ran multiple responses to different questions together, and that someone had asked Elijah about his history with spousal abuse. It seems possible that Martha had mentioned Elijah's violent history to the court, prompting the questions to him. By bringing this issue before the court, then, Martha sought redress for a particular incident and sought to force her husband to accept her physical boundaries generally within their marriage when other efforts to do so had failed.

Two other cases evidence Black women's efforts to determine the boundaries of their marriages through different means. Edward Smith brought his wife, Harriet Smith, to court under a charge of desertion. In her defense, Harriet testified that "her husband treated her so shamefully she was compelled to leave him." She had endured his abuse as long as possible and was "not willing to take up with him again as she knows he would again abuse her." Harriet had remained firm on this matter, as Edward claimed that she had "left his house over a year ago and that he has tried by all means in his power to prevail on her to return but she . . . refuses."[29] According to the court records, the judges "after giving each of the parties good advice," commanded that they live together and if another instance of abuse occurred they should come before the court again. Rulings such as this in which bureau agents ordered spouses to live peaceably with one another were also common. Paul Cimbala observed similar patterns with the Georgia Freedmen's Bureau and attributes agents' seeming desire to turn a blind eye toward abuse to their overwhelming desire to enforce an orderly society. Agents believed that family units were the basis of well-ordered society and further believed that allowing marriages to dissolve would make dependent family members a burden on the bureau.[30]

Similarly, Thomas Carey brought his wife, Nancy Carey, to court for desertion and like Harriet, Nancy refused to return to a marriage where her individual rights were not protected. In leaving Thomas, Nancy had "taken most of his things with her" and told him that if she was forced to live with him "she would kill him when asleep." Unlike Edward Smith, Thomas Carey did not desire to have his wife return to him, but rather seemed to agree with her assertion that they were not "suited for each other and would like to separate." In coming before the court, the Careys asked that the government acknowledge their decision and dissolve their marriage. Instead, the bureau court "lectured them on the sacred relationship existing between man and wife and ordered them to try and live amicably together."[31]

That the courts ruled against Black individuals' right to dissolve their marriages speaks to the way in which white reformers' intentions for newly free people and newly free people's own visions of freedom often clashed. In both cases, the judges felt it necessary to inform the litigants about the nature of marriage, assuming that their difficulties arose from a lack of experience with the institution rather than a problem with husbands' physical violence. Moreover, given that in both cases wives initiated the separation, these incidents indicate how the boundaries of bodily autonomy could differ between Black men and Black women. Women carved out an independent place for themselves in the body politic by seeking to bring federal authority to bear on their personal safety.

Bureau court records also testify to a diversified and complicated economic system that the Black community had already built by the end of the Civil War. Where the Friends continually celebrated their own efforts to induce Black refugees to work, and bureau agents bemoaned the lack of industry they thought they saw, bureau court records suggest that these accounts provide an acutely imperfect picture. While the truncated nature of bureau court records makes it difficult to know the intricacies of business relationships, and raise far more questions than they answer, collectively they testify to an important reality and begin to map the contours of the postwar economic landscape Black residents were building.

Additionally, the various cases that came before the court testify to the interconnectedness of the Black community in York County. Often, individual settlements such as Slabtown or Newtown are portrayed as independent communities. This is particularly true in histories of Slabtown, which tend to treat it as an autonomous entity. Yet bureau court records suggest that it is more accurate to think of Slabtown and Newtown as neighborhoods within a larger landscape of freedom that incorporated all of York County and ultimately most of the Tidewater area.[32] Transactions, and consequently court cases, occurred between individuals who lived in various places within the county. Even before the war ended, bureau agents commented on the consistency with which Black residents moved between communities, noting that as a result it was difficult to get accurate population statistics. This suggests that not only did economic relationships extend throughout the county, but that people also did not necessarily remain settled in one location during or after the war.

Various cases brought before the court related to default of payment or nonpayment for labor, and their brief details provide a sense of some of the business activities in which Black residents engaged. John Taylor, an oysterman living at Indianfield Farm, brought a case against Sally Green for failing to pay for her husband's casket. Sally and Samuel Green had been living together at Darlington Farm where Samuel worked as a sawyer before his death.[33] John Wyatt, another Black resident, had crafted a coffin for Green's husband, Samuel, and then transferred the account to John Taylor for payment of a debt. This type of transferring of debt was common during this period, and both Black and white residents routinely transferred the balance of debts to others who owed them money as a way to pay off their own debts.[34] Taylor wanted the amount "credited on account of judgment held against him by Sally Green." This suggests that Taylor owed Green money and wanted to officially use the debt he had received from Wyatt to offset what he owed Green.[35] Given that Green acknowledged the debt and testified to her intention to pay it, it appears that there was no conflict in this case. Rather, Taylor brought the somewhat convoluted situation before the court to ensure that the debts could be properly recorded, and payments made official. It is possible that Taylor chose to do this because the county register of deeds at the time was both unreliable and well known for being an unreconstructed rebel.[36]

In the same court session, Joseph Price brought suit against Thomas Gibbons and William Pryor for nonpayment for labor. The type of labor for which Gibbons and Pryor owed Price was not specified but both acknowledged that they owed him a debt and would pay as soon as possible. Again, the lack of details of the case leaves much to be desired, but it is clear that Price was transacting with multiple people for his services of some kind and that their business was official enough to bring before the bureau court.[37]

Records also testify to Black community members leasing out land and equipment, usually for farming but also frequently for oystering. Jesse Mayo brought suit against William Wooten, a white man, because Wooten borrowed one of Mayo's plows and had not paid to rent it. Mayo had allowed Wooten to borrow the plow with the understanding that Wootten would "use it on shares." In this agreement, Wootten would use Mayo's plow to cultivate three acres for himself and one for Mayo. Mayo and his wife, Sarah, appear on the 1865 census living on Tinsley Farm. According to the census, Mayo was a farmer and worked at Fort Magruder.[38] Wooten testified that while at Mayo's house, he saw two plows and "said to him he had better lend me one to break up my ground to which he [Mayo] consented." "I took the plough home," Wooten claimed, "but nothing was ever said about paying for it." Sarah Jane Burk, a witness in the case, testified that she was present for the agreement and Wootten had agreed to use the plow on shares.[39]

Similar cases of unfulfilled business agreements like Mayo and Wootten's came through the bureau court when payment was not made in a timely manner. Griffin Becket brought Daniel Stanley to court for nonpayment of services Becket performed "doctoring" Stanely's horse.[40] In 1865, Becket lived in Williamsburg with his wife Kate and three children, Elton, Mary, and Oney. Like Mayo, Becket appears to have been engaged in various economic ventures, as according to the census he was a laborer, but he apparently also worked providing medical care to animals.

Robert Christian presented a particularly interesting situation when he brought Abram Stark and Tillman Carter to court for debt. Christian, a Black man, had leased land to both Stark and Carter, and both men owed him the previous year's rent. Stark had leased two acres and owed a balance of three dollars and seventy-five cents. Christian stated that he had asked Stark for the rent repeatedly "and it seems as if he did not want to pay it." Court records did not indicate how much land Carter had rented, but he owed Christian a balance of seven dollars and twenty-five cents.[41]

This case suggests that by 1867 Robert Christian owned a sufficient amount of land to be able to rent out portions of it to other members of the community. None of the people in question in the case appear on the 1865 census, so it is difficult to know where they were living in 1867 and by extension where Christian may have owned land. However, in 1870 a Robert and Letta Christian appear on the York County census as landowners in Nelson Township. That year's census recorded Robert owning $105 worth of real estate and $200 of personal property.[42] This is likely the same person, but it is unclear when he acquired the land.[43]

Letters and reports from the Friends who lived at Yorktown at times outright obscured the presence of Black businesses. In 1864 the Friends operated a store for refugees in Yorktown under the supervision of one of their members, Alfred B. Cranstone. It opened in June and, as *The Friend* ensured its readers, was "intended only for Blacks—the laborers among them, agents of our own and other similar associations, being the only whites allowed to purchase."[44] This stipulation that only a few white people could be allowed to purchase in the Friends' store was quite serious, as in another issue *The Friend* reminded its readers to be vigilant in not allowing "illegal trade with disloyal people through the medium of the negroes."[45] In November *The Friend* celebrated the accomplishments of this new store, opining, "it is difficult to estimate the advantages already derived by the freedmen for the so recent establishment of the stores under the direction of our Board, in South-eastern Virginia." Many people would find this surprising, the author thought, but their surprise would be "greatly lessened when it is remembered there are nearly six thousand in the neighborhood of Yorktown, now almost entirely dependent upon us for supplies."[46] A different report from November celebrated the sales at Yorktown in September which amounted to $6,373.71 and reached $866.15 in a single day. These figures testified to the buying power of the Black population around Yorktown, though *The Friend* celebrated it as an act of charity that enabled refugees to "support themselves" rather than depend on government handouts.[47]

Within a year, the Friends felt they had ample cause to celebrate their store venture. In July of 1865, *The Friend* reminded its readers that they intended the stores to "aid such [people] as have recently emerged from slavery, in their self-support" and that to that end they had "endeavored jealously to watch the improving condition of our customers." They watched the "improving condition" of their customers to ensure that once their condition had improved enough, the Friends would not "unprofitably or unnecessarily" prolong their labor and could turn their attention, "experience," and "benefit of our capital" to other settlements.[48] By September of that year, the Friends felt they could move on because "all restriction on trade in the late rebel States having been removed" they could discontinue their store in Yorktown. Consequently, they were offering it for sale to another Friend "to do a very good trade and at the same time confer a great benefit upon the coloured people."[49] Though they offered their store for sale, the Friends still felt that its continued operation by white proprietors would remain a benefit to the Black population.

In their estimation and depiction of the economic situation at Yorktown, then, the Friends suggested that without the help of benevolent white businessmen, the Black population at Yorktown would be left to the mercy of government aid. Their reports in 1864 indicated that no stores in Yorktown existed where Black residents could go for fair prices, and that without the monetary investment of the Friends, refugees would have to rely on the army for support. This image left an important fact out of the equation that was the business market at Yorktown. The Friends were not the only store operators in the city.

Whether or not the Friends were aware of this fact in 1864 when they opened their store is impossible to know. But in May of 1873, Robert Ruffin, a Black business owner, appeared before the Southern Claims Commission to receive compensation for articles in his store that the Ninety-Ninth New York Volunteers had plundered in June of 1863. At the time of the taking, Ruffin had presented his case to the provost marshal at Yorktown who had assured him that he would receive compensation from the federal government later. In 1871, Ruffin listed Reverend Thomas Napper, Reverend Peter Dorcy, Washington Banks, Washington Fields, and James B. Mitchell as witnesses who would testify on his behalf.

Ruffin explained to the commission that he had been enslaved by Colonel Alexander Fleet in King and Queen County, Virginia, but in June of 1862 had gone to the Army of the James as a waiter for a major in the One Hundred Twenty-Third Pennsylvania. The commission asked Ruffin a variety of questions about his enslavement, and though he said he felt he was treated well, when asked why he left he replied, "I thought freedom was better than anything else." Early in 1863, Ruffin told the commission, he got word that his father, a storekeeper in Yorktown, was sick. Ruffin's father had also been enslaved but purchased his freedom prior to the war and "carried on more business . . . than any other colored man in our section during the time of slavery." Ruffin's father died in March of 1863, at which point Ruffin took over the store in Yorktown. Ruffin estimated that he had saved about $125 himself while working for the Union army, and that his father had acquired about $800 by the time of his death.[50]

Ruffin described his store as something of a grocery that serviced both civilians and the army. His store was located outside of the garrison of the fort, "out with [the] colored people," and Ruffin was "the only person that had a store out there." Ruffin stocked "a large lot" of cheese, sugar, cakes, crackers, preserves, watches, shoes, and "other things.". Ruffin estimated he had about $1,500 worth of capital in the store, with which the New York soldiers walked away.[51]

Based on Ruffin's description of the theft, it is possible that he stopped operating his store after this incident. He concluded his testimony by stating, "They took all that was really of any use to them & there were a great many other little things that were used around there among the women such as dry-goods, that were destroyed or trampled upon." Though these items were destroyed, he did not request compensation for them because they were not taken. Most of the commission's questions centered around the types of goods the soldiers took, and whether they could be considered for army use—a stipulation of compensation by the Southern Claims Commission. The commissioners never asked Ruffin if he was able to reopen his store, and thus the record remains silent on that point.

Whether or not Ruffin was operating his store in 1864, however, reliance on Friends' reports about Yorktown would suggest that no store had been in operation at Yorktown since refugees began to arrive. Moreover, their constant celebration of their stores as vehicles for Black uplift ignore the efforts formerly enslaved people like Ruffin had already made to create a functioning, independent economy. That Ruffin had increased his father's operation so quickly by May of 1863 suggests that his business was ultimately successful and would have remained so had the store not been looted.

By 1866 two stores were still in operation at Yorktown, one of which was in Slabtown. It is possible this was Ruffin's original store, and that he either continued to operate it and sold it or sold it after the theft. In March of 1866, Sarah Cadbury described the store located inside the fort as "Galligher's store." This establishment was likely owned by Charles Gallagher who appeared on the 1870 census for York County as a "general merchant" originally from Delaware.[52] Gallagher and his family were living in New York in 1860, so more than likely he began operating this store during or after the war.[53] Possibly Gallagher bought the Friends' store they advertised for sale in 1865.

However, in April of 1866, Cadbury noted that after visiting the store in town, "Mary introduced me to a Slabtown store." This was Daniel Norton's store. Cadbury mentioned meeting Norton in the store and found shopping in a Black man's store so amusing that she "laughed outright, in the colored Dr's face." She dismissed this store as "only a cabin with shelves round, a counter."[54] Later letters evidence Cadbury's preference for shopping at Gallagher's store rather than Norton's, though Norton's would have been located much closer to her home.[55]

That Cadbury found a Black man running a store so comical is likely evidence of her own newness to the community at Yorktown rather than indicative of its novelty. Theft and disagreements over pay brought another Black man's shop into bureau court records, suggesting that Norton and Ruffin were not the only men operating independent storefronts during and immediately after the war. In January of 1866, Frank Cook sued John Taylor for default of payment for labor Cook had performed while working in Taylor's store in 1864. Taylor testified that "his business in 1864 was a shoemaker at Fort Yorktown," but at the same time he operated his store, he was also preparing farmland for cultivation at Darlington's farm. Based on Taylor's testimony, he ran his shoe shop at the fort while living at Darlington's farm "just above the church and schoolhouse." Moreover, it appears Taylor employed multiple other shoemakers as John Ruff testified that he lived at Slabtown and worked for Taylor as a shoemaker, and in 1865 Cook's occupation was listed as shoemaker in the census.[56]

Cook contended that Taylor owed him money for working in the shop, but Taylor asserted that his shop had been robbed while under Cook's care and for that reason he had not paid Cook. Taylor felt that the robbery occurred because of Cook's negligence and that the property stolen had a higher value than what Taylor owed Cook in pay. Thomas Napper, Shiloh's pastor, testified that Taylor and Cook had asked him and three other men to settle the matter. One of these additional men, David Yetman, was only ten years old at the time, living at Newtown with his father, Daniel, who was a carpenter.[57] Based on the testimony of these various witnesses, the court decided that John Taylor should pay Frank Cook thirty-six dollars, a portion of what he contended Taylor owed him.[58]

Again, the details of the case remain murky, and given the time that had passed from the robbery in 1864 to the hearing in 1866 the specifics were unclear even to the witnesses involved. However, the case presents important information about the state of Black businesses in Yorktown before the war ended, and the ability of Black residents not only to own businesses but employ other skilled laborers. Moreover, as with Ruffin's case, Cook and Taylor's situation suggests that at times Black businesses failed not for lack of industry or profit, but because of a failure of the US Army to protect them.[59]

Despite the setback of losing most of his inventory in his store, Robert Ruffin engaged in a variety of business ventures in the immediate postwar period. Ruffin came before the bureau court at least fourteen times, both as a plaintiff and as a defendant in various cases involving businesses that he owned or leased. In December of 1865 John Burnbridge brought Ruffin to court for default of payment. Burnbridge contended that his son had been working for Ruffin since December of 1864 but had not been adequately compensated. Ruffin had paid Burnbridge's son some money and had compensated him with clothing and bushels of meal. However, Burnbridge felt that the total balance of what Ruffin had agreed to pay his son had not been met. Daniel Norton appeared as council for Ruffin but his role in the litigation of the case is not recorded. As with many other cases, the details of the case are not provided, and the record text does not specify what Burnbridge's son was doing for Ruffin. However, a witness in the case, Robert Pollard, testified that he too had worked for Ruffin, and knew of another boy, Alpheus Rhone, who had done the same.[60]

In January of 1866 Robert Ruffin again appeared in court when Thomas Brown contended that Ruffin owed him back pay. Again, at issue in the case was the total payment. Upon hiring Brown, Ruffin had agreed to pay him a bushel of corn a day for twelve days. In this case, the court records specified that Brown had gone to work for Ruffin at his mill.[61] Other cases gave more details about Ruffin's mill operation. When Ruffin brought Robert Tibbs to court for theft, Ruffin testified that he was an "owner of a Grist Mill about two miles from Yorktown Va" where he had employed Tibbs as a miller. Two other men, Richard Wilkinson and Clayborne Holmes, also worked for Ruffin and testified in the case.[62] Clayborne Holmes likewise brought Ruffin to court and brought another employee of Ruffin's, Peter Cole, as his witness.[63] A handful of other cases regarding Ruffin's mill make clear that Ruffin employed quite a few men at his mill and that numerous Black men in the community were professional millers.[64]

Yet this was not Ruffin's only business venture, which is why it is hard to know for sure whether John Burnbridge's son worked for Ruffin at the mill or elsewhere. In November of 1866 Nathaniel Taylor brought Ruffin and his business partner, Henry Fergerson, to court for nonpayment of a contract. Ruffin had approached Taylor numerous times to buy his ferry between York and Gloucester. Taylor finally agreed to rent the ferry to Ruffin and Fergerson, and according to Fergerson they had operated the ferry since August of 1865. Fergerson insisted that he and Ruffin had in fact bought the ferry and never had any intention of renting it. Rather, they had paid Taylor the sum he requested at the time of the agreement and did not believe they owed him the "rent" he was now requiring. Ruffin's testimony does not appear in the court records, suggesting that he was not present at the hearing. The court ruled in favor of Taylor and gave Ruffin and Fergerson twenty days to make their payment.[65]

One of the most common types of cases that came before the bureau court involved issues of personal property. Black residents regularly sued to protect their property or demand compensation for property that had been destroyed. These cases indicate a handful of important realities that are unseen in other records. First, by 1866 and 1867, Black residents of York County had acquired considerable personal property in the form of farming equipment, boats, oystering supplies, livestock, and home furnishings. Where Friends' teachers frequently complained that Black residents' homes were spartan, their personal possessions few, and as a result their lives in freedom undeveloped, bureau court records tell a different story. Black residents not only acquired personal property, but they also defended their right to claim it as their own and protect it from interference by others. Second, these records add another layer to the image of Black industry already in operation at Yorktown by the war's end. In many cases, suits involved equipment required for private industry, and litigants sought to protect not only their property but also the utensils they needed to labor independently.

Such was the case when Daniel Cook brought Frank Taswell to court for destroying private property in December of 1866. Cook and Taswell had come before the court two months prior, having bought a boat together for oystering. Rather than working in the boat himself, Taswell wanted to "put a man in the boat in his place," to which Cook objected. Taswell, a shoemaker, testified that working as a shoemaker he could "do better . . . than oystering."[66] Cook offered to buy Taswell's interest in the boat, but Taswell refused to sell to Cook. Moreover, Cook told the court, he wished "to earn his living but cannot oyster without a boat," indicating that the boat was key to his desired occupation as an independent oysterman. The bureau court required the two men to sell the boat at public auction.[67]

In December, Cook brought Taswell back to court because after Cook bought the boat at auction outright, Taswell had destroyed it. In late November, Cook had left the boat in its usual place on the shore after working all day and found it missing the next time he went to work. Upon looking for the boat, he found it "cut a piece a piece was cut off about three feet and it was split."[68] Henry Janas, a witness, told the court that "Taswell said if the boat was sold and he did not get eighteen . . . dollars for his share, he would cut his share out of her." After listening to the testimony of multiple witnesses, and cross examinations by Daniel Norton who represented Taswell in the case of destroying private property, the court reserved its decision.[69] Though court records do not indicate the ultimate outcome of the case, in 1870 Daniel Cook's occupation was listed as oystercatcher, indicating that despite the setback with the boat he remained independently employed as he had wished.[70]

David Jones likewise sought the bureau court's authority when James Elliot mistakenly took his boat for three days. Jones told the court he was the "owner of a skiff" that went missing after he left it onshore following a day of fishing. He reported this matter to the provost marshal and upon looking for the boat found it in the possession of James Elliot. Elliot had apparently taken the boat mistakenly, believing that it belonged to William Goodin. Goodin testified that he had sent Elliot to retrieve a boat Goodin had loaned to another man, Wesley Hughes, the year prior. The entire case appears to have been a simple misunderstanding as Elliot went looking for a boat he was not familiar with and accidentally took the wrong one.[71]

Still, the facts of the case yield valuable insights into the various business dealings and personal property of the men involved. David Jones sued under a "claim for damages," which the court ultimately awarded him. Unable to use his personal boat for three days, Jones wanted to be compensated for use of his boat. For his part, James Elliot was apparently paying William Goodin to rent his boat, presumably to fish himself. Goodin either owned multiple boats or was engaged in another occupation that did not require him to regularly use the boat he had rented to Wesley Hughes.[72] By bringing the case before the bureau court, Jones claimed a right to his personal property and to the protection of his business operations from interruption, both of which the court upheld in their final ruling.

Similarly, John Willis and Miles Sewell sued I. Baker for "refusal of payment for use of a skiff" when Baker used their boat without permission. Baker had apparently said after the fact that "he would pay for use and damages" but then said "it was too much and refused to pay." Baker, a white man, did not appear in court and the judges unanimously decided that he owed Willis and Sewell one dollar a day for use of their boat.[73] Based on the 1865 census, Willis and Sewell were neighbors at Slabtown, which is perhaps how they came to purchase a boat together. Willis was only seventeen years old, and lived at 52 Slabtown with, presumably, his younger brother Isaac Willis, age twelve. Isaac attended school, suggesting that John made enough to support them both. Sewell lived at 64 Slabtown with two children, Carolina and Robert. The census taker indicated that Sewell made enough money to support his family.[74]

Oyster tongs were also a recurring issue in bureau court proceedings, as like boats, owners frequently loaned them out to others for use and sought redress when they were damaged or otherwise lost. Like boats, oyster tongs were essential equipment for individuals engaged in independent labor as oystermen. John Adams sued John Carter for damage to private property when Carter broke his tongs after borrowing them and refused to pay Adams for their cost. Adams and Carter were also probably neighbors, as they both lived at Wormsley Creek at the time of the 1865 census. According to Carter, he had paid for the use of the tongs already and they broke as a consequence of normal use. The court dismissed the case. Both men were listed as oystermen on the 1865 census. Adams lived with his wife, Mary, and two children, Simon and Mary. Carter supported an especially large household composed of Ann, age thirty; Susan, age twenty-six and recorded as "crippled"; William, age seventeen; Katy, age fifteen; J. H., age thirteen; Lucy Ann, age ten; Thomas, age eight; Richard, age six; and Emma, age three.[75]

Another form of personal property disputes that came before the court involved animals, both livestock and animals used in farm labor. Enos Washington and Gustavis Harris came before the court over a conflict involving the recovery of a horse. Enos Washington explained that two years prior a horse was stolen from him, and that having recently visited Yorktown he spotted the stolen horse in Gustavis Harris's possession. Two men, Stephen Allen and

Abram Williams, testified on Washington's behalf that his horse had been stolen and that the horse in question was the same horse. Gustavis Harris explained that he had traded a mule for the horse from Oliver Macklin. Macklin, in turn, explained that he had purchased the horse from "a private soldier at Fort Magruder."[76]

This particular case demonstrates the intricacies of wartime occupation and personal property ownership that plagued many people after the war ended. Macklin testified that he had been careful "to take writing from the soldier showing that he paid for the horse" because he too had "two horses taken from him before" resulting from the fact that "he had no receipt to show for them." In a place like York County where many white residents had fled, thousands of Black residents accumulated, and Union soldiers moved in and out of the area frequently, personal property was sure to become an issue. Productive property like horses were important for army use and could be taken from loyal residents for military purposes, leaving the postwar situation confused. How Washington's horse came into the possession of the soldier from whom Harris bought it cannot be known, but the fact that it changed hands so many times yields insights into the way in which the market for productive property was active after the war. All the owners involved in the case, Washington, Harris, and Macklin, had accumulated the capital to own and trade in horses, and likely used both the horse in question and the mule to farm or engage in another type of labor. Ultimately, the court decided that the horse should be returned to Washington and that Macklin should return the mule he traded Harris for the horse. This uneven outcome further suggests how the contingencies and complications of a postwar landscape could deprive Black individuals of investments they had made into their futures.[77]

In another instance, E. J. Wynn, a white man, brought Fill Travers to court for default of payment related to "one yoke oxen" and a cow.[78] Travers had apparently purchased the animals with a note, and when Wynn presented Travers with the note, Travers had refused to pay. For his part, Travers confirmed that he had purchased the cow, but that one of the oxen had died and the other ox he had returned to Wynn. Travers was not willing to pay for the ox he returned.[79] Again, the details of the case are missing from the hearing transcript, but the evidence recorded suggests that Travers returned the second ox after the first one died—either because he feared both oxen were unsound or because he wanted to save his capital to purchase a new pair of oxen. That Travers was willing to stand up to Wynn and refuse payment suggests that perhaps Travers suspected that the oxen were unfit and was unwilling to pay for subpar livestock. Regardless, the case testifies to Travers's eagerness and ability to invest in animals that would have been productive for independent farming.

Black residents also used the bureau court to defend their right to personal belongings they had accumulated prior to their flight from slavery. Jackson Tolliver sued Buck Cook for retaining private property in the form of two bedsteads belonging to his wife. Tolliver, age thirty-five, appears to have been living at Newtown with his wife, Lucy, age twenty-five, though Lucy is not identified by name in the suit.[80] According to Tolliver, "his wife during the rebellion came in the Union lines and on leaving home left two bedsteads with Cook to take care of," suggesting that even at the moment of flight, Lucy was preparing the belongings she would want in freedom. Cook agreed that this was the case and that he was willing to give the Tollivers their beds, but that he wanted the money he had expended for transportation of the items. Presumably, Cook had paid to transport the bedsteads from wherever Lucy left them to Yorktown. The court agreed that Tolliver should pay Cook for transportation costs.[81] It is further worth noting in this instance that when Lucy Tolliver arrived on the US lines, she may have looked empty-handed. White workers in camps frequently commented on destitute refugees arriving with nothing but the clothing on their back. Lucy too may have appeared destitute upon her arrival because her preparation would not have been immediately obvious to observers. Yet prepare she did, and that preparation served her well in creating the Tolliver family home in freedom.

In another instance, Mira Ann Goldman sued Robert Armstead for larceny, contending that he had stolen her personal belongings while she was trying to transport them across the river to Gloucester. Goldman stated that she "moved from Newtown to Gloucester" in January of 1867 but upon arriving in Gloucester was unable to move all of "her effects" because she was waiting on her brother to meet her. Leaving a portion of her belongings until her brother arrived the next day, Goldman found that some of them were missing. Goldman then "complained to the Asst Supr [Massey] who sent a guard with her" to the house of Robert Armstead, at which point she found blankets and sheets that belonged to her. A series of witnesses testified that the blanket and sheets in question were indeed Goldman's while Armstead's wife testified that she had made them herself. Ultimately the court decided in favor of Goldman and sentenced Armstead to "sixty days hard labor . . . on account of bad character which he bears and that he not be allowed to return to the County of York."[82]

Goldman's efforts to retrieve her belongings exhibit a willingness to leverage the bureau's authority, and at times its muscle, to protect the lives individuals were building in freedom. The court's sentence said nothing about returning the items or monetary compensation, presumably because Goldman had already retrieved her possessions while protected by Massey's guards who accompanied her to Armstead's house. By continuing to pursue the matter as a criminal charge in court, Goldman was helping construct the norms for her new, free community by insisting that personal belongings left unattended could not be taken and ensuring that people who were willing to engage in theft would not be welcome in the community.

Occasionally issues regarding home ownership came before the bureau court, indicating that Black residents were actively seeking out permanent homes for themselves and transacting with one another—as opposed to white landowners—to do so. Like cases involving productive property, those involving home ownership demonstrate the difficult circumstances in which Black residents operated in the immediate postwar period. Land ownership remained an issue, and with questions of land ownership came questions about the buildings that stood on that land which residents had built during and immediately after the war. Again, though the records reveal that it was a confusing period that could deprive newly free people of hard-won property, the records simultaneously reveal the way in which Black residents continued to strive for the means to support freedom against an everchanging and often uncertain backdrop.

Richard Jones sued Martha Lane for default of payment on a house he claimed to have sold her for four dollars. Lane explained that she had not purchased a house from Jones and in fact could not purchase the house in question from him because it did not belong to him. "The house he claims never belonged to him," she noted, "but belongs to the owner of the land." Multiple people had apparently been attempting to get Lane to pay them for the house, "but it does not belong to any of them."[83] Records do not indicate where the house in question was. Two Richard Joneses appear on the 1865 census, one age fourteen and employed as an oysterman, and the other age sixteen. Both Joneses appear to have been living in the Buck Point section of York County in 1865. Martha Lane does not appear on that census.[84] While it is impossible to know if either one of the Richard Joneses were the same man in court with Martha Lane, in 1865 both men were living in households with multiple other people, suggesting that they could have been the person in court and that all of the residents may have tried to claim the house.

Regardless of where the house was located, this case suggests that while the issue before the court was ownership of the house, Jones probably claimed compensation for it because he had invested in it somehow. Most likely, Jones and the others who requested payment from Lane had paid to construct the house on the landowner's property or even constructed it themselves. If they did so before the war ended, they may have believed that the house they were building would belong to them into perpetuity—indeed, as residents' complaints against the bureau indicated later, many believed that they would retain the land on which the bureau placed them. Again, the transcript of the case was not provided, but the summary of Lane's comments suggest she bought the house from the landowner and believed that this meant that she had already paid the lawful owner for it. The court unanimously decided that Richard Jones "had no claim to the house" and dismissed the case.[85]

Black residents also used the bureau court and the Freedmen's Bureau's authority to defend their rights to their families, especially their parental rights over their children. In many cases these issues came before the bureau when parents or family members sought the bureau's help in retrieving children from the hands of white residents. Paul Cimbala notes that Black Southerners' identity as free people "required that they assert their right to determine the destinies of their families in the face of planters who were still trying to reassert their mastery" by exploiting vulnerable children. Such instances were usually cases where Black residents found a reliable ally in the bureau.[86] In late 1866 and early 1867, multiple cases involving children came to Massey's attention. Henry Williams, a resident of Gloucester County, had sought Massey's assistance to retrieve "his wifes grandson named Isaac Stubbenfield" who had "been bound out by the civil authorities without his wifes consent." As Stubbenfield's nearest kin, Williams's wife sought redress for the situation because "the boys consent was not obtained and by the terms of the indenture he will be allowed no wages."[87] Similarly, Henry Wormley had contacted S. C. Armstrong at Fort Monroe because "two of his children" were being "held in slavery on the line between King & Queen & Gloucester."[88] Massey followed up immediately on the matter, writing to a "Mr. F Sincoe" that Wormley had reported that he desired to obtain his children and that he never gave his consent for the children to be bound out to Sincoe. "You evidently have no claim to their service," Massey explained, and he hoped "the children will be delivered up to the father . . . and thus prevent any unpleasant circumstances which might arise."[89]

Richard Milby, a shoemaker living at Buck Point, also petitioned Massey for the return of his children from a "Mr Blakey" in Middlesex County, Virginia.[90] "I am informed," Massey wrote Blakey, "that you have in your possession several children of a colored man named Richard Milby, now a resident of this county which you have refused to deliver to their father on his application for them." If he continued to refuse to give the father his children, Massey told Blakey, "you hold yourself liable for disobedience of Orders of the War Department."[91] Milby was likely not the only one seeking his sons but simply identified by Massey because he was considered the head of his household. Louisa Wilkinson sought to claim two of her nephews, Major Derrick and John Isom Taylor, because both of their parents had died. Wilkinson and her husband, Richard, lived in Newtown with five children identified as their own.[92] As in the other cases, Louisa Wilkinson had attempted to retrieve her nephews herself but "was unable to obtain them" and in the intervening days Major and John had "been bound out by the Asst Supr of New Kent Co." Wilkinson, Massey stated, wished "to take care of them herself" because she was their next of kin.[93]

In some cases, parents did not know the whereabouts of their children and enlisted the bureau's help in locating them. Thomas Anderson applied to W. H. Sloan on his behalf to locate his sons, Joseph and Thomas, who "were formerly owned by Mr. Isaac Vinder" of New Kent County, Virginia. Henry Vinder, Isaac's son, had held Joseph and Thomas "shortly before the close of the war," and Anderson had "not heard of them since." The issue came before Massey because Anderson's daughter, Elvi, "was held by Mr Ben Vinder of James City Co."[94] Though Anderson did not know exactly where his children were, he made a claim on the bureau as a citizen of the United States for the responsibility of the federal government to assist in the locating of missing children and the restoration of citizen's families.

Ultimately, it easy to see the uneven and at times seemingly unfair outcomes of bureau hearings as further evidence of the way the federal government failed newly free people after the war ended. The Freedmen's Bureau Court records are certainly a testimony to that. But they are also evidence of the conflicted and confusing landscape of freedom that the Civil War and the violent death of slavery wrought and the uncertainty Black Southerners had to navigate. Moreover, and more importantly, these records reveal integral information about the lives Black residents were building in freedom, and they are evidence of the tenacity with which Black people struggled to carve out independence and autonomy in freedom. These were not people unprepared for freedom or in need of direction. They knew the directions they wanted to go, and they wanted the support and protection of the federal government to get there.

CHAPTER 5

★ ★ ★ ★ ★ ★ ★ ★

"We Have a Right to the Land"

Resisting Relocation in the Postwar Period

In December of 1866, Peter Dorcy and Philip Tabb wrote to General Oliver Otis Howard, head of the Freedmen's Bureau on behalf of the Black residents of York and James City Counties.[1] A "large mass meeting of the Colored people of York and James city County Va met to hold consultation together to see what was the proper course to pursue relative to our grievances," they explained to Howard. After this discussion, the meeting's participants determined that their best course of action was to send their reports to "one who we know is a friend to this down trodden race," and "[c]hief over all the affairs of the Colored People." Government officials had, they explained, returned abandoned lands to their former Confederate owners and "poor people know not where to go having been living and is at present living upon lands which was claimed to be Government Lands." Despite having promised to pay the newly instituted rents required of them "a large portion of us have been ordered to move right a way and we have not where to go." They had taken their case to Lieutenant Massey, the bureau officer in charge at Yorktown, but Massey had informed them that if they were told to leave, they must do so. This was worse treatment, Dorcy and Tabb noted, than they received at the hands of "they who are represented as our enemies."[2]

"Our treatment in some respects is worse than it ever was," they continued, and detailed individual cases that demonstrated this truth. "A man at the age of sixty five years," for instance, "was put in a house" on the Saunders Farm by Massey's predecessor. Then, "after being there a while . . . [he] was ordered to pay rent." But the white owner of the property, Robert Saunders, had advised him not to pay rent until forced to do so.[3] When another man, "Mr Shields" approached the man for rent, Massey followed up by ordering him to pay rent without consulting Robert Saunders. There were other cases of a similar kind, Dorcy and Tabb noted. The confused nature of the situation this man confronted demonstrated the shifting tides of postwar land ownership. It was not yet apparent to the Black resident or the landowner, Robert Saunders, who could charge rent for the property. In the aftermath of the war, lands previously confiscated by the federal government and administered as government lands reverted back to their prewar ownership, and in York County, as elsewhere in the postwar South, Black residents were caught in the middle. The situation in York County was further complicated by the fact that long-term US occupation meant that Black residents had remained in relatively fixed locations for a long period of time. When the war ended, they expected to retain the land upon which they had settled. Shifting government policies contradicted this notion, and as the meeting of Black residents in York and James County demonstrated, they refused to accept such outcomes without an attempt at negotiation.

Dorcy and Tabb's letter, however, also reflected the perspective from which Black residents of York County approached the situation. Rather than wait for federal officers to tell them what their future would be, they sought to craft and control it themselves. Moreover, they believed they had a legitimate claim to the land because so many enslaved people had worked that same land all their lives. Thus, Black residents did not ask for a redistribution of wealth so much as an acknowledgment that their labor gave them a legitimate claim. Black petitioners expected the federal government to heed their calls for consideration and were not willing to settle for being ignored. When their local Freedmen's Bureau agent did not cooperate with their efforts, they went above him, addressing themselves to the head of the Freedmen's Bureau, a man who they believed was responsible for safeguarding their best interests.

Samuel C. White, a white landowner in York County, similarly addressed himself to the head of Virginia's Freedmen's Bureau, Orlando Brown, in 1867. White wrote to request payment of rent for the years 1865 and 1866 for his 475-acre farm known as the Temple Farm. His description of the state of the farm illustrates how drastically Yorktown's landscape had changed during and immediately after the war. "I have made out the above amount as near with your instructions as I can," White explained, "the above amount I consider reasonable." He justified the $1,900 bill by describing what was left of his property in the wake of federal occupation. The Temple Farm included a "mill and a large orchard," which had been "in the occupancy of the government for the last four years." During those four years, all of his timber had "been destroyed houses gone enclosures destroyed and I should think at least 1000 yards of fortifications thrown up on said farm." "My very yard," White noted, "was taken for a slaughter pen for the army and my farm grazed by large quantities of stock for the Army." He concluded his letter by noting his own destitution in the wake of the war, "I hope you will approve the account as I much need the money."[4] White found himself in a similar situation to many white landowners in York County who returned home to find the landscape irrevocably altered.

Dorcy and Tabb's petition and White's letter paint a poignant picture of York County in the wake of the Civil War. Emancipation had ensured that there would be no return to the status quo, and the destruction and revolutionary transformation of the county's physical landscape likewise guaranteed that York County's farming operations would be entirely different from how they were organized before the war. Moreover, occupation by Union forces and thousands of refugees from slavery had turned the landscape into what many described as a barren wasteland, especially on the farms closest to Yorktown proper. In the immediate aftermath of the war then, all residents of York County whether Black Virginians, US soldiers, or former Confederates had to devise a new system of residency and farm labor. Unsurprisingly, these different groups often clashed. But the nature of the destruction also forced white landowners to work with the bureau and Black residents.

Histories of refugee communities often end with the disestablishment of those communities as the US Army rapidly demobilized in 1865, while histories of the Freedmen's Bureau generally characterize the transition of 1865 to 1866 as a moment of lost opportunity, especially with regard to land distribution.[5] Although established to guard the rights of formerly enslaved people, the bureau under the Johnson administration quickly became an unlikely ally of white planters in their mutual effort to revive the Southern economy. One of the primary markers of this effort was Andrew Johnson's decision to return "abandoned" lands to their former Confederate owners, often dislocating newly free people from those lands in the process.

An investigation of this postwar period from the ground level instead of the level of federal policy reveals the continuity in Black residents' efforts to establish their lives during and immediately after the war. Despite frequent changes in authority, shifting regulations of land ownership, and white actors whose considerations for formerly enslaved people were mixed, Black Southerners found ways to make their needs and desires heard. Taken from a national view, it is easy to see the dynamics of white planters, Johnson's administration, and the Freedmen's Bureau as the forces that dominated and ultimately determined the course of this transition. Observed from a small place such as York County, however, that power appears diluted, and the efforts of Black Southerners to resist supervision and chart their own course to economic and social independence becomes evident once more. The transition from wartime occupation to the oversight of the Freedmen's Bureau was by no means straightforward, and in the twisting and turning of immediate circumstances there was space for negotiation and innovation. Black residents in York County took advantage of that space as Dorcy, Tabb, and their fellow petitioners did, believing that the federal government should respond to their needs. Within this space they began the process of preserving the communities they had established and homes they had built through formal means such as petition as well as in everyday acts of resistance. An evaluation of their efforts reveals that Black residents sought recognition of the work they had already done both in slavery and in freedom. They had earned a right to the land, they believed, and during the Freedmen's Bureau's tenure in Yorktown from 1865–1868, Black residents held on to a hope that the federal government might compensate them for the labor that had produced the crops and bought the land they now claimed as their own.

Tracing these shifting policies and land occupation status during this period is difficult. Bureau records testify to the confused nature of the moment and often only provide snippets of complex interactions between agents, landowners, and Black residents. Generally, the end of the war and the return of confiscated lands meant that properties Black residents believed would remain in their possession were returned to their prewar white owners. But "returning" legal title did not necessarily mean white landowners were able to physically repossess the land. Some white landowners agreed to rent land to Black residents, others wished to rent to only some Black residents, and still others initially agreed to rental systems and then changed their minds in subsequent years. For multiple years after the war landowners pushed the bureau to remove Black refugees, Black refugees resisted, and federal policies changed. A letter from a white landowner demanding removal did not mean that removal happened, and so questions about the future of land status arose year after year. Similarly, Black residents might have agreed to pay rent at the beginning of the year to remain in place, but they did not necessarily pay those rents when the end of the year came around. Moreover, dynamics and rental agreements differed from farm to farm. Consequently, the narrative that follows is not straightforward but attempts to weave together pieces of information that, taken collectively, testify to the tenacity with which Black residents retained their claims to the land they inhabited.

Yorktown's initial organization of farm labor on confiscated lands during the war loosely followed patterns established elsewhere, especially further down the peninsula at Fort Monroe. The Friends were key organizers in this effort, soliciting from among their followers individuals to relocate to York-town and supervise individual farms. Their vision mirrored that of many other Northern workers in refugee communities across the South and met with many of the same constraints. Convinced that the best way to help Black Southern-ers was to "help" them to labor, the Friends provided farming implements and sought to direct farming efforts within the old plantation complexes. Yet to focus exclusively on the Friends' effort as the organizing force of the system that emerged in Yorktown during and after the Civil War would be a mistake. Friends and Freedmen's Bureau records reveal that Black residents sought to make the system work for them, utilizing the opportunities provided by be-nevolent workers while maintaining autonomy over their lives. What emerged in York County was more than a system of supervised farming. Black inhabit-ants rooted claims to land ownership after the war in the labor they had already expended and the crops they had produced. In this way, Black residents began constructing meaningful lives for themselves and their community before the war ended and before their freedom had been formally recognized in the law.

Initial efforts on the part of the Friends to organize farm labor in York County focused on a system of "industrial allotments" where white supervisors assigned Black refugees plots of land to work. Organizing the plots within the same boundaries that had defined the prewar plantation landscape, the Friends hoped to assign a white supervisor—usually a Friend—to each farm. This orga-nization along lines of prewar ownership signaled the contingent nature of this arrangement. Lands could be used for such purposes only after the US Army had confiscated it as land abandoned by disloyal white owners. In York County this included not just farms, but other productive property such as grist mills.[6] The Friends believed that they could disperse the destitute Black population to these farms, relieving the pressure on the city of Yorktown and rendering Black people "most speedily self-supporting, intelligent, and law abiding."[7]

In early 1864, the Friends advertised for "two or three young men to go upon plantations in the neighbourhood of Yorktown, to direct and assist the freedmen in their farming operations."[8] Though the article stated that Friends would be preferred, anyone interested in the "cause" were also welcomed to apply. They would receive a "moderate" salary and would find it necessary "to work with the people." These advertisements implied that without the Friends' help, Black refugees would remain dependent on the government for support. Moreover, the Friends believed that without their insight and direction, Black people's farming efforts would fail.

John C. Tatum, one of the Friends who arrived in Yorktown at the beginning of their efforts, further advised that "one of the best modes of helping the freedmen [would] be the furnishing of some aid in their work on the ground allotted to them."[9] They would also supply farming implements. In addition, the Friends sought to establish a store where refugees could obtain seeds and other necessary goods at fair prices rather than the exorbitant prices characteristic of army sutlers.[10] Despite appearances, this was not strictly benevolence for the sake of benevolence. The Friends planned for Black residents to "refund" them the cost of the various supplies they provided "when they harvest[ed] their season's crop."[11] Black residents would pay for the aid they received.

Each advertisement for supplies and report submitted to their peers in Pennsylvania suggested that the Friends arrived in York County to find a desperate situation and that without their efforts the land would not reap a harvest. Yet elsewhere in the occupied South, by the time Union forces or US-sponsored organizations arrived, Black refugees had already taken over the work of cultivating the land white planters had abandoned. This was likely the case in York County too, though the Friends did not comment on it. Given the situation Isaac Wistar described upon arriving to take over Fort Yorktown, it is apparent that Black refugees wasted no time getting back to the business of providing for themselves. If Black residents had so quickly returned to oystering and other business ventures, they likely had returned to farming as well.

Such was the case famously at Davis Bend in Mississippi where in the absence of any white people claiming control of the plantation, Black residents created an independent colony. By early 1864 three thousand residents were producing cotton and a profit.[12] Elsewhere, such as Port Royal, South Carolina, Black residents produced staple food crops for themselves but avoided expending their efforts on cotton, which required a yearlong commitment to reap a financial profit.[13] Similar instances of Black residents applying their labor on their own terms as soon as the opportunity arose could be found along South Carolina's coast.[14]

The cessation of armed conflict brought more questions and uncertainty than it did answers to the situation in York County and the rest of the occupied South. United States policies preceding the Confederate armies' surrenders had left many Black refugees with the impression that the newly established Freedmen's Bureau would become an agent for permanent land confiscation and redistribution. In the spring of 1865, the Freedmen's Bureau administered more than eight hundred thousand acres of confiscated land across the South, and Black refugees believed that having been the cultivators of that land, they were its rightful possessors.[15] As Chandra Manning has noted, permanent freedom had yet to be established in the spring of 1865 and there was no way of knowing if emancipation would remain permanent.[16] Moreover, historian Greg Downs has argued that before the war was even over, the federal government was preparing for a rapid demobilization as a result of a brief financial panic in the early spring of 1865.[17] In an effort to save money, the federal government discharged soldiers from the army quickly, a move that "played havoc on the Freedmen's Bureau" whose agents were often soldiers and who relied on the military for any type of enforcement.[18]

Still, the situation was anything but predetermined, and within the uncertainty opportunity for negotiation could be found. In May of 1865, President Andrew Johnson issued two proclamations extending civil and property rights to most former Confederates who took an oath of loyalty to the United States.[19] Land restoration began almost immediately as returning white landowners sought to reclaim their property. In many locations in the South, refugee camps also disbanded rapidly with the army's demobilization. Still, pockets of resistance remained.[20] Realizing that dispersal meant a loss of power and believing that their labor had paid the price for the land they now farmed, formerly enslaved people in the South Carolina Sea Islands, the Virginia Peninsula, and the lower Mississippi Valley defied the bureau's efforts at their removal.[21] Their exertions complicated the intentions of federal officials who believed that economic revival in the South depended on the rejuvenation of market crops and in turn hinged on access to sufficient, cooperative labor.[22]

In this context, the Freedmen's Bureau sought to convince Black refugees of the necessity of agreeing to labor contracts with white landowners and attempted to institute a system of paid farm labor. Formerly enslaved people though, challenged these efforts, and in September of 1865 the central bureau office in Virginia issued a circular stating that "reports [have] been received at these Head Quarters that the freedmen, in some part of the State, refuse to enter into just and reasonable contracts for labor, on account of the belief that the United States Government will distribute lands among them." Superintendents throughout the Virginia bureau, the circular ordered, should "take the earliest opportunity to explain to the freedmen that *no lands will be given them by the Government.*" Furthermore, bureau agents should "explain to [Black refugees] the advantages of at once entering into contracts for labor for the coming year, and that the system of contracts for labor is in no way connected with slavery, but is the system adopted by free laborers everywhere."[23] Black Virginians had uniformly refused to acquiesce to a system of paid, supervised labor and in presuming it was because of its resemblance to slavery, bureau agents failed to appreciate formerly enslaved people's desire to direct their own futures.

Such orders, and indeed the complaints on the part of bureau agents across the South of their inability to convince Black refugees to enter contracts, suggested that the case was clear: The war was over, white landownership had been restored, no land would be redistributed. Casting Black resistance as misguided, such framing suggested that Black people simply did not understand the situation at hand. Yet Black Southerners had good reason to hope for land in 1865 and good reason to retain that hope even after policies shifted in favor of white landowners.

Formerly enslaved people faced the end of the war believing that the federal government would redistribute land. Such convictions were not confined to a single area, such as the South Carolina Sea Islands where some redistribution had already occurred, but were widely observed and reported on by bureau agents from Virginia to Georgia and elsewhere.[24] In Georgia, Black leaders such as Aaron A. Bradley encouraged refugees to stand firm in their hopes of land ownership and to resist signing labor contracts with white planters.[25] In Hampton, Virginia, Calvin Pepper, a white lawyer, assured audiences that they could all have lands and "their rights should be secured to them."[26] Along with the Sea Islands, some land redistribution occurred in Mississippi, and as historian Lynda Morgan has pointed out, observers could reasonably conclude from both law and practice on the part of the US Army that land redistribution was on the horizon. "Several pieces of legislation," Morgan has noted, "coupled with the actions of the bureau and the military, clearly indicated that Congress seriously considered land redistribution plans and in some cases had even implemented them." Indeed, Congress's orders establishing the Freedmen's Bureau authorized such land redistribution.[27]

Moreover, Black Southerners, having experienced the shifting tides of US policy through four years of war, had no reason to think that any one government stance would be permanent. In South Carolina, US General William T. Sherman's famous promise of homesteads for formerly enslaved people had proceeded in a haphazard way, and its implementation changed every time someone new took control of Union forces in the area.[28] In Virginia, Oliver Otis Howard, head of the Freedmen's Bureau, issued Circular No. 3 in May of 1865 reminding agents that they should not restore any land to returning Confederates and two months later Howard ordered the implementation of the bureau's land allotment system.[29] President Johnson rescinded these orders in September and redistribution never started.[30]

Such dramatic shifts in policies and conflicts at different levels of government made it entirely reasonable for Black residents to bide their time to see what the next month might bring. This was, as Steven Hahn has argued, anything but a misinformed reluctance on the part of Black Southerners, but rather a strategy through which Black refugees avoided committing themselves to an unwanted system of labor before they were certain what the future might hold.[31] By continuing to hold fast to these beliefs, and circulating rumors that contradicted official policy, Black Southerners maintained their solidarity and their conviction that "just compensation for the travails of enslavement" required providing future security through land ownership.[32]

It was within this context of shifting policies and expectations that Black residents of York County confronted the end of the war and began the process of establishing a postwar system of farming.[33] Rather than submit to a system of paid labor, Black residents of York County participated in a program of land leasing wherein they entered contracts to rent the land on which they had already established themselves from white landowners.[34] An October 1865 report of lands rented in the county recorded six hundred people living at Slabtown and renting from Doctor Frederick Power. The report identified 396 of those residents as "self-supporting" and noted that they were "engaged as storekeepers, mechanics, oystermen, & c." It further noted that though 218 acres of the property was cleared, only thirty acres of land were under cultivation. These figures suggest that residents did not farm this land but rather had established a community that resembled a neighborhood or small town.[35] A similar system existed in Hilton Head, South Carolina, where Black residents who pursued independent work such as truck farming—selling produce directly to consumers—or fishing lived in rented homes with garden plots.[36]

In February of 1866, the situation had evolved and Uniontown's future on Powers's land appears to have become uncertain. Assistant Bureau Commissioner F. J. Massey identified further considerations at work in Yorktown. The Friends, Massey explained in a letter to Robert Powers, the county magistrate and brother of Frederick Powers, had "erected a number of buildings at considerable expense to them for use as School Houses and churches in 'Slabtown.'" If Robert Powers would not "execute and sign an agreement allowing [the buildings] to remain" they would be removed, and the result would be "considerable material injury to the best interests of the freedmen and probably effect the proposed leasing of the 'Farm.'"[37] In other words, the Friends had built the structures for the benefit of refugees and if Powers would not guarantee that the buildings could remain, Massey suspected that Black residents would not want to lease Powers's land for the next year. They were willing to rent from Powers because they valued the community they had created. With this appeal Massey also revealed the complicated state of affairs that persisted after the war. Stripped of much of its power to protect the rights of Black Southerners, the Freedmen's Bureau appealed to civil authorities to intercede on behalf of Black residents. In this case, Massey's request further emphasized the political power that local landowning white families continued to wield. The county magistrate was also the landowner's brother.

A month later Massey informed Slabtown's residents that the issue was resolved for the time being. Massey did not specify what caused the disturbance in the first place, but it appears there may have been a disagreement between Powers and the Black community over rental agreements for the coming year. An unidentified "committee," presumably of Friends, had advanced the first quarter's rent for the entire property, and Black residents would be expected to rent their individual plots from the committee. None of the buildings would be removed, and if anyone wished to relocate elsewhere, they would have to pay back rent for the time they had occupied a lot in the village. This agreement suggests that Slabtown's residents had refused to pay rent for their lots and that the Friends circumvented the issue by paying the initial rent themselves. Massey concluded his message to Black residents by stating that he "hoped the Freedmen will see the justice of this order and will display in their promptness in responding to the same their appreciation of the generosity of the 'Committee' for their kindness in coming to their relief when it was necessary that some party . . . should accept the responsibility of renting the land."[38] Massey's note that he hoped the residents of Slabtown would see the "justice" in this situation hinted that he anticipated resistance to this new state of affairs and perhaps understood that the agreement simply delayed resolution of the heart of the problem: that Black residents did not agree that they should have to pay rent. Elsewhere in the county, Massey informed Black residents that they would have to pay rent to individual landowners if they wished to remain where they were then living.[39]

Despite Massey's attempt to clarify the situation it remained complex. In some instances, former Confederates had not signed oaths of loyalty. On July 31, 1866, Massey reported that three thousand acres of land belonging to Colonel George Blow remained in federal hands because Blow was "an unpardoned rebel" who had made "no effort for 'Executive Clemency.'" The population residing on Blow's property must have been large as Massey lamented the fact that had the government previously been aware of the situation, Blow's farm could have been a "great source of revenue for the Bureau."[40]

Black residents of York County faced a complicated situation in the immediate aftermath of the war, and policies affecting their future rarely took their best interests into account. Land restoration, the implementation of contracts, and the restoration of civil authority all coincided to create a situation unconducive to Black independence. Still, Black residents found ways to maneuver around and resist these polices. In the process they continued to work and advocate for their vision of the future.

In some cases, Black residents resisted this new land and labor system by simply refusing to comply. In February of 1866 Massey found it necessary to issue a circular explaining that the terms of the lease for the Bellfield Farm specified that residents could only utilize fallen timber. Apparently Black residents had continued to cut standing trees because Massey went on to direct that "standing timber is not to be cut for wood until this supply [of fallen timber] is exhausted." "It is hoped," he concluded, "that the 'Freedmen' will promptly live up to the contracts which they have made as it will prevent trouble and annoyance and to the best interest of all concerned."[41] Though Massey framed this situation in terms of "living up to" the contracts they had made, Black residents continued to insist on their right to the resources at hand by ignoring restrictions on the use of the land they were renting. During the war, all the physical resources of the landscape had been at their disposal, and they would not simply accept a reversal of policy.[42]

Others found ways to help their neighbors within the confines of the land-lease system. George Taylor sued William and James Roberts in the Freedmen's

Bureau Court for nonpayment of rent. Taylor rented ten acres from a white man, "Mr McCandlish," and had paid the whole rent upfront. He then rented two thirds of the land to the Roberts brothers "at the same rate that I rented it for but they refused to pay me." That Taylor paid the entire rent up front and then leased a portion of it to the Roberts brothers for the same rate suggests that he did them a favor by advancing the rent with capital he had available and only charging them the amount he had expended once they had cultivated the land and made money.[43]

Major Fields found a less benevolent way to navigate the system and ensure he did not lose the money he had invested in his home. Sally Cook sued Fields after Fields sold her a house and told her there would "be no trouble" with her staying in the house for a year, as he claimed to have already paid the year's rent. Shortly after occupying the house, Cook discovered that the rent had not been paid and she could not stay. Forced to move out, Cook insisted that she would not have bought the house if she had known the truth of the matter. For his part, Fields explained that he knew he was going to have to move off the land, but he had "built the house there and wanted to make something of it."[44] With this statement, Fields exposed a problem that would plague Black residents throughout the county: Many had invested their own resources in building homes on land they thought they would get to occupy indefinitely. When landowners returned and refused to continue renting the land, those resources would be lost, and homes torn down. Though his methods were underhanded, Fields had devised a way to recoup some of his financial losses before his house was demolished.

A Freedmen's Bureau circular issued in May of 1866 pointed to still another way Black Virginians were influencing the system and exerting control over their lives. Citing "An Act to regulate contracts for labor between white and colored persons and to impose a fine on persons enticing laborers from the service of their employees under such contracts," the circular defined several regulations. Chief among them was a directive prohibiting "any person" from enticing "away from the service of another employer any laborer employed by him under a contract as provided by this Act knowing of the existence of such a contract."[45] As Steven Hahn has explained, Black residents of the Virginia Peninsula found multiple ways to direct and withhold their labor to maintain some bargaining power. In some cases, as this circular suggested, individuals would enter a labor contract but then leave it if a better opportunity presented itself. They also resisted signing long-term contracts in order to have the flexibility to pursue a higher paying situation at will.[46] In other cases, maintaining hope that the land redistribution policies would change, Black people collectively refused to sign labor contracts, creating a temporary labor shortage that "weakened the landowners' attempts to tie them down and dictate the terms" of labor contracts.[47] Newly free people throughout the postwar South utilized similar methods to control their immediate circumstances in the aftermath of the war.[48]

By the end of the war, the Black community in York County had spent at least three years building homes, cultivating land, and creating the institutions, such as churches and schools, that sustained them. In their eyes, what they were building was meant to endure long after the US Army and the Freedmen's Bureau left. Many of these residents had been enslaved in York County before the war and felt that through years of uncompensated labor they had earned the right to retain the land. Others had not originally lived in York County but sought refuge there because the presence of the Union army guaranteed a level of stability not replicated in many other places. Still others came because the growing community beckoned, and in community there was protection and strength.

Yet when Northerners, whether agents of the bureau or teachers for the Friends, looked at the sprawling landscape of freedom York County had become, they saw something that was necessarily transient. Even before the war ended, white workers had made attempts to convince the Black community to disperse. Lucy Chase had visited Yorktown from her post at Hampton in July of 1864 and observed, "Efforts are constantly made to induce the negroes to remove from their huddling places upon government farms."[49] To the eyes of these white onlookers, there was little to hold on to in communities like Slabtown and Newtown, where newly free people seemed to be cramped together in crowded dwellings and dependent on government support.

Inherent in this situation was a tension between how Northerners envisioned Black people's freedom, and the freedom Black residents were building for themselves. Adding to this tension was the fact that at least during the war and immediately after, resources were scarce.[50] This was not a problem particular to Black civilians. All civilians in the war-torn South, especially Virginia, faced scarcity. Yet when white benevolent workers took in the embodiments of Black freedom visible before them, they saw poverty and a lack of will to labor where they could have seen resilience, determination, and hope.

In the immediate aftermath of the war, Freedmen's Bureau agents at Yorktown actively sought to help newly free people stay on the land while paying fair rents. Their willingness and commitment to this effort testifies to the fact that already by 1865 and 1866, Bureau agents believed that if given the opportunity, formerly enslaved people would quickly become industrious and independent of government support. Consequently, these initial efforts were not so much about moving people out of York County, but rather moving them from the densely populated neighborhoods of Slabtown and Newtown to farms in the area where they had a better chance of laboring for themselves. Many residents of these communities already worked in independent fields such as fishing and oystering, but those who could not find outside work could not support themselves through farming the relatively small plots of land within these two neighborhoods. Thus, believing that newly free people needed to become self-supporting, bureau agents also thought that they would be better suited to do so on outlying farms than in settlements where they would need to go elsewhere to find work.

Yet the rapid changes that occurred in Union command and authority at the end of the war also unsettled this process, leaving Black residents unwilling to walk into situations where their interests were not guaranteed protection. In May of 1865, the Industrial Committee of the Friends' Association of Philadelphia for the Relief Freedmen reported that they had begun helping families from Slabtown build homes on outlying farms. A change in the superintendent of the department, however, had quickly slowed down this effort, leaving newly free people "unsettled" and "fearful to leave their settlements."[51] Just as the constantly shifting tides of US policy could give Black residents hope for positive change, it also made them wary of committing to arrangements that might not be permanent.

In other cases, the Freedmen's Bureau protected Black residents' right to remain on farms, having first assisted in negotiating rental contracts with returned white landowners. In September, C. B. Wilder, in command at Fort Monroe, wrote to the agent at Yorktown, requesting that he look into a case of unauthorized removal. J. A. Jones, a white landowner, had been "ordering off the colored people from the place occupied by them by direction of the Government."[52] At this point, bureau agents protected Black residents' right to remain on land for which they had negotiated rental contracts and did not take kindly to landowners such as Jones who attempted to break those contracts.

While the Freedmen's Bureau at Yorktown also helped negotiate rental agreements with willing landowners, this process depended on precisely that: the willingness of landowners to rent their property to newly free people. This created a problem that would plague residents for years after the end of the war, as landowners changed their mind about rental agreements or attempted to change the terms of those agreements. For their part, white residents believed that they were dealing with an issue of overpopulation. Too many people had made York County their home during the war and, for a variety of reasons, York County could not or would not support that population. To these white residents' eyes, the solution was simple: Black residents needed to go somewhere else. This was a problem common to many settlements that endured by war's end, but the outcomes at Yorktown were decidedly different. Whereas at places like Roanoke Island Black residents ultimately had to leave in large numbers, at Yorktown they stayed in large numbers. Try as the Freedmen's Bureau might to coerce formerly enslaved people to relocate, they fought back, negotiated the terms of their living conditions, and held on to the community they were building.

Consistently bureau agents and benevolent workers failed to recognize the reasons Black residents clung to their community, tending to underappreciate that people had already established lives in freedom before the end of the war and before the passage of the Thirteenth Amendment ensured that freedom. Sarah Cadbury summed up the problem in a letter home explaining, "People do not like to go away and find work, schools keeping some."[53] On one hand, this observation touched on an accurate reason why Black residents chose to stay: They had built schools and wanted to continue taking advantage of the educational opportunities available to them only in the places where refugee settlements had taken root. Massey's letter to Robert Powers indicated as much, when he argued that if the schools and church were torn down, many people would likely not want to enter rental contracts and continue residing in Slabtown. This desire to retain access to education would remain constant. On the other hand, though, Cadbury also dismissed the tangible efforts newly free people had already made towards building their lives by assuming that people "do not like to go away to find work." This too would be a constant refrain. As far as white workers were concerned, the question was clear: Leave and labor elsewhere, or stay and remain "dependent" upon the government.

Underneath Cadbury's observation lay an assumption that if Black residents were to relocate to the surrounding area, they would have reasonable opportunities for labor. Yet in a different instance, Cadbury admitted hearing a woman contradict this assumption when she expressed her desires at a public meeting. This woman stated that "she would go if they would tell her where she was to go," and another woman agreed that she too would go "if they would ensure her good wages."[54] This was not an aversion to labor keeping people in place, but rather a desire to ensure that the terms of that labor were fair and an unwillingness to go where they could not be guaranteed fair situations. To leave Yorktown to find work was not only to move beyond the bureau's reach. It would also mean losing the consolidated Black community that ensured individuals' bargaining power.

In a report to the bureau's office at Fort Monroe, F. J. Massey further explained, "One of the great difficulties I have to contend against is the fear in the minds of the freedmen that when they go back to their former homes they will receive no justice and have their rights constantly tread underfoot."[55] Large numbers of Black people were still moving in and out of the area at this time, and those who came in from other places brought "most doleful accounts of their treatment by the whites." If they could be "assured that justice would be given them outside of this County," Massey thought, "one of the greatest difficulties would be surmounted regarding their removal."[56] In this explanation, Massey revealed two reasons newly free people chose not to relocate. Not only were they fearful of mistreatment by those who had formerly enslaved them, but they also did not want to lose the protection proximity to the bureau could afford.

This was a practical concern. Massey frequently reported on tensions between the Black and white populations of the county and acknowledged that Black residents were unlikely to receive justice at the hands of civil authorities. In June of 1866 Massey wrote again to Robert Powers, the presiding justice of the county, that Black residents were "daily complaining at this office that offences of various character have been committed against them by either other freedmen or white men and ask that action be taken upon the same." All such cases were now outside of his jurisdiction and since having shifted back to civil authorities, incidents of crimes and outrages had increased dramatically. Massey further acknowledged that Black residents held little trust in civil authorities, mentioning, "I presume it is unnecessary for me to refer to the present feelings of the 'Freedmen' toward the civil authorities as their past reactings are well known to you." Still, Massey hoped that Powers would take decisive action to ensure that law and order could be restored.[57]

Beyond York County on the greater Virginia Peninsula, violence was also an endemic problem in the immediate postwar years. As historian Robert Engs has detailed, "lawlessness was rampant and clashes between" white and Black residents "were almost daily occurrences."[58] In nearby Surry and Isle of Wight Counties, bureau agents permitted former Confederates to hire out Black laborers on the same auction block used during slavery. As if that was not enough, the auctioneer carried on the proceedings dressed in a Confederate uniform.[59] Massey likewise noted that Black residents outside of the county had reported conditions that looked considerably like slavery. "Accounts of harsh and cruel treatment by the Whites in the neighboring counties" had proved to be one of the biggest obstacles to convincing Black residents to relocate. Those who did move were "compelled to call their employers 'Master' and 'Missus,' [were] not paid promptly if at all and that . . . cuffs and oaths [were] meted out to them without measure." Thus, Black residents preferred to stay within York County because, Massey acknowledged, "here they say that they know the Whites dare not treat them with impunity."[60] Remaining in York County meant not only remaining closer to the bureau's center of operations, but also benefiting from and maintaining the strength of a large, concentrated Black community.

Newly free people frequently leveraged the bureau to accomplish their goals, petitioning local agents and at times "going above their heads" to superior officers when their needs were not met. In one instance, Black residents went all the way to the Washington, DC, office of the bureau to make their needs known. The "free people now living upon lands of a Mr Cook and Mr Hogg near Yorktown Va" had complained to the Washington office that they had been "ordered to leave the place immediately and are threatened with forcible expulsion seizure of crops &c."[61] Their efforts met with success and Massey received orders to protect these Black residents' rights.

Over the course of 1866 many of the rental agreements made at the beginning of the year broke down, and the bureau transitioned from protecting Black residents' interests to enforcing the desire of white landowners to remove them. Still, Black residents made their desires known, and their voices of resistance survive in the archive, testifying to what was a concerted community effort to negotiate the terms of their freedom. In March of 1866, Margaret Newbold Thorpe described interacting with residents of the Warren Farm who refused to accept the landowner's desire to remove them. "We told them that Mr. Warren did not want them to live any longer on this land," Thorpe recalled, "but they declared they would not move, the land was theirs, they had toiled on it all their lives, without wages." Moreover, "the Union soldiers had told them they might remain there as long as they lived."[62] In declaring that the land was theirs by nature of the fact they had cultivated it "all their lives without wages," the residents of the Warren Farm challenged the idea that only white landowners could claim the confiscated property and established their claim on the basis of their work. That they established their claim to the land based on their work ran in direct opposition to those who attempted to claim that newly free people would not move because they did not want to work. Instead, they articulated another reason they did not want to move, besides the access and protection guaranteed by the bureau: They had already paid for this land with their labor.

To ask the residents of the Warren Farm to relocate was no small object. In an 1865 census of the Black population of York County, the Freedmen's Bureau recorded nearly 140 people living at the Warren Farm. As their testimony suggests, some of this number were people who Warren had enslaved, but others were newly free people who had relocated there likely at the behest of the federal government.[63] Some bureau records indicated that they had arranged for Black residents to move the Warren Farm as recently as early 1866. During the war and into 1865 and in some cases 1866, the bureau juggled confiscated lands that had not been claimed. Where possible, they moved Black people to land they thought they could retain, creating a problem as bureau policy continued to change and the federal government mandated that all confiscated land should be returned. Moreover, at the Warren Farm, some residents were engaged in farming, others were oystermen, and still others US veterans. Wyatt and Emily Carter lived at the Warren Farm, and Wyatt, now disabled, had recently been discharged from the army. Mingo Goodwin, another disabled veteran, lived at the Warren Farm with his wife Mary and sister Alice. Families such as these had given more than their labor to claim this land. They had also offered themselves in service to the Union cause.[64]

Others at the Warren Farm had just finished building homes at the time of the 1865 census, clearly believing, as they stated to Thorpe, that the land was theirs and there they would remain. Jesse and Ann Williams had just completed their house for their six children in March of 1865. George and Elizabeth Weeks were newcomers to the Warren Farm that year, but they too had already begun building a home.[65] Asking residents of the Warren Farm to relocate was asking them to give up the work they had already put in building their lives in freedom. It is no wonder then that Thorpe found "we failed to convince them of the justice of it all," because it likely did not seem like justice at all. Thorpe tended to agree with those who felt it did not seem like justice, concluding, "Our arguments seemed as weak to them as they did to ourselves."[66] Thorpe's passing reference to the weakness of the arguments hinted that Black residents had expressed their unease with the situation and made their opinions known, enabling Thorpe to comment that she and the residents of the Warren Farm saw similar flaws in the policy.

By the end of the year, M. D. Warren was still working to remove Black residents from his farm. In October Warren informed General S. C. Armstrong, who oversaw the peninsula operations from Fort Monroe, that he no longer wanted to maintain the leasing situation that had governed his property for the past year. "From what I have heard," Warren explained, "it would be doing none of the parties good, for the Farm to remain longer under bad cultivation which it has received." Consisting of fifteen hundred acres, Warren insisted that the property could produce a much better harvest than it had in 1866. In fact, the money Warren had gained from the crop yields was too low to even pay the taxes or interest of the farm. Warren wanted to shift oversight of the labor system at his farm to his own supervision and informed Armstrong that he intended to "make an election of such as I employ," keeping the labor of only the Black residents he wanted. "If the place had been properly cultivated," Warren concluded, "I might have been willing to a different course."[67] Warren's suggestion that the farm had not been properly cultivated reflected the assumption that plantation labor after the war should produce the same yields as it had before the war. Moreover, he assumed that Black residents would submit to demands that they labor as much and in the same way as he desired, as if they were a pliable labor force who could be directed at the discretion of white planters.

Warren used the apparent poor crop production for the year to justify shifting from a land-lease system to supervised paid labor. However, in early 1866, residents of Warren's farm made their contracts with Massey, not Warren. Contracts varied by person, but generally renters agreed to pay Massey three-fourths to one barrel of shelled corn per acre at the end of the year. Renters likely made their contracts with Massey because Warren had not yet claimed his land at the beginning of the year and the bureau expected to retain it.[68] Regardless, between the lines of Warren's assertion was also a further implication: He did not want to make a fixed amount of profit from his land, but rather wanted to have enough control over production to ensure he could maximize his profit.

Additional factors had contributed to overall poor crops yields in York County in 1866. In November, Rhoda Smith, a Friends teacher in Yorktown, reported to *The Friend's Review* that "the severe drought experienced last summer destroyed either entirely or partially the crops of many who rented the land, and they are consequently deprived not only of the means of paying their rent, but of sufficient breadstuff for the coming year." Restoration of abandoned lands had further made it impossible for residents to forage for supplies—especially trees—to provide for their basic needs such as fuel to heat their homes.[69]

Three families on the Bellefield Farm, owned by Rebecca McClandish, expressed similar sentiments when approached by Agent Massey regarding removal in early 1866. According to Massey the families "were notified that it would be impossible to rent them lands on said 'Farm' . . . but they have repeatedly refused both stating that the Govt had placed them there; and there were going to remain."[70] One of the families resisted the bureau by force, and Massey reported that when he sent a guard to the farm "the wife of Richard Roberts (col'd) openly defied him with an axe and words of bitter enmity towards the Govt."[71] According to the 1865 census, Richard Roberts' wife was Lucy Roberts, and they resided in their home with their daughter, Fanny Christian Roberts.[72] Baffled, Massey explained that he had offered them the chance to relocate to the Warren Farm, but they wished to remain where they were. Small wonder that they mistrusted the government's efforts, as the situation at the Warren Farm was no more secure. Though bureau agents often complained of Black residents' resistance as if it were an unnecessary complication, they had to accommodate their wishes, revealing how underneath the complaints lay a dialog of negotiation.

Roberts's decision to defend her claim to her home with force was not as irregular as Massey's comments made it seem. Willie Lee Rose observed that at Port Royal, South Carolina, Black residents would meet white visitors and "guard him with their guns" until they confirmed the individual was a friend to their cause.[73] Further down the Virginia Peninsula, Robert Engs also detected Black refugees refusing to give up their land and opposing efforts to make them do so with armed force. In such instances their resistance was so strong that US soldiers had to evict them at gunpoint.[74]

Massey reported that he feared "strenuous measures" would be necessary to convince Black residents that they could not stay on the land they inhabited in York County. One landowner had told Massey that upon finding residents of his land still occupying it he asked them why they had not begun preparations to relocate. "He was asked into one of the Cabins," Massey related, "where two or three chapters of the prophesies of Daniel was read to him, proving to their minds that the millennium, to the colored race was coming, that the lands would soon be theirs &c."[75] Interpreting political events along the lines of a Biblical narrative was also not uncommon. As Matthew Harper has detailed, Black Southerners understood emancipation as part of a larger Biblical narrative that allowed them to chart their future and gave them confidence to engage resolutely in politics.[76] Again, this was more than a simple act of resistance; it was a calculated decision to wait for a reversal of policy that would affirm their right to the land.

Coordinated community acts complemented these individual acts of negotiation, as Sarah Cadbury's passing reference to a public meeting indicates. In December of 1866, the Friends widely published a speech given by Bailey Wyatt, a resident of Newtown. According to the 1865 census, Wyatt worked as a carpenter and lived at Newtown with four other family members, Elsey, Moriah, Lucy, and Lewis. In 1866 Wyatt signed a contract with Stafford G. Cooke, who owned the land on which Newtown stood, thus renting his home within the neighborhood.[77] Wyatt gave his speech at a meeting Black residents held for the express purpose of responding to a previous meeting in which bureau agents and the Friends' superintendent had advised them "to seek homes in the adjoining counties, and elsewhere."[78] Clearly standing as a representative chosen to speak for the community, Wyatt started by stating that "if we turn back to them counties or the lands we came from . . . we shall forever be made hewers of wood and drawers of water."[79] However, "We now, as a people," Wyatt declared, "desire to be elevated, and we desire to do all we can to be educated, and we hope our friends will aid us all they can." Echoing the same sentiments expressed by individuals on outlying farms, Wyatt explained, "we have a right to the land where we are located . . . Our wives, our children, our husbands, have been sold over and over again to purchase the land we [are] now located upon. For that reason we have a divine right to the land."

More than that, Wyatt went on, US soldiers had told residents the land had been confiscated from Confederates, "who was fighting the United States to keep us in slavery and to destroy the Government." By proclamation of the president, he continued, they would have their freedom and "you shall have the confiscated lands." This was a promise the government had made to people who had supported the efforts of the US Army to end slavery and save the Union. To change this policy now and insist that confiscated lands must be returned, Wyatt contended, the government was contradicting itself and breaking an agreement it had made with a people who had remained loyal to the Union cause. "We feel disappointed," Wyatt said, "that they have not kept their promise." These new orders to leave the land were an outright reversal of the policies under which federal agents had been operating. And from Wyatt's perspective, those policies kept changing despite efforts on the part of Black residents to meet whatever was required of them. "We was first ordered to pay rent," he insisted, "and we paid the rent; now we have orders to leave, or have our log cabins torn down over our heads."

Wyatt's speech was more than an appeal to the sense of justice of his audience or a rebuke of the ever-changing policies of the federal government toward newly free people. It was a carefully constructed argument that addressed not only the inconsistencies of policies and unkept promises but laid out a careful argument for the right of formerly enslaved people to the land they had paid for with their labor. Their work had created the profit with which white landowners had purchased the land, and not only the South but the North had grown wealthy on the back of their forced labor. "Didn't we clear the land," he asked, "and raise the crops of corn, of cotton, of tobacco, of rice, of sugar, of everything?" Bringing home his point he went on, "And didn't them large cities in the North grow up on the cotton and the sugar and the rice that we made?" Black Southerners had not just helped save the Union during the war; their labor built the nation the war saved.

Clearly aware of his audience and calculating his words to prompt their advocacy for a change in the government's current course, Wyatt was careful to acknowledge the work of the Friends who would subsequently publish his speech. "The Quakers of the North," he noted, "we . . . consider our best early friends, for the great sacrifice they have made and is making for us, we . . . thank them most kindly." Not only the Quakers but "the great North," he thanked for "the great sacrifice of lives, and of blood . . . we heartily thank them." Wyatt addressed his speech to more than the bureau agents in front of him. He included the Northern public at large, in hopes that by appealing to them the Black community might sway the government's policies once more.

This too was a political calculation. Jacob Vining, the superintendent of schools for the Friends, was in the audience and subsequently quoted Wyatt's speech. It appeared in print in both *The Friends' Review* and *The Friend.*[80] As historian Amy Taylor has argued regarding refugee camps, the act of being overheard and having a speech repeated and disseminated made "an aural claim to space in the camps."[81] Now, Wyatt utilized a similar strategy to make a claim on the American nation and calculated his words to encourage his Northern audience to sympathize with his cause.

That the points Wyatt made in his speech so closely echoed the sentiments expressed by individuals in their encounters with Northern teachers and bureau agents suggests that what appears in the historical record as individual acts of resistance were in fact a coordinated effort to affect the direction of the bureau. Moreover, the sentiments he articulated were an expression of community beliefs regarding justice and what they were owed because of slavery. Black residents of York County were well connected to one another through their churches, their economic ties, and their broad community network. Wyatt gave voice not just to a desire not to be removed but to a collective understanding of the best avenue of approach to negotiate with the federal government. If bureau policies would not change, then Black residents would find other ways to determine the course of their own freedom and retain ownership of the land generations of enslaved people had already earned through their uncompensated labor.

This ability to coordinate their efforts to make their wishes known to the bureau became especially evident when agents attempted to convince Black residents to elect a delegate to travel to Texas and consider the option of relocating there at government expense. In August of 1866, Oliver O. Howard, head of the bureau, ordered Virginia agents to "allow the Freedmen of Norfolk Fort Monroe and Yorktown to assemble and elect a delegate from each settlement to visit plantations in Texas or other States where in the estimation of the assistant commissioner renumerative [sic] employment can be obtained." Transportation would be provided by the bureau, and Howard hoped the results of the trip would "induce the people of the large and destitute settlements to remove to such places as may offer employment."[82] At Yorktown, Lieutenant Massey responded by calling a "Meeting of the 'Freedmen' in York County" in Slabtown in order that they might "recommend a delegate to this office in whom they have implicit confidence as their future welfare may depend materially upon the report he renders."[83] That the bureau agents acknowledged the need for delegates in whom the community placed their trust already indicated the extent to which bureau agents had realized they needed to accommodate the desires of the people. In an effort to make their relocation attempts successful, agents understood that a good report coming from a member of the community, rather than assurances from a government agent, would be more favorably received by Black residents.

Massey called three separate meetings and was unsuccessful each time. On September 8 he reported that not only had the Black community not elected a delegate, but they had also refused to even show up to the meeting to entertain the idea of removal. Explaining the situation, Massey noted, "Some counter influence is at work and the bare thought of removal to the 'Freedman' is an idea which he will not for a moment entertain himself and he will make every effort in his power to not allow it to take root in the breast of those around him."[84] In this, again, Massey underestimated the situation. Believing that relocation was best, Massey attributed people's refusal to entertain relocation to a "counter influence" who did not want to move and therefore convinced other people not to consider moving. Yet as the individual encounters testify, most people had no desire to leave the land they felt they had already earned. Rather than a "counter influence," the failure of Massey's attempts to assemble a meeting indicate Black residents' coordinated effort to maintain their bargaining power as a community united on this issue and for others that would arise later.

Still, Massey believed he could be successful, and assured his superior at Fort Monroe that a fourth meeting would "no doubt" produce a delegate.[85] Unsurprisingly, he was mistaken. For a fourth time, the Black community of York County refused to show up for a meeting whose purpose was to consider relocation. This refusal to even elect a delegate further testifies to the degree to which residents did not want just any land, but wanted this land on which they had already begun building their futures. They did not want to elect a delegate because no matter how much potential Texas or another state had, they had already invested their time and labor in this place. Exasperated, Massey appointed two delegates himself, but "for various reasons they have refused to act."[86] Massey did not explain what those reasons were, but more than likely his selected appointees knew better than to contradict the will of their community. As Steven Hahn has explained, elevating Black political desires "demanded the mobilization of entire communities."[87] In the post-emancipation South, Black communities utilized a variety of methods to ensure solidarity in political participation and if those methods failed, often employed coercive measures to do so. Political success demanded discipline and strong community backing.[88]

Three months later, in December, the situation had not changed, and Massey had to acknowledge that it was not because people were averse to laboring elsewhere. "Wedded to the land on which they were placed by the Government they do not wish to change their homes," he admitted, "but remain here doing an occasional job, instead of providing themselves with comfortable homes in other neighborhoods." Their resolution to stay was clear, and they resisted "all efforts which tend to their removal to other points."[89] Key to the efficacy of their strategy was their unified front and the ability to coordinate such decisive community action.

Policymakers believed that by stopping rations they could force the issue of removal. Surely, in their eyes, once people could no longer depend on being fed by the government, they would go somewhere else. Oliver O. Howard issued orders to this effect in August of 1866, stipulating that after October 1 the bureau would cease issuing rations "except to the sick in regularly organized hospitals, and to the orphan asylums for refugees and freedmen already existing."[90] This order took effect on the Virginia Peninsula later that year, and S. C. Armstrong stipulated in November "rations are to be issued only to prevent death by starvation, and in the overpopulated Counties of this District Asst Suprs will be careful not to encourage by issuing rations the longer stay therein of those who belong and can go elsewhere."[91] Here again, Armstrong misidentified the reasons Black residents chose to stay, believing they only stuck around because the government offered them food.[92]

Still, as 1866 drew to a close, Black residents of York County continued to resist the bureau's efforts to make them relocate. For his part, Massey acknowledged that perhaps this was because they had crops in the ground that they did not want to abandon. Many residents, Massey noted, "have now small plots of ground under cultivation and it is hoped when their crops are gathered that greater success will attend efforts for their removal."[93] In December, Jacob Vining reported to *The Friend,* "Some excitement is just now caused by an order to remove the coloured people from Acretown, Slabtown, and other rented lands." By the end of 1866, Black residents were renting these lands from their white owners, not occupying them at government expense. According to Vining, those who paid their rent would renew their leases and remain.[94] Vining believed that forcing those who had not paid rent to move was a just decision. However, viewing such a decision as just failed to consider circumstances in 1866 that had contributed to the difficulties of newly free people experienced which made it almost impossible for some to pay rent.

In December, Massey summarized the year in a letter to S. C. Armstrong, acknowledging that outside forces had made the situation difficult for Black residents trying to carve out independence from a hostile landscape. "I regret exceedingly to report that the crops have been so poor during the past year that the 'Freedmen' have suffered severely," and consequently many had not been able to pay their rent. However, it was not for lack of a desire to pay rent that they had failed to do so. In fact, Massey noted, it had "embarrassed them greatly." With winter quickly approaching, Massey believed, suffering would increase for a people already struggling to get by.[95] Despite the bad conditions, however, people continued to struggle to hold on to the lives they were building in York County rather than give up and move elsewhere.

The year 1867 opened with something of a stalemate, as bureau agents continued their efforts to disperse the large population of Black residents, and Black residents in turn resisted their efforts. Oliver O. Howard ordered in February of 1867 that bureau agents at Yorktown should immediately "proceed to effect the distribution of freedmen now collected in camps or colonies in this Subdistrict viz at Newtown, Slabtown, and on the [Winn] Farm, James farm, Saunders farm, Warren farm, and Isley farm, and at such other points where they have been placed by Government officers."[96] That Howard chose to refer to places such as Newtown and Slabtown as "camps or colonies" belied the perspective with which he and his fellow bureau agents approached the issue of collected Black communities. Refugee camps and colonies, during the war, had been places where the US Army and its partners attempted to manage populations they perceived as destitute. In referring to these places in York County with these terms, Howard suggested that they were still fundamentally dependent and temporary settlements rather than autonomous communities. Yet, the fact that Howard even had to mention places such as the Warren Farm indicates that thus far residents had been successful in resisting the bureau's efforts and in so doing demonstrating that they were, as they had declared in 1866, "independent of the Bureau."[97]

To some degree, the postwar years did witness a decline in the refugee population at Yorktown. Massey reported on this population reduction triumphantly, framing it as a success of the bureau in redistributing Black laborers. In February of 1867 he noted that Slabtown's population, which had been close to 1,000 in 1864, was only 540. Newtown had also experienced a population decrease.[98] More than likely, however, this was not just about people seeking outside employment as Massey believed, but rather a reflection of individuals' desire to return to their families or move on at their own accord.

Bureau records document that a small amount of people requested transportation to return to their former homes. In many of these cases, petitioners wished to travel to coastal and northeast North Carolina and Virginia counties bordering York. In December of 1866 Massey had reported that "requests for transportation are daily made at this office to Counties on the river or others not very far distant." He needed help, however, because the bureau office did not have the resources to get them there. Around the same time, John and Argin Bowen specifically requested to return to their home in Plymouth, North Carolina, taking with them three children, MC, Emiline, and Hannah Pyanus.[99] In February of 1867 Massey noted that "large numbers" of people living in Newtown "desire to be removed immediately (to the neighboring Cos of Warwick James City and New Kent) in order that they may have an opportunity of breaking up ground and planting for the present year."[100] Though these individuals had chosen to leave York County, they still wished to remain close by rather than leave the state, as the bureau had previously urged the community to consider. By remaining near York County these would-be farmers ensured they could still readily access the community they had built. Moreover, though Massey claimed people requested transportation at his office daily, his records do not suggest that this represented a large number of people. More than likely he received such frequent requests because the same people had to ask more than once, and it took time for Massey to arrange for their transportation with the bureau's limited resources.[101]

By March of 1867, Massey acknowledged that Black residents generally still resisted efforts to make them leave, and white residents frequently complained of this at the bureau office. This marked a key reversal from earlier years when Black residents could petition the bureau for support when white residents attempted to make them move. Yet in the same letter in which Massey reported this dilemma, he also acknowledged that in James City County, the next county over, "a strong protecting arm is needed to guard jealously the right of the Freedmen and secure them justice."[102] Despite the fact that outside of the immediate supervision of the bureau, Black residents could not be assured of justice, Massey believed resistance to removal was about to give way.

In a second report that same month, Massey assured General Armstrong, "the Freedmen now more fully understand their proper position and what the general government expects of them and above all their minds have been disabused of the idea of 'divine right' to the land."[103] While Massey identified this as an "incalculable good," more than likely what he observed was a growing recognition among the Black population that the Freedmen's Bureau was not going to be the friend Bailey Wyatt had hoped for. Massey also made an important observation about the issue of nonpayment of rent that remained from 1866. He informed Armstrong, "I do not believe that during the present year land owners will complain so loudly of nonpayment of rent," indicating that rents would be paid more consistently. This observation on Massey's part suggests that at least in previous years, Black residents had not paid rent not because they could not, but rather because they did not believe they should have to. Withholding their rent was another method of getting their point across that they were entitled to the land they had already paid for. But, having been "disabused of the idea of 'divine right' to the land,"—or perhaps more accurately, convinced that the Bureau would not support that right—Massey believed those who had used this method of resistance would submit to the requirement of paying rent.[104] Still, that Black residents had accepted that rental policies would not change did not mean that they would give up the land in which they had invested, or their aspirations of independence.

By May, Massey reported that "there has been a great reduction in the number of unemployed 'Freedmen' in this county."[105] Massey felt confident that "removal of Freedmen to other counties is now complete," but he did not mean that the Black population had been dispersed and reduced to its prewar levels. Rather, "the present tenantry of the several farms are now settled for the entire year."[106] Though Massey read this as an accomplishment of the bureau against the will of Black residents, it can also be read as a degree of victory for the former refugees who wanted to retain hold of the property they had been cultivating during the war and the homes they had built in freedom. This retention of these communities, even in the form of tenantry, would serve them well after the bureau departed.

Massey's report may appear to suggest that the story of Black freedom begun during the war had come to its conclusion. For his part, Massey would seek reassignment, claiming his productivity had waned and his successor would undertake the business of shuttering the bureau's operations. Though the bureau would remain in Virginia until 1870, its operations after 1868 strictly involved coordinating educational efforts.[107] But the story at Yorktown would continue to evolve and Massey's depiction of removal as complete belied the landscape of freedom Black residents had built and would continue to defend in the ensuing decades.

CHAPTER 6

★ ★ ★ ★ ★ ★ ★ ★

Landscapes of Freedom,
Landscapes of Memory

In 1902, a "Southern woman" published an account of her visit to Yorktown in the *Richmond Dispatch*. She wrote of the ride to Williamsburg and then the drive to Yorktown, which she described as "a stretch of country replete with historic associations, before the magnificent monument commemorating Washington's victory looms in sight." It was a striking experience for this traveler; "How impossible to describe the feeling that overwhelms one as one draws near to it," she exclaimed, "Hallowed spot where Cornwallis laid down his sword, and Washington founded a nation." With these words, this visitor summed up the way popular white discourse framed Yorktown in the last decades of the nineteenth century and into the early twentieth. It was the place where "Washington founded a nation," and "the ghosts of the past seem to rise and stalk over the green fields and winding road."

Yet, as much as the author wished to depict this "hallowed spot" as caught in days past, there were other present realities she could not help but notice and comment on. "But what amazed this tourist was that nearly all the land between Williamsburg and Yorktown" she continued, "appears to be inhabited by negroes; and a thrifty lot they seem to be, judging from their creditable homes." The author and her fellow travelers determined to converse with a few of these inhabitants and spoke with a woman who "told us she was going to Uniontown."[1] When the visitors asked where Uniontown was located, the woman pointed "to our sacred Carcassone" and explained that that was "where the 'colored folks' lived." After the visitors proceeded to "our sacred Carcassone"—Yorktown—the white traveler concluded that indeed "perhaps [the local woman] was right (except for blessed memories)." Lest her readers miss her meaning, the author explained, "Of the 150 inhabitants of which York-town, muddy, dilapidated, forlorn-looking Yorktown, to-day can boast, all but twelve families are negroes. The streets swarm with them." Moreover, "both postmaster and custom-house officer (thanks to our Republican President!) are Black."[2] Except for the memories of white inhabitants of old, Yorktown, the traveler revealed, was the exclusive domain of Black residents.

The reality that the white Southerners' sacred city was primarily inhabited by Black Southerners hit the author with even more force when she and her companions "stopped at the ancient custom-house building." Taking a special interest in this building because it was the first established in the United States, they "were greeted by a negro woman who was conducting a school. The structure she told us was the property of her father." Making no secret of her feelings on the matter, the author described, "swarms of little pickaninnies sat around the room in which once gay cavaliers in knee breeches and velvet coats clinked their glasses . . . for here was the trysting place of those proud aristocrats of old Virginia." With her loaded terms, this "Southern woman" attempted to communicate, and perhaps generate outrage, that this hallowed place, the rightful home of "proud aristocrats of old Virginia" was now the domain of Black Americans.

Concluding her article, she noted, "I must not forget to mention the pretty national cemetery on the outskirts of the town, nor the fortifications begun by [Confederate General] Magruder and completed by [US General] McClellan."[3] Though she spent less time reflecting on the meaning of these sites—all of which dated from the Civil War—than she had the Revolutionary-era sites, the author gestured toward the many histories visible on York County's landscape in the postwar era. In this gesture, though, she shared with her fellow white Southern women her concern about the way the landscape of this Revolutionary historic site was progressively yielding to the forces let loose by the Civil War, most notably, Black Americans' freedom and independence. Such descriptions of the confluence of Revolutionary War and Civil War histories evident in York County were common, though often white commentators ignored the reality of Black freedom so plainly evident around them.

In the post–Civil War era, what this "Southern [white] woman" called the "hallowed spot" where George Washington "founded a nation" would be the political stage on which Black citizens of York County continued to stake their claims to a place in the nation. One of the primary ways Black residents accomplished this was by firmly establishing their presence in York County through land ownership and occupation so that by 1902 visitors could not help but notice them. Their ability to achieve this was uncertain in the immediate postwar era, as conflicts between Black residents who wished to stay and white authorities who wished them to leave, continued. In the wake of the Freedmen's Bureau's departure, Bayley Wyatt, Peter Dorcy, Philip Tabb and the community they represented were left with little in the way of answers to one of their most pressing questions: If forced to leave the land they had spent years inhabiting and cultivating, where would they go? What would become of the community they had painstakingly built in freedom—the one they had defended through petition, negotiation, and force? Despite Lieutenant Massey's assurances that the Black population of York County had dispersed, his letters on this matter are misleading. York County's Black population would remain relatively stable between the end of the war and 1870 rather than significantly declining.[4]

Freedmen's Bureau reports from 1865–1866 recorded 765 individuals residing in Slabtown and 795 residents at Newtown.[5] In 1867 the bureau recorded 550 people living on Frederick Powers's farm—Slabtown—and 700 people living on Stafford G. Cooke's farm—Newtown.[6] Black residents continued to occupy other farms in the area, but Slabtown and Newtown remained the largest concentrated communities. This situation may have seemed unremarkable to Massey because by the time the bureau left York County in late 1868, agents had negotiated rental situations in which Black residents rented the plots of land on which they resided, and in some cases also rented land to farm. Black residents were, in the eyes of white workers, self-supporting. While Massey may have understood his work as complete, Black residents did not. For them, the most pressing question of how to obtain full control of their lives and livelihoods by achieving land ownership remained unanswered.

Because the bureau's primary concern was the Black population of the county, from 1865–1868 their lives were consistently documented, and those documents have been preserved. After 1868, when the Freedmen's Bureau left York County, it becomes more difficult to piece together the story of the community. Nevertheless, the efforts of Black residents to achieve land ownership and control their futures remain discernable. Although the written record provides an incomplete picture that leaves far more questions than it answers, what we can know about the efforts of Black residents in the decade after the Civil War to achieve land ownership testifies to the resilience and success of a people determined to make freedom look the way they had always hoped.

It would be difficult to track the reorganization of all the land in York County after the Civil War and document every Black person who achieved land ownership during that period. However, by examining three case studies, each surrounding the land of a prewar white landowner—Frederick Powers, Edward Darlington, and Stafford Cooke—a sense of the success of Black residents in acquiring lands and the efforts they took to protect that investment becomes discernable. Residents of the farms of each of these owners took different paths and faced different obstacles to land ownership, largely related to the actions and circumstances of the white landowner. Frederick Powers had to sell his land at public auction to pay for debts he had incurred—a problem that plagued many white landowners in the postwar period. A duo of Northern investors purchased his property at auction shortly after the war and it was from these two men, Lob Wolf and Daniel Heyman, that Black residents eventually bought parcels of land.[7] Edward Darlington appears often to have been an ally to the Black population of York County. He served on the Freedmen's Bureau Court and seemingly voluntarily sold parcels of land to Black individuals beginning almost immediately after the end of the war. Conversely, bureau agents acknowledged that Stafford Cooke, despite his own protestations to the contrary, was particularly disagreeable when it came to interacting with the Black residents who rented land from him. Indeed, both during and after the bureau's tenure, Cooke made numerous attempts to remove Black residents from his property.

All three cases are incomplete. Records of land sales appear sporadically in county deed books, sometimes appearing in the clerk's office years after the sale took place. In other cases, reference to landowners suggest that they had purchased land previously, but the deed books do not document their sales. Court records also present a partial picture of the many situations, especially when white landowners took Black residents to court in attempts to remove them from their property. They provide little to no narrative of the individual circumstances in which people found themselves, and often group similar cases together, flattening any variation between people's situations. What is clear, however, is that Black residents prioritized land ownership and when possible, purchased the land they inhabited or cultivated rather than continuing to rent. Moreover, the Black community at large seems to have achieved a substantial level of economic independence, if not security. And, perhaps most importantly, the majority never chose to go somewhere else. Rather than take the money they had earned and buy land in an outlying county or migrate to another state, for the most part Black residents in York County remained in the community they had built during the war. In doing so, they maintained the ties that had lent them strength in their postwar dealings with the Freedmen's Bureau and continued to use that position of strength to advocate for their futures. Their success in these efforts are reflected in turn-of-the-century accounts from white travelers like the "Southern woman" who commented on the fact that this bastion of white aristocracy was now almost exclusively inhabited by the very people white Confederates had attempted to permanently enslave and bar from citizenship.

Slabtown and Frederick Powers's Farm

Black residents and the Union army established the Slabtown settlement on the farm of Frederick and Caroline Powers, outside of the city of Yorktown.[8] This neighborhood is perhaps the most well documented in York County because the Friends established their initial schools and churches here and described it extensively in letters. According to Freedmen's Bureau records, Frederick Powers had weathered the war outside of Richmond and had not taken part in the rebellion. In the wake of the war, Powers found himself in a situation similar to many of the white landowners in York County—in debt. Powers's creditors initiated a suit to sell Power's property, sometimes called the "Belle Farm" at public auction. Two hundred and eighteen acres of the property went up for sale in 1869 with the exception of the land embracing the Yorktown National Cemetery, which Powers had already sold to the federal government.[9]

Lob Wolf and Daniel Heyman purchased Powers's farm at auction in 1869 and gained title to the land on December 6, 1872, having by then paid the purchase price in full.[10] But well before that date, Wolf and Heyman had begun the process of subdividing and selling portions of the Slabtown property to individual owners. York County's *Deed Book* recorded a deed of trust between Robert Christian, a Black resident, and Robert Sheild [sic] for 348/100 acres of land in Slabtown, identified as lots seventeen and eighteen.[11] These lots were part of the original property purchased by Wolf and Heyman, so Christian had certainly purchased them prior to using them as collateral for a loan from Sheild.[12]

Wolf and Heyman's motivations for purchasing the Powers's farm are unclear, but it appears they may have seen it as an immediate revenue source. Residents were already paying rent on the property, and at an early date in January 1870, Wolf and Heyman had the Slabtown section surveyed with an eye, presumably, towards sale. Other county records indicate that Wolf and Heyman were operating multiple business ventures in York County by the time they purchased the Powers's farm. Their ventures included logging and considering that part of the Powers's property was uncultivated, they may have intended to cut and sell the timber that remained on site.

The surveyor of Wolf and Heyman's new property divided it into lot A, composed of 59 acres; lot B, composed of 47.7 acres; and fifty-six smaller lots varying in size from just under 2 acres to just over 5 acres.[13] This plat map offers the most comprehensive image of the landscape of Slabtown as the fifty-six small lots are identified as a "plan of Slabtown." However, these lot lines most likely did not correspond exactly to conditions on the ground. The Freedmen's Bureau's 1865 census recorded 388 independent residences in Slabtown, significantly more residences than were represented by the fifty-six lots on Wolf and Heyman's survey. Many of these residences included nuclear families as well as additional dependent occupants. Their relationships were not recorded, but many appear to be elderly parents, children of siblings, and adult siblings. The presence of similar last names ascribed to multiple families in dwellings in numerical order also seems to suggest that residents lived next to or nearby extended family relatives. Slabtown's population exceeded five hundred people in 1867, and bureau agents noted that everyone paid rent and would be allowed to remain.[14] More than likely, then, the fifty-six lots subdivided by Wolf and Heyman's survey included more than one home, or at least more than one household, per lot.

Records of purchases by Black residents picked up in 1873.[15] In March, John W. Thomas, Celia Fields, Washington Fields, Louisa Coffin, and William Washington all purchased plots of land from Wolf and Heyman.[16] Interestingly, none of these individuals appear on the 1865 Freedmen's Bureau census of York County living in Slabtown. Bureau agents recorded a Washington and Catherine Fields living at "Stumptown," a William Washington living at "Sugar Hill," and a John Thomas living at "Indian Field," while individuals by the names of Celia Fields and Louisa Coffin do not appear at all.[17] That none of these early land purchasers seem to have lived in Slabtown at the war's end suggests that they may not have been renting the land they bought since the end of the war. Given that lots likely included multiple dwellings, it is possible that those who purchased land also became landlords to the people living on the property and collected rent from them directly. It is also possible that when these new landowners purchased property it forced others who were already residing there to relocate.

A map of the Yorktown National Cemetery produced by the army's Quartermaster Office around 1866–1867 further supports this conclusion. While the map did not note other settlements in the area, it did provide an image of Slabtown—likely because of its proximity to the cemetery. This map depicts "huts" sitting along neatly ordered roads within the community. When compared with the survey produced for Wolf and Heyman, it is clear that more than one "hut" sat within the boundaries of the designated lots, suggesting that lots did not correspond to individual homesteads.

Perhaps most importantly though, this series of sales suggest that land in Slabtown may have been coveted real estate, so much so that individuals relocated from other places within York County to reside at Slabtown. Owning property in Slabtown would have provided individuals with ready access to the businesses and especially shops that Black residents had established within the neighborhood. It would also have put residents in close proximity to the institutions they had built—their churches, schools, and a "Freedmen's Seminary" identified on the contemporary map of the Yorktown National Cemetery.[18] Additionally, Wolf and Heyman may have been more willing to sell to any Black resident with the means to buy land than were former planters who sought to handpick the Black people they allowed to rent on their farms. If this was the case, Black landowners may have become landlords for individuals already residing on their lots and by doing so protected their community's claim to the landscape they had built.

Around the same time, Daniel and Robert Norton also purchased lot number two in Slabtown from Wolf and Heyman for forty-five dollars.[19] Deed book records testify to the fact that the Norton brothers purchased multiple parcels of land in various locations in York County, and sold parcels almost as frequently. Like Robert Christian, the Nortons used their landholdings to acquire loans from local white planters. At some point Daniel purchased the title of lot number two from Robert, because by 1875 Daniel and his wife Sadie had sold the lot to a man named Joseph Lewis for $300—more than six times its purchase price.[20] Joseph Lewis did not appear on the 1865 census nor did he appear in the 1870 census for York County. However, the location of the lot and the increased purchase price provide important insights. First, this lot was located on the outskirts of Slabtown, near a Black cemetery and near a church according to the quartermaster's map. That Joseph Lewis was willing to pay such an increased price for the land suggests that during their period of ownership, the Nortons had improved the property, possibly by building a more substantial

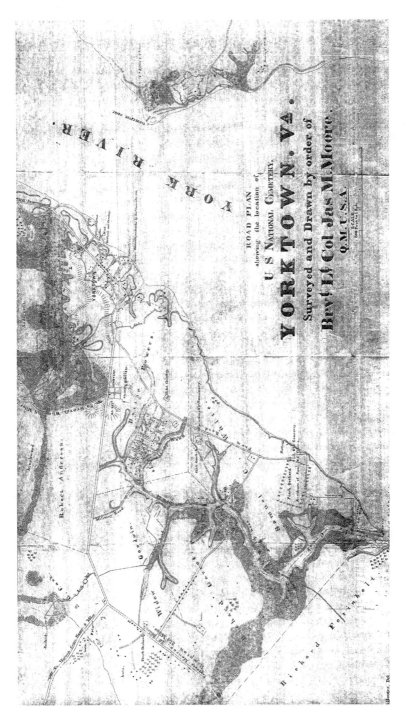

Figure 6. Map of Yorktown National Cemetery and surrounding area. Produced by the
US Quartermaster Office. National Archives. Copy of image provided by Diane Depew.

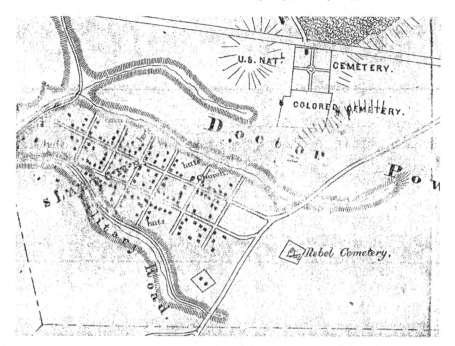

Figure 7. Detailed view of Yorktown National Cemetery,
Produced by the US Quartermaster Office.

residence. In 1875, Wolf and Heyman sold the neighboring lot, lot number one, to David L. Shively, the superintendent of the Yorktown National Cemetery. Though this lot was larger than lot number two, it sold for $100 less.[21]

Deed book records continue to testify to Black residents purchasing and selling land in Slabtown in the decades that followed. However, the sporadic nature of the registration of deeds and sales makes it difficult to comprehensively track the community. What is clear, however, is that Black residents retained ownership of Slabtown. Whether they had originally resided in the neighborhood during the war or not, they spent their first decade of freedom gaining clear title to the land they had fought so hard to preserve during the tenure of the Freedmen's Bureau. By doing so they maintained not only legal claims to their homes but to the community institutions they had constructed in Slabtown. Whether it was their intention or not, by holding control specifically of Slabtown, Black residents also created a dramatic narrative landscape in the postwar era. Located just beyond the walls of the Yorktown National Cemetery,

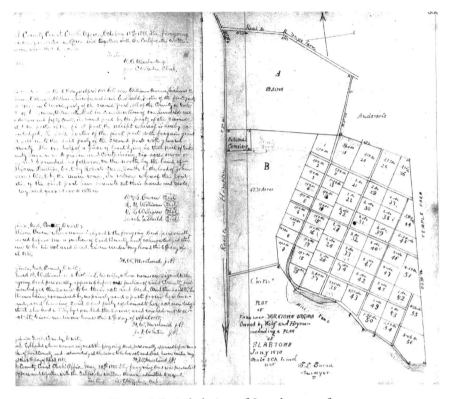

Figure 8. Detailed view of Snead survey for
Wolf and Heyman. York County *Deed Books.*

Slabtown stood as a visual reminder of what the Civil War had wrought that
visitors to the area could not possibly miss.

Edward Darlington's Land

In contrast, Edward Darlington began selling parcels of land to Black residents
as soon as the war was over. Darlington appears to have owned multiple properties in York County at the end of the war, though inconsistent naming makes
it difficult to track individual properties. The Freedmen's Bureau 1865 census included listings for Darlington's Farm, Darlington Mill, and Darlington Woods.
An inventory of farms on which the bureau collected rents listed "Baptist
Land" as entirely rented but did not list a farm under the name "Darlington."[22]
Given that subsequent deed book records identified lots of land Darlington sold
as "formerly known as Baptist Tract," it is possible that the sales that appear
in the deed books represent land that was all part of a single original holding.

However, even these records inconsistently identified land by its former name, so it is difficult to know for sure.

What is certain is that as early as 1866, Black residents began buying large lots of land from Edward Darlington. In contrast to the small lots purchased at Slabtown, these lots ranged in size from ten to twenty-five acres. This suggests that the lots may have included a home as well as farmland and that in purchasing this acreage, Black residents were also securing an independent livelihood. Additionally, a single reference to a "survey made by TJ L Snead in 1866" suggests that Darlington, like Wolf and Heyman, had his property surveyed for sale and then proceeded to dispose of parcels of his property over a period of multiple years.[23]

Records of sales began in late 1866 and represented lots of land that bordered one another, creating something of a Black farming community. In November of 1866, William P. Taylor bought ten acres of land from Darlington for one hundred dollars. The deed specified that this land was bounded by land belonging to Washington Fields and Robert Pollard.[24] It further stipulated that Taylor purchased "the reversions and remainders, rents, issues, and profits thereof," suggesting that others may have been renting land within his lot and he would begin collecting the rent therein.[25] According to an application for a homestead deed Taylor submitted later, in 1869 he purchased an additional six acres of land from Charles Gallagher, whose property bordered Darlington's.[26]

The following month, December 1866, Armistead Taylor purchased twenty-five acres for $150. His property bordered the land of William P. Taylor and Washington Fields.[27] In some cases, purchasers may have been acquiring farmland while living elsewhere. For example, in December of 1866 Washington Fields purchased twenty-five acres of land from Edward Darlington for $250.[28] Fields and his wife Catherine appeared on the 1865 census living at Stumptown, and in 1875 Washington Fields purchased lot number thirty-nine in Slabtown from Louisa Coffin.[29] It is possible, then, that the Fields lived at Stumptown and then Slabtown while acquiring farmland elsewhere.[30] In 1868 Peter Carter joined the ranks of Black farm owners by purchasing twenty acres of land from Darlington for two hundred dollars. Carter's acquisition also bordered the "lands of Charles Gallagher, Bolivar Shield, and others," suggesting that it was close to the properties of the aforementioned landowners.[31]

No records exist to suggest that Darlington sold his land under duress as Frederick Powers had. In fact, Darlington had served on the Freedmen's Bureau Court, filling the space that the Black community had elected Daniel Norton to occupy. Though Darlington was likely a second choice, agent Massey at least described him as a friend to the Black community. It is unclear how Black residents felt about Darlington's commitment to their interests, but they were at minimum willing to do business with him.

While the case of Darlington's land sales leaves many questions unanswered, just as with Slabtown it is clear that Black residents in York County prioritized legal acquisition of land over renting. Moreover, they acquired land close to home rather than take their resources elsewhere, maintaining a tie to the community they had built close to Yorktown. An inventory of farms from 1865–1866 noted that 350 lived at "Darlington's Farm." If this is the same property, it is also reasonable to conclude that the Black landowners listed above acquired land that others were already renting and in doing so became landlords themselves.

Newtown/Acretown—Stafford G. Cooke's Farm

Residents of Newtown faced an entirely different situation. Newtown sat on land owned by Stafford Cooke. In July of 1866, Cooke notified Lieutenant Massey that he did not wish to lease his property for the ensuing year because he wanted to occupy it himself. He inquired "what action the Bureau [would] take in causing the freedmen to vacate his lands at the end of the present year."[32] Residents of Newtown had apparently only begun paying rent earlier that year as a circular alerting them to the necessity of paying rent appeared in February of 1866. Those who could not pay rent, the bureau informed them, would be offered assistance and then "removed elsewhere."[33] Unwilling to wait for the bureau to act, Cooke also brought suit against numerous residents for default of payment in the bureau court. In November of 1866 Cooke attempted to sue Beverly Graves, Major Fields, Samuel Washington, Daniel Cook, and Fleming Butler for not paying rent. The court acknowledged that these individuals owed rent and ordered them to pay but did not order their removal.[34]

In February of 1867 Cooke wrote Massey again wishing to make exceptions to his request for removal of all Black residents occupying his land. "The undersigned wishes the following exceptions to be made in said removal who can rent a portion of his land by complying with his terms," he informed Massey. His terms stipulated that renters would pay fifteen dollars for one and a quarter acre of land for a residence and firewood. They would need to pay rent quarterly, in advance, or vacate the property.[35] Cooke listed sixteen individuals by name, which represented a small fraction of the people residing at Newtown.[36] In 1867 the bureau had recorded seven hundred residents in Newtown. In a subsequent letter Cooke further stipulated that if tenants failed to pay their quarterly rent on time they would be "subject to ejectment from the premises in ten days" time and further their house would be "pulled down and all property they may have liable for the rent which such ejected tenant may own without the privilege of claiming the benefit of the civil law of exemption from distress or levy."[37] In other words, residents would continue to reside in homes they had built under precarious terms that would not accommodate financial distress and, if Cooke had his way, deprive them of any form of redress.

Massey refused to accept these terms, citing his authority "to interfere with the terms of leases 'to prevent imposition and injustice to Freedmen.'"[38] Undeterred, Cooke took his case to Massey's superior officer, General Samuel C. Armstrong at Fort Monroe. Listing his reasons for objecting to the bureau's new stipulations, Cooke insisted that such terms would have "the unstatisfactory influence on such freedmen as remain . . . causing the belief in their minds that they occupy lands more by compulsion on the part of the Bureau than by the permission of the land holder." Additionally, Cooke rationalized that he did not believe anyone should be allowed to remain on terms other than his own because Black residents had "the privilege of going elsewhere."[39] Black residents could move away, Cooke reasoned, and thus did not have the right to stay where they pleased, even if they had established a community and built homes.[40]

Despite his nearly constant efforts, however, Stafford Cooke failed to keep only the renters he had handpicked. In 1870 and 1872 Cooke once again tried to sue numerous residents for unlawful detainer, claiming that they illegally held premises that belonged to him. Many of the residents named in these suits lived in Newtown in 1865, indicating that they had remained in place, resisting Cooke's efforts to force them to leave. Some of the individuals Cooke sued, including London Cooke and Robin Gale, were veterans of the United States Colored Troops. London Cooke would eventually move to Grafton Township, another section of York County, but upon his death would be buried in the Yorktown National Cemetery.[41] Using tactics similar to those they had employed against the Freedmen's Bureau, none of the Black residents Cooke attempted to sue appeared in court. They refused to entertain the idea that Cooke or white authorities could make them leave their community. Though the court repeatedly ruled in Cooke's favor, he brought the same individuals back to court multiple times, indicating that residents refused to comply with the court's orders to turn the property over to Cooke.[42]

Again, many of the particulars of the situation at Newtown remain unclear and largely undocumented. Cooke's suits against Black residents appeared as a list of names with little information to distinguish one case from another. However, the sporadic references to Cooke's attempts to remove people from his property testify to a determination on the part of Black residents to retain the community they had built at Newtown in the face of an uncooperative white landlord. Moreover, that Black residents were willing to defy the court by not showing up to these cases suggests that they were calculating that they had enough power to resist white policymakers. As Robert Engs has observed, York County would become known as a stronghold of Black political power and a place where Black residents could openly defy white neighbors' attempts to restrict their futures.[43] At Newtown, like at Slabtown, they had much to protect—not only their individual homes, but their community, its institutions, and the businesses they had built in this relatively urban space.

In the decades after the Civil War, Black residents of York County would purchase parcels of land outside of the properties previously owned by Frederick Powers, Edward Darlington, and Stafford Cooke. They also continued to rent property until such as time as they could buy. Deed book records offer glimpses of these realities, but little detail. In 1867 John Banks bought sixteen acres of land adjoining the property of John Roberts, another Black resident, from Thomas Tinsley.[44] In 1873, William Ashby likewise bought ten acres of land from Thomas Tinsley.[45] Instances abound of Black residents purchasing land from other Black residents, suggesting that the owners selling the property had acquired it at some time after the war.

Robert Anderson's estate, which was located across from the national cemetery and bordered portions of Frederick Powers's farm, presents a particularly intriguing case. Deed book records noted that John H. Gilmer appointed Peter Halstead to "demand, collect, & receipt for all rents due by the occupants of the lots houses tenements of the real estate of Robert Anderson." The 1865 census recorded thirty-five people living on "Mrs Anderson's land" which may have been identified as such by the bureau because her husband had died. Regardless, county deed books later recorded that the power of attorney given to Peter Halstead was revoked because Halstead had "not collected or accounted for any rents."[46] Peter Halstead was the county postmaster and a general merchant originally from New York. It is impossible to know why he had not fulfilled his duties to collect rent, but whatever the reason, residents had not paid it, perhaps because they remained committed to the belief that land in York County rightfully belonged to them.

In another telling instance, Washington Banks, Frances Ross, and Daniel Norton registered an indenture with the county clerk in August of 1868. According to the text of the indenture, Frances Ross had previously been married to George Ross who had died and left Frances "considerable personal property." Banks and Ross would occupy said personal property upon their marriage, but the property would remain "at the sole and only disposal of the said Frances Ross notwithstanding her coverture." To avoid ownership of the property being transferred to Banks at the time of their marriage, Ross conveyed title to Daniel Norton for one dollar under the condition that Norton would ensure that Ross dictated the future of the property.[47]

James B. Mitchell registered a deed of trust in January of 1875 conveying a parcel of land he had purchased from Edward Darlington to John Carter with a similarly specific stipulation. The deed required that Carter and his successors permit James' wife, Henrietta, to "occupy possess and enjoy the said tract or parcel of land and the rents issues and profits thereof . . . for and during the term of her natural life for her support."[48] Presumably, James Mitchell sought to ensure that his wife would be taken care of and could benefit from his land even after he had died.

In each situation, Black residents navigated different circumstances defined in part by the preferences and financial situation of the white landowner as well as their own material circumstances. Yet in each case, Black residents pursued the same outcome with equal determination: gaining permanent ownership of the homes and community they had built in freedom. Though the historical record presents an incomplete picture of Black landownership in the immediate postwar years, it is undeniable that Black residents prioritized the acquisition and protection of land. It is also clear that the two settlements, Slabtown and Newtown, persisted in the postwar era, remaining centers of the community. According to the 1870 census, forty-two of the 515 Black households in Nelson Township—where Slabtown and Newtown were located—owned some amount of real estate. Seventy-seven households owned private property. Though it is likely that Nelson Township was not representative of the entire county, 42 percent of the county's Black population lived in Nelson in 1870, making it an apparent community center. Even though the majority of Black households did not yet own real estate, 91 percent of the households identified a woman as "keeping house" while a male head of household labored in some capacity.[49] This suggests that even when they had not yet acquired land, Black households had the economic means to maintain a level of security without a woman needing to work outside of the home.

Undoubtedly, the landscape of York County had irrevocably changed in the wake of freedom. Where there had once been farms or plantations there were now Black settlements made up of renters and owners and their families. More than likely, white planters recognized that given the amount of development that had taken place, their former plantation fields would never again yield the profits they had in the antebellum era. More importantly, where the majority of Black residents had once been enslaved, independent Black labor remained. Visitors to Yorktown could not have missed what a difference war and the postwar effort on the part of formerly enslaved people had wrought, and they likewise could not miss the reality that newly free and enfranchised Black people were actively claiming a permanent space for themselves. Visitors to the area continued to search for the "ghosts" of "aristocratic Virginians" who might linger in this historic spot, but to do so required sifting through other realities evident within this drastically altered landscape.

Landscapes of Memory

When US soldiers had arrived in Yorktown in 1862, they too could not help but reflect on the connection between the Revolutionary history of the place and the battle they were then fighting. Like the white Northern teachers who would arrive later and the "Southern woman" who visited at the turn of the century, Union soldiers were unimpressed with Yorktown's appearance and expressed surprise that such a famed city could look so insignificant. In 1862, a correspondent from the Fifty-Third Pennsylvania explained, "I strolled through the famous old town which has gained such celebrity in *two* wars. The general appearance of the town would indicate that it was founded before the Revolution," but despite its age, "nothing has been added . . . except the rebel barracks." Indeed, "a few squalid, old houses" remained, "a few old chimneys, a court house, remarkable only for its extreme old age" constituted the whole of Yorktown.[50] Another writer from the Oneida Cavalry was similarly unimpressed and noted, "there are but few houses and I am positive none pretending to have an appearance of once having been painted."[51] Though Yorktown was "a small place . . . containing about twelve or fifteen houses," another Union soldier thought "the fact that it has been twice selected as a place of defense, and to check the advance of a large army, makes it a place of interest second to none, excepting Bunker Hill . . . in the United States."[52] To the eyes of US soldiers, Yorktown's lack of development since the Revolution did not disqualify it as one of the most important places in the United States.

The convergence of these two moments in US history were clearly visible on the landscape. A soldier from the Fifth New Hampshire described his unit's camp to readers of his hometown newspaper as "on the ground where Cornwallis surrendered, and almost under the same tree, which stands in all its glory as of old. Many of the breastworks that were thrown up in the days of the Revolution are still plainly visible, and some of the rebel fortifications are in the same places."[53] Soldiers made a point of exploring the Revolutionary landscape and commented on the confluence of historical events. Describing the fortification of Camp Winfield Scott, a soldier from the Sixty-Second Pennsylvania assured readers at home, "the men have worked assiduously, night and day, as did our good old Revolutionary forefathers, with picks and shovels in hand and guns and ammunition on their backs."[54] A soldier from the Fifth New Hampshire noted, "A party of us visited the identical house where Cornwallis signed his surrender—the building is still in a good state of preservation . . . a tree nearby . . . is pointed out as the spot where his doughy lordship delivered up his 'ancient blade,' not to Washington, but to the brave Lincoln."[55] The soldier referenced the mythologized circumstances of the surrender at Yorktown, alluding, in his reference to the "doughy lordship" surrendering his sword to "the brave Lincoln," to the fact that Cornwallis refused to surrender his sword in person and in response Washington likewise appointed General Benjamin Lincoln to accept the sword as his proxy. That the author chose to refer to the incident with such indirect language demonstrates that he expected his audience to be so familiar with the event that they would recognize his veiled reference. A soldier from the Eighth Pennsylvania likewise described his historic tour to a hometown audience, relating, "Yesterday we visited the spot where Washington had his Headquarters in his time at Yorktown." He assured his readers, "It has got a beautiful fence around it, and a poplar tree, which I have no doubt was planted while his Headquarters was there."[56] The presence of physical objects that remained from the historic event, like the tree, seemingly added to Yorktown's authenticity.

Some went as far as to collect token relics, including soldiers from the Twenty-Second Massachusetts who inadvertently dug up the body of a Revolutionary War soldier, and upon realizing what they had uncovered, "secured quite a number of the buttons from his vest" before reinterring the body.[57] Another soldier from the Eighty-Fifth New York assured his readers that the Army of the Potomac would, like Washington's army, be successful in securing the future of the United States. "In the conflict which is ere now taking place upon the classic and rather muddy fields about Yorktown," he noted, "even in the very spot as evidenced by the relics that are found of revolutionary heroes, where in years gone by the fate of a nation was determined . . . we report *not all quiet, but all well* with the Army of the Potomac."[58] Matters may not have been settled yet, but this soldier assured readers at home, once again the Union would survive.

Occupying Yorktown on the anniversary of American independence, correspondents for the army newspaper *The Cavalier* reflected on the meaning of the location in light of the present struggle. "Day after to-morrow is the 86th anniversary of American Independence," the author reminded readers. He reflected, "What thrilling thoughts the occasion awakes in every loyal breast." He too could detect the ghosts of the nation's founders: "Here, where the spirits of patriotic heroes still linger, where Patrick Henry might once have been heard, and where now the treasonable dagger is drawn to stab that same principle to the heart, that was once so nobly here defended." That the "foul plot" of disunion could "mar the spot where the patriotic defenders of the Union fought and died," the writer noted, "gives rise to sad reflections . . . and when history shall record the story of our nation's struggles, it will be proudly said that we handed down the heritage of our forefathers untarnished to the hands of the following generation."[59] Writers for *The Cavalier* took great interest in describing to their readers the history of the place they occupied, and were summarily unimpressed with what Southerners had accomplished since the Revolution. "The military history of Yorktown is a bright page in American records," one author opined, "but her social and civil history for the last fifty years had better been a blank." Following the Revolution, the author explained, "Yorktown degenerated into a place of little importance . . . from one of the most important places in America, it was reduced to a mere village." Most offensive of all was the choice of the inhabitants, "descendants of the original 'F.F.V.'s' [First Families of Virginia]" whose fortunes "consisted in land and negroes; but they dealt more in their slaves than in the produce of their soil."[60] By turning away from industry in favor of a life of leisure maintained by enslaved labor, this author thought, the descendants of the founding generation had failed to do justice to the legacy their forefathers had left behind.

Missionaries likewise noted the intersection of historical moments written across Yorktown's landscape. In 1864, Lucy Chase, wrote of a visit to Yorktown with delight. Upon approaching Newtown, Chase described, "We were very much excited by the spectacle of rebel earthworks in the neighborhood." She went on, "Long lines of parallels, with zig-zag communications, protected by forts, all so complete as to be intelligible." Newtown, for its part, was "well-built, of uniform size, not crowded, fence-inclosed, with the door-ways within the gates, the acres adjoining, and nothing unclean to be seen either in front, or in the rear."[61] Sarah Cadbury wrote home in 1866 similarly enamored with the "real scenes of war" and the opportunity to dine within a fort. Yet, she noted, "Everything is mighty desolate looking."[62] Inside the city of Yorktown, Cadbury was surprised to find desolation rather than life. "Inside the fortifications a few straggling houses 2 or 3 old brick ones," she commented. No one was around, she noted, except for a "crowd of darkies." Bewitched by the idea that battles had occurred in this place, Cadbury explained, "The earth works were very interesting & we drove inside the inner works . . . It made it more interesting as Edd Holway . . . tells us all sorts of interesting news of the place & at Fort Magruder where the battle of Williamsburg was fought we saw the ground of slaughter."[63] Like many who would tour Civil War battlefields in the decades after the guns fell silent, Cadbury felt an intense connection to the events that had transpired on a landscape that retained physical reminders of the "slaughter" that had occurred there.

Northern missionaries also made a point of seeking out Yorktown's historic sites and commenting on their visits. Lucy Chase noted that during her trip to Yorktown she and her party "visited the house where Washingtons terms of capitulation were signed by Cornwallis. It was McClellans head-quarters also."[64] Sarah Cadbury likewise sought out this storied structure noting, "We gradually made our way to the Capitulation House . . . we visited the house, going inside and fancying which was the room where Cornwallis and Washington met."[65] Cadbury and "Mr. B" also attempted to "hunt up Cornwallis' cave," where Cornwallis had taken shelter during the Revolutionary siege.[66] Throughout the Civil War and after, visitors to Yorktown sought to connect with the nation's future by visiting the famous sites of its past.

Visitors to Yorktown were not the only ones captivated by the significance of the city during the Civil War. In October 1862, A. P. Smith's reply to President Lincoln's colonization plan appeared in *Douglass' Monthly*. Smith reminded the president that the Black man was "here in the infancy of the nation, he was here during its growth, and we are here to-day." "If through all these years of sorrow and affliction," Smith continued, "there is one thing for which we have been noted more than all else, it is our love of country, our patriotism." Black Americans had never "been found wanting in the times that have tried the souls of men." Rather, "We were with Warren on Bunker Hill, with Washington at Morristown and Valley Forge, with LaFayette at Yorktown, with Perry, Decatur, and McDonough in their cruisings . . . battling side by side with the white man for nationality, national rights and national history." When this new "atrocious insurrection" was over, "the historian will record; whoever was false, the Blacks were true." "Are you an American?" Smith asked, "So are we." "Would you spurn all absurd . . . propositions for your colonization in a foreign country?" by nature of his status as an American he further queried, "So do we."[67] Black Americans, Smith reminded the president, had fought just as hard to maintain the nascent nation as white men had, and as a result to consider leaving the country that was their home was nothing short of illogical. Black Americans *were there* Smith asserted, at Yorktown and Valley Forge, and through their presence and effort had carved a perpetual place for themselves in the American nation.

J. T. W., a soldier from the Third United States Colored Troops, similarly deployed the imagery of Yorktown and the Revolution to assure his audience of Black troops' devotion to the Union, and American, cause. "I do firmly vow," he wrote to *The Christian Recorder*, "that I will fight as long as a star can be seen in our old flag—the star-spangled banner." This war had brought men from all over the country "shoulder to shoulder—heart to heart—in this great struggle for a nation's life." The battles he and his comrades were now fighting were worthy of association with "Bunker's Hill, Yorktown, and the like" and remembering them had "magic powers in making the heart of every true patriot in the land beat quickly." Such sites of Revolutionary significance had the power to wake the soul of all true Americans. "Thank God that [war] was won," he exclaimed, and most assuredly "the Confederacy, founded upon treason and rebellion, will itself soon fall."[68] Not only did J. T. W. believe that Revolutionary sites could stir the souls of men, but he also made a thinly veiled assertion: These sites and their legacy did not belong to treasonous Confederates.

As much as Americans were captivated by the historical legacy of York-town, they also could not miss the fact that its storied landscape had irrevo-cably changed. Old earthworks mixed with new, and cannons, ammunition explosions, and the convergence of thousands of soldiers and refugees had wreaked havoc on the already declining town. Yet in place of the seemingly quiet and sleepy Revolutionary city a new reality took root, one that com-municated revised narratives of freedom and union. In the twentieth century, interested parties would take pains to restore the Revolutionary landscape to Yorktown, erasing the Civil War's legacy. But the very necessity of "restora-tion" meant that something else had been built on top of and around the Revo-lution's legacy in the area. A different landscape of freedom, and a competing narrative of the nation, had emerged. This new narrative, as J. T. W. noted, had to acknowledge the participation of Black Americans.

Landscapes of Increased Devotion

One of the most significant memorial spaces that emerged from the Civil War was the national cemetery system. Prior to the Civil War, the federal govern-ment did not maintain a formal system of burial grounds for soldiers. On July 17, 1862, the same month that the federal government issued its Second Confis-cation Act, Congress enacted legislation authorizing the president to purchase cemetery grounds for use as national cemeteries for soldiers who died in service.[69] As historian Drew Gilpin Faust has argued, the scale of death in the Civil War and the pervasiveness of violence demanded that meaning be made of the loss. Consequently, "Americans had to identify—find, invent, create—the means and mechanisms to manage more than half a million dead." This "work of death" was one of the Civil War's most fundamental undertakings.[70] One of the ways the federal government created new mechanisms for imagining and assigning meaning to the US dead was through the national cemetery system. Though the 1862 act authorized the purchase of lands for soldier cemeteries, in many cases during the war field commanders established cemeteries in battle zones and simply confiscated land.[71] The federal government would not take up a formal burial program until after Lee's surrender at Appomattox, at which point it initiated a system of identifying and disinterring Union soldiers and moving them to official national cemeteries.[72] By 1870, nearly three hun-dred thousand Union soldiers had been laid to rest in seventy-three national cemeteries.[73]

As an established military outpost, Yorktown required a cemetery from the moment the Union army began its occupation. As with most other field cemeteries, the US Army did not purchase land outright, but rather confiscated a portion of Frederick Powers's property for use as a cemetery.[74] The federal government would not formally purchase this plot until after the war.[75] Union soldiers took pains to note that they located the Yorktown National Cemetery in a specific spot: the spot where Cornwallis had surrendered to Washington. In 1863, "Ignatio, Jr." a writer for *The Cavalier,* noted that upon Lafayette's return to Yorktown after the Revolution, celebratory exercises took place in the spot "where the Union Cemetery is now located."[76] In April of 1863 when Union soldiers' bodies needed to be retrieved from Williamsburg, "Lieut. Wildie, of Fort Magruder, sent a detail of contrabands to perform the labor of disinterment."[77] This was one of the few instances during or immediately after the war that Union personnel would comment on who performed the labor of caring for soldiers' bodies, but it was common for Black laborers to be responsible for disinterment and reburial throughout the years that the national cemetery system took shape. At Yorktown, Black residents would continue to care for the Union dead long after the army left.

Union soldiers could be sure that they had properly located this historic spot because over the years various individuals had marked it with monuments, testifying both to their perception of its importance and the veracity of the oral record that passed on this information. In May of 1862, a US soldier noted while reporting home that "Between the rebel and federal fortifications is the spot where Cornwallis surrendered his army to Gen. Washington." This spot, he explained, was "enclosed by a cedar fence . . . and is filled with beautiful trees." Anxious to take a piece of US history home with them, "visitors [had] plied their jack-knives into the fence, so now it presents a somewhat shabby appearance." Near this spot a monument had once stood, marking "the spot where the British sword was given up." However, "the rebels [had] lately shot off the monument."[78] A year later, a correspondent for *The Cavalier* visited the location and determined that the "rebels" had removed the monument before their evacuation "because it was in the range of their guns." They had left the monument's base though, and soldiers had "carried [it] off piece-meal," again testifying to the significance that both US and Confederate soldiers placed in this monument and its meaning.[79]

Decades later, in 1920, Sydney Smith wrote a book detailing the history of "Old Yorktown" and described this short-lived monument. "A monument was erected in the town in 1860," she explained, "to commemorate the surrender." Made of granite and white marble, it bore the inscription "erected the 19th day of October, 1860, by the regimental and company officers of the Twenty-first Regiment of Virginia militia of Gloucester county, and the volunteer company attached hereto, to mark the spot of the surrender of Cornwallis' sword on the 19th day of October, 1781." The monument's creators had authenticated the site through "several marks of identification" including "a heap of ballast stones . . . supposed to have been brought over from England."[80] Around fifteen years later, the superintendent of the national cemetery, John Shaw, would rectify the loss of the surrender monument by furnishing his own. This new monument read, "On this spot: Lord Cornwallis Commanding British Forces Surrendered to General Washington 19 October 1781." According to Godfrey Harrod, a Black laborer in the cemetery and resident of Newtown, Shaw erected the monument "with the understanding that it would be taken care of [by] some of the citizens of Yorktown." Given that so few of the residents surrounding the cemetery were white by this time, it is likely that Shaw understood that his Black neighbors would continue to care for the monument.

Black residents of York County had also found significance in this site, and the national cemetery was not the only notable burial ground that would grow on this legendary spot. From the end of the Civil War and into the twentieth century, Black residents of York County used this location for their own burial purposes. It was such a popular site for burials that by 1920, when the new superintendent of the national cemetery, A. H. Ackley, reported on the issue, he wrote, "There is a colored grave yard [*sic*] on the east and north of the monument and on the north side." Shaw's monument was surrounded, so much so that it appeared to be part of the cemetery: "There [are] graves three feet from the fence around the monument—sixty feet from the south east corner of the cemetery wall."[81] The "cemetery wall" he referred to was likely the national cemetery wall, which consisted of brick by that time. Thus, three significant memorial sites existed alongside one another, mixing the Revolutionary War history with the varying legacies of federal authority and Black freedom left by the Civil War.

In the wake of the Civil War, the federal government was careful not just to create a system for formally caring for Union soldiers' bodies but also to craft places of significance and meaning that could be interpreted by anyone entering a national cemetery. Bureau agent F. J. Massey would report in 1865 that the Yorktown National Cemetery consisted of "about two acres of land belonging to Mr Fred Powers." "It has a good substantial fence around it and every inch of the enclosed ground is filled with graves of fallen braves," he stated. But it would be impossible to identify each of the men buried there because "the headboards have been destroyed or otherwise disposed of."[82] The problem of lack of identification of soldier dead would never be resolved. Elsewhere in Virginia, at Fredericksburg National Cemetery, less than 20 percent of Union dead would ever be identified.[83] Faust notes that of the United States Colored Troops buried in national cemeteries across the system, only a third were ever identified.[84]

As the federal government formalized the national cemetery system, sites like Yorktown would transform from sites enclosed with a "good substantial fence" that lacked headboards to uniform public spaces whose aesthetics testified to the restored nation and the supremacy of the Union cause. They were not just places of rest for the dead but also nationally significant public spaces for the living. John Neff has noted that national cemeteries fulfilled the impulse to express meanings of the war—and the massive loss of life—through commemoration of the dead. As Quartermaster General Montgomery Meigs, who headed the project asserted, "All care for the dead is for the sake of the living."[85] For the federal government, Neff argues, national cemeteries were the "quintessential forum for engaging and expressing the war's meaning."[86] Historian Catherine Zipf explains further that "these cemeteries not only honored the fallen dead of the Union army but also served an ideological agenda as a permanent, systematic embodiment of Federal authority within the former Confederacy." This agenda, Zipf argues, was "easily understood by northern and southern audiences" because of the careful construction of the built environment.[87] They were "architectural monuments to the Union cause."[88] Yorktown's national cemetery, moreover, could not be missed even by travelers who came looking for George Washington's ghost rather than the ghosts of the recent past. Located on what was then called the Hampton-Yorktown Highway, the national cemetery was visible to everyone who entered the city.[89]

Prior to 1867, most national cemeteries resembled Massey's description of Yorktown—unmarked mounds surrounded by fences. In 1867, however, the federal government undertook a beautification process directed by Montgomery Meigs.[90] Meigs sought to create uniform narrative spaces that would speak to the renewed authority of the federal government and the righteousness of the Union cause. To accomplish this, he designated formal elements and directed their arrangement to highlight the common identity of all national

Figure 9. Photograph of central flagstaff at Yorktown
National Cemetery. 1873–1912. National Archives.

cemeteries.[91] Cemeteries would be enclosed by brick walls, and near the entrance of each cemetery contractors erected a lodge, where superintendents—always Union veterans—would live as well as receive visitors to the cemetery. Meigs selected a Second Empire French style for these lodges, which replicated the design of new federal buildings also constructed under his direction in Washington, DC.[92] Seeking to unify the nation's identity through a uniform building style, this design became known as the "General Grant mode" because so many buildings constructed in Washington during Grant's administration utilized this form.[93]

National cemetery lodges, moreover, reaffirmed this connection because they replicated the new State, War, and Navy Building in Washington, creating, as Catherine Zipf describes, structures that could be read by visitors as "little war departments."[94] Cemeteries also featured a central flagstaff and rostrum for speakers to utilize during public ceremonies, signaling again the federal government's intention that these would not just be places for the dead, but for the living.

Updates to the national cemetery design further affirmed this connection between restored federal authority, Union victory, and the significance of the soldiers' deaths. In 1905, the Washington office directed all cemetery superintendents to replace the printed copies of Lincoln's Gettysburg Address, which

Figure 10. Photograph of Yorktown National Cemetery with
Cemetery Lodge visible in the background. 1873–1912. National Archives.

hung in superintendents' offices, with an updated version. These printed copies
of the oration were to be "hung in a conspicuous location in the public office."[95]
Four years later, the Washington office replaced these printed copies of the address with iron tablets and mandated that superintendents place them on the
exterior of the cemetery lodges.[96] Yorktown's tablet was in place by January
1910, ensuring that visitors to the cemetery could not mistake the significance
of this place.[97] Lincoln's words dedicating the Gettysburg National Cemetery
to the "unfinished work" of the nation's "new birth of freedom" reminded visitors what these Union dead had died to achieve and call them to carry on that
undertaking.

Records from the superintendents of the Yorktown National Cemetery
reveal many of the same characteristics that the "Southern woman's" article
noted about the town. In the first fifty years of the cemetery's existence, a
thriving Black community surrounded the cemetery. One superintendent took
issue with this reality upon his arrival at his post at Yorktown in 1912. Writing to his superiors he demanded that the administration install a phone line
because, he claimed, he and his wife were virtually stranded and without help
because they were one of the only white families in the area. Generally, though,
other superintendents seem to have accepted this, and Black laborers frequently worked in the cemetery caring for the Union dead.[98] Godfrey Harrod

Figure 11. Modern view of the entrance to Yorktown National Cemetery
with the superintendent's lodge located just inside the main gate.
Author photograph, 2021.

labored in the cemetery for more than forty years and was so well respected
by the various white superintendents that when they left the area, he acted
in their stead. At various times when Harrod and the superintendent needed
additional help, other Black laborers worked in the cemetery, including fellow
residents of Newtown. Sometimes superintendents found it difficult to employ
additional labor, indicating that Black residents did not need the paid work the
cemetery could provide because they maintained other, more desirable options.

More notable, however, are the burial patterns in the Yorktown National
Cemetery in the decades after the Civil War and prior to its closure, for lack
of space, in the twentieth century. The vast majority of veterans buried in
the national cemetery in the decades after the Civil War were veterans of the
United States Colored Troops, many of whom cemetery records noted "died in
the area." Family members of the deceased decided the disposition of soldiers'
bodies, meaning that in each case of a USCT soldiers' death, his family chose
to bury him in the Yorktown National Cemetery.[99] In many cases, wives chose
to be buried with their husbands after their deaths as well. Especially in the
case of soldiers buried in the twentieth century, this was a calculated choice
on the part of family members and the cemetery superintendent, because by
then Yorktown had run out of space inside its brick walls. In 1904, the cemetery
superintendent reported that "there is no vacant plots in this cemetery . . . so

Figure 12. Yorktown National Cemetery Superintendent's Lodge.
The Gettysburg Address tablet is located to the left of the
lodge entrance. Author photograph, 2021.

we have to burry [*sic*] our dead on top of those unknown graves." Since beginning his tenure at Yorktown four years earlier, he reported that "I have interred
four (4) bodies 3 colored men and one white man."[100] Still, family members
chose to bury their loved ones in this cemetery in already occupied graves
rather than at the larger national cemetery in nearby Hampton.

In at least one instance, Godfrey Harrod retrieved the body of a USCT
soldier after his burial elsewhere when it became apparent that he was a veteran. In February of 1905, the superintendent recorded sending an additional
payment to Harrod for "services rendered in dis-interring and removing from
burial place . . . near the National Cemetery and re-interring the same . . . the
remains of Joseph E. Turner late Pri of Co 'B' 41 USCT."[101] The superintendent
confirmed Turner's identity as a veteran through consultation with his sister,
Mary F. Smith, who appears to have been residing in Nelson Township, where
the cemetery was located, and suggesting that Turner had lived there too.[102]
No explanation was given as to why Turner was not originally buried in the

cemetery when he died on January 5, 1905.[103] It is possible the family could not furnish proof of his service until the later date.

During the course of his tenure with the national cemetery, Godfrey Harrod became responsible for another commemorative space in Yorktown, the Yorktown Victory Monument. On April 6, 1882, Robert Norton, the Black senator representing York and Elizabeth City Counties in Virginia's General Assembly and Daniel Norton's brother, introduced a motion to give consent of the State of Virginia to the United States for purchase of a tract of land in Yorktown "for the purpose of the erection thereon . . . of a monument to commemorate the surrender of Lord Cornwallis and his forces to the allied army commanded by General George Washington in October, 1781."[104] Five months prior, Virginians had laid the cornerstone for this monument during an elaborate multiday celebration commemorating the centennial of Washington's victory.[105] Democratic governor of Virginia, Frederick Holliday, declared at the dedication that "History [had] no parallel" to the event this monument marked. The monument would "proclaim to future generations," he continued, "the surrender of Force and the triumph of Law [speaking] with its own structure with more than mortal eloquence of how so many States and interests have been blended into one by the magic of the Republic's Life." He concluded his speech by celebrating the preservation of the Union, exclaiming, "God reigns and the government at Washington still lives! . . . We build this Monument to perpetuate the recollection of that work. We will guard it with pious hands and hearts and transmit it to the countless generations who will follow us to show how in God's ways a brave and noble deed evolves its own triumphs." Finally, he continued, "May the principles this Monument is intendent to represent not fail from the memory of men!"[106] With this exhortation, Holliday made plain that the purpose of this monument, like the purpose of the national cemetery, was to speak to people—present and future—about the nature of the American nation. The monument's very form, Holliday asserted, could attest to this legacy. Yet despite Holliday's exclamation that the people of Virginia would guard the monument with "pious hands," its care fell to the cemetery's superintendent, and by extension, his employees. In the decades after its completion, Godfrey Harrod patrolled its grounds and performed routine maintenance on the fence that would eventually surround it. Black residents became the keepers of this monument and preservers of its meaning.

The same year that Robert Norton introduced his bill authorizing the federal government to purchase land for the completion of the Victory Monument,

Daniel Norton purchased his own historic piece of real estate: the famed Yorktown Custom House. Daniel Norton, who also worked as a doctor, used the Custom House as an office and opened the school for Black children that the "Southern woman" encountered on her visit in 1902.[107] In the twentieth century, interested parties of white women would set their eyes on reclaiming the Custom House and other historic sites in Yorktown and repopulating them with the ghosts of the "proud aristocrats of old Virginia." But from the end of the Civil War until the coming of the National Park Service in the 1930s, Yorktown's historic memorial landscape remained decidedly in the hands of its Black residents. Fully aware of the meaning of these sites and their relationship to the ongoing process of reformulating the nation's identity after the Civil War, Black York County residents used these landscapes to make their own claims on a place within the nation.

CHAPTER 7

★ ★ ★ ★ ★ ★ ★ ★

"We Build Our Memorial in Our Lives"

Postwar Politics and the Continued Fight for Equality

In March of 1870, Robert Norton, who was then a delegate representing York and Elizabeth City Counties in Virginia's House of Delegates, declared that "They had had enough of the military in that county." Norton was responding to a report regarding "the resistance made by colored persons in Norfolk, Elizabeth City and York counties, to the civil authorities" which resulted from the fact that Black residents "were put in possession of the lands by military power, and refused to leave them when required to do so by civil authorities." A resolution submitted to the House of Delegates requested that the president send the military to "enforce the laws of the State and prevent the bloodshed which will ensue if the civil authorities endeavor, unaided, to carry out the laws." The first delegate to respond, Robert Norton insisted that "as far as York county was concerned, there was no disturbance, and the military were not needed there."[1]

Such a statement might at first appear strange coming from a Black delegate in a Southern state just a few years after the end of the war. Generally, the federal government in the postwar years is framed as a resource upon which Black citizens depended. Moreover, unlike other Southern states, by 1870 Virginia had not produced a Republican regime and remained under white conservative rule.[2] Yet as Black residents in York County had experienced firsthand, their efforts to craft their own freedom often conflicted with the structure the federal government or US military wanted to impose on the defeated South.[3] As Robert Norton assured his peers in 1870, Black residents in York County were prepared to enact and protect freedom for themselves. When their white allies—whether US forces or white Republicans—did not honor Black citizens' equality or expectations, Black residents found new avenues through which to make their voices heard and their strength felt. To do so they mobilized the same community networks and organizations such as the Lone Star Society, the secret organization Lieutenant Massey had identified, they had utilized to negotiate with the Freedmen's Bureau.

That an issue related to land occupation came before the House of Delegates in 1870 indicates that Black residents on the peninsula continued to hold onto their claims to land ownership after the departure of the Freedmen's Bureau despite hostile civil authorities. Robert Norton's insistence that they had had enough of the military further suggests that Black residents strongly opposed the federal government returning to York County to meddle in their affairs. The land question might not yet have been settled, but residents no longer believed that the federal government would settle it in their favor. Claims of unrest were certainly founded in local tensions, but Norton, for his part, was content to let local residents work out their problems for themselves. Though he did not mention it in front of his fellow delegates, Norton likely also understood that by maintaining their large population base as they had throughout the end of the 1860s, Black residents maintained their political leverage. If federal authorities became involved, the balance of power would shift, and Norton clearly had no faith in the federal government's ability to act in the best interest of Black citizens. This belief was likely founded in the disappointment Black residents had already experienced with local white Republicans who controlled federal offices.

In the postwar era, Black residents in York County continued to leverage their community strength to maintain political power. Patterns of political action largely reflected the same trends and strategies they had employed during the US Army and Freedmen's Bureau's tenure in the county. Unwilling to cede authority to white actors, even those who claimed to represent the interests of Black Southerners, Black York County residents negotiated postwar politics with an acute awareness that if their needs were not met, they could take their votes somewhere else. Political alliances remained fluid in Virginia for much of the latter half of the nineteenth century. The Republican Party experienced difficulties maintaining the support of the Black community in the state, and sometimes Black voters chose to align themselves with white voters in third parties who wished to dislodge the Democrats. By 1877, Virginia's legislature contained twenty-two individuals who identified as "independents," and in 1879 the most successful coalition party, the Readjusters, formed.[4]

Robert and Daniel Norton's political careers provide a useful window into the politics of Yorktown's postwar community. The Nortons continued to wield power and make calculated decisions based on the interests of their neighbors despite the fluctuating political landscape of the postwar South. Black leaders who rose to power after the Civil War remained, in historian Steven Hahn's words, "fulcrums around which local politics pivoted" for decades after the war.[5] This observation holds in York County as the Norton brothers remained at the center of postwar politics in the latter half of the nineteenth century. Moreover, the Nortons' shifting political allegiances and readiness to criticize their own party when that party failed to treat Black candidates equally, demonstrates the political uncertainty of the postwar decades.

Black residents also continued to deploy commemorative activities for political ends and adapted ongoing memorial displays to meet their evolving political needs. This was common across the South, but such activity took on added weight in Yorktown because of its Revolutionary history. These were more than expressions of commemoration; they represented an effort to construct a useful past from which Black Americans could continue to make claims on the nation. They were also intentional efforts to assert the central role Black Americans had played in the history of the nation, a history that established their present belonging and rightful claim to citizenship. In the latter decades of the nineteenth century, various actors in York County embraced its Revolutionary legacy and deployed it to construct Yorktown as the heart of the American nation. Historical memory was never far from the rhetoric of political debates, and politicians, Black and white, used those memories to make political arguments, indicating both the flexibility of those memories and their political utility. How Black residents deployed this rhetoric also highlights a key strategy they used to navigate the postwar political landscape.

As historian Jane Dailey has noted, Black Southerners did not see the last decades of the nineteenth century as a prelude to Jim Crow but rather participated in a dynamic period of political contestation.[6] Black residents of Yorktown and the Virginia Peninsula continued to be politically active even after they were disfranchised through the stipulations of the 1902 state constitution. In the early years of the twentieth century, as Hahn elaborates, "bases of substantial Black political activity . . . managed to survive, albeit in more vulnerable forms."[7] One of those forms was expressions of public memory through memorial events that reaffirmed a successful Black political past and elaborated on the fight for full citizenship still underway.

Daniel and Robert Norton's Political Careers

In May of 1868, *The Virginian-Pilot* reported that "the carpet-baggers and negroes are at open war in many parts of the State." Black Virginians were growing disillusioned with their white allies and taking a stand to assert their right to political autonomy. "[Daniel] Norton and [Thomas] Bayne have gone to work in this region," the Democratic newspaper continued, "with a resolute purpose to defeat their white friends."[8] Daniel Norton planned to "settle the question of [Black men's] admissibility to Congress" by running on the peninsula against the white Republican candidate. According to *The Virginian-Pilot,* many had expected Thomas Bayne, another Black leader, to be the one to test Black politicians' eligibility for Congress, but "the District which boasts the remains of Virginia's colonial greatness" would instead "have the honor of sending the first colored Representative to the Congress of the United States."[9] York County, home of so much Revolutionary history, would make history again. Given the newspaper's known Democratic alliances, it is likely that the author commented on York County's Revolutionary history to galvanize the white electorate and inspire horror that this place marked by the history of the United States' white founders would shift so drastically to Black political rule. Yet the point was still monumental: A place storied for its ties to the nation's beginning would once again be a stage for a new birth of freedom.

That *The Virginian-Pilot* reported as early as May on the congressional election and assumed that Daniel Norton would carry the field indicated that white residents on the peninsula understood that Norton wielded considerable political authority within his Black majority district. Moreover, that the paper acknowledged that Norton would "settle the question" reflected a strategy like the one he and his followers had employed during the tenure of the Freedmen's Bureau. Though white Republicans had not extended an invitation for Norton to run for Congress, and despite the fact they apparently were not receptive to the idea, Norton placed his name in the field anyway, claiming the right of Black politicians to represent their peers at the highest levels of government. By May of 1868 Norton was already serving in Virginia's state constitutional convention, where his actions led *The Virginian-Pilot* to describe him as a "moderate man" who consistently sought to reassure white Virginians that their Black peers had no intention of starting a war but rather wanted their rights acknowledged.[10] That Norton felt it necessary to assure his white neighbors of these intentions further indicates the success of his efforts. He likely understood that white Virginians would perceive the success of his political career and his continued rise to power as a threat.

That a white Democratic newspaper reported as extensively on Black politicians as *The Virginian-Pilot* did is, of course, suspect. However, in an editorial published in the paper in 1874, Robert Norton charged that the only Republican newspaper on the peninsula was owned by a white Republican politician who refused to acknowledge the equal candidacy of Black Republicans.[11] Members of the Norton brothers' campaign committee routinely used the newspapers as an outlet for their political statements and advertisements for political rallies. Undoubtedly writers for *The Virginian-Pilot* reported on the divide between Black and white Republicans on the peninsula because splits in the party could also split voting returns and enable Democratic candidates to carry the field. Still, the paper's extensive reporting on these difficulties within the Republican Party provide important insights into the political strategies employed by Black politicians during this period.

In September of 1870, the question of Norton's candidacy for Congress returned, indicating a widening divide between white and Black Republicans in the county. Despite the fact that it was a Democratic newspaper, *The Virginian-Pilot* reported that "we would sooner see [Norton] elected to a seat in Congress than some of the miserable creatures from Ohio or Pennsylvania, who only cajole the [Black man] to gain votes." The "Douglas" faction represented Dr. W. W. Douglass, of Richmond County, whose candidacy against Norton reflected an early split in the Republican ticket. The following month, a group of "certain lewd fellows of the Douglas faction" broke up a meeting of "the Norton party" in Hampton.[12] Among the crowd of roughs was one Jerome Titlow, "the Radical sheriff of the county, who, the reporter suspected, could not tolerate the idea that the [Black residents] should have a will of their own."[13] Again, despite its Democratic allegiances, *The Virginian-Pilot* pointed to the heart of the matter. White Republicans were not willing to share authority with Black Republicans. Though Daniel Norton received the votes necessary for his nomination in September, in November *The Virginian-Pilot* reported that "Governor [Henry] Wells, as Chairman of the Radical State Committee, has issued a bull to the Radicals of the first district declaring Dr. Douglas the Radical candidate." Unsurprised by this development, the editorial author commented, "The carpetbaggers have no idea of letting a colored man go to Congress." Moreover, in the eyes of the Radicals it seemed "colored men are good enough for voters, but it is impertinent of them, these white brothers think, to expect fat offices."[14] At the local level, however, voters elected multiple "Norton men" to offices such as clerk of the court and treasurer of the county.[15]

Norton's experience with the 1868 congressional election mirrored his treatment at the hands of the Freedmen's Bureau. Acting as citizens in a democracy, his peers had chosen him to represent them in the Freedmen's Bureau Court. Unwilling to allow a Black man to occupy such a seat of authority, however, white leaders got involved at the state level and disqualified Norton. That the white Republicans' response to his run for Congress fit into this same pattern was surely not lost on Norton.

Unwilling to allow white party leaders to keep him from the field, Daniel Norton again entered the race to represent the Forty-Third Congressional District in 1872. Norton first attempted to join the race by gaining a nomination at the Radical Republicans' official convention. However, the Radicals apparently held the convention in Portsmouth, Virginia, prematurely before new members of the district could properly organize for it. Attending this convention in person, Robert Norton condemned this decision on the part of the Radicals. He contended that the party should not make a nomination yet because "the people in his part of the district (the Peninsula) had been recently transferred to this district, and had not had sufficient notification to prepare for it." Moreover, Robert Norton argued, "It was illegal because it was called by the Executive Committee of the district as it formerly stood, and whose powers expired by the change of the districts, and a new Executive Committee should have been chosen, representing the new district." Norton pointed out that the convention and its executive committee did not fairly represent its constituents, including the Black-majority district of York County. Moreover, he asserted that voting districts had only recently changed, and voters in his locality had not received proper notification to allow them to participate in the nomination process. Declaring Norton's commentary out of order, the convention moved on to nominate a white man, James H. Platt. In response, someone in the crowd cried out, "Give us a Black man." Mr. Hubbard, another representative from York County, agreed with Norton that the convention was illegally called, but the convention proceeded.[16] Norton's treatment at this initial convention reflected tensions that plagued Black voters on the peninsula. Though Norton seemed to have a reasonable objection, convention delegates unilaterally dismissed his input.

In response, the Nortons held an alternative convention in June of 1872 wherein voters unanimously nominated Daniel Norton. This convention elected a committee for canvassing the district composed of Robert Norton, Dr. J. H. Riddick of Norfolk City, and K. G. W. Jones, of Charles City. That the committee members represented more than just York County demonstrated the expansive nature of the Nortons' influence by 1872. This alternate convention also passed "a series of resolutions declaring themselves to stand by and support the nominees of this convention against the nominee of the office-holders' illegally called and packed convention in Portsmouth." A decision to hold an alternative convention reflected the Nortons' and their supporters' firmly held belief that as enfranchised citizens, they had a right to participate in the selection of their representative. If the white faction of the Republican Party would not honor that right, they would find an alternative way to ensure their voices were heard.

After nominating Daniel Norton, the convention further determined to hold what they called a "jollification meeting" and circulated an invitation entitled, "Sic Semper Tyrannis—Grand Rally of the Republicans of Norfolk." Constituents were to meet at city hall where "distinguished speakers" would address the crowd. Reporting on this event, *The Virginian-Pilot* noted that the speeches given "were strongly indicative of undying hostility to the office holders' ring, and of a determination to best Platt at all hazards."[17] With this jollification meeting Black residents of the peninsula did not just rally around their candidate. They also demonstrated their power by collecting in large numbers and reminding white Republicans who could control the vote in Black-majority counties.

Such events were also more than celebrations of political victories. They were expressions of citizenship and belonging, and in this way an embodiment of the change the Civil War had produced in the American nation. As historian Patricia Clark points out, "By taking over public spaces," especially spaces that had previously been off-limits to Black Southerners, processions and celebrations "forcefully altered the social geography of southern towns and cities." They gave "concrete meaning to freedom."[18] These events not only helped establish a collective Black identity from which to draw political power, but they also called on white neighbors to respect the "full range of rights . . . to which Black people were due."[19] Throughout the end of the nineteenth century and into the twentieth century, Black residents of Yorktown and the peninsula would continue to use these strategies to contest their place in the postwar civic order.

True to their word, Daniel Norton and his supporters held their ground through the fall election, opposing Platt and repeatedly calling out the hypocrisy within their own party. In September, Daniel Norton declared at a convention composed of representatives from Nansemond, Suffolk, and York Counties that he intended to "do all in his power to elevate his race and his party, and to fight corruption and maladministration as long as he had the power to speak." He impressed the newspapers' correspondent who commented that Norton was "a natural orator" who used "choice language, producing a fine effect upon his hearers" and would, no doubt, prove "a dangerous foe for Mr. Platt to encounter."[20] Clearly, Norton was already a skilled politician, and the power of his influence could be read in the reaction of his audience.

That same month, Daniel Norton published an open letter in *The Virginian-Pilot* countering charges made against him by his white Republican opponents. Platt had accused Norton of taking bribes to run for office to split the Republican ticket, suggesting that Norton was seeking to aid the interests of white conservatives. Norton replied directly to Platt's charges, noting that he did not hold public office during the period to which Platt's accusations applied. "The whole charge is FALSE," he declared, "not only false, but a downright lie, and no one knows it to be so better than J. H. Platt." Moreover, unwilling to let baseless accusations remain fodder for damaging his reputation as a politician, Norton assured Platt he would "soon have to answer in the courts of this State for this base slander."[21] Norton rejected the idea that a Black man could seek political office against a white Republican only for personal gain. And he further insisted that his rights as an American citizen should be protected by the law.

Apparently, writers for *The Virginian-Pilot* understood what Platt and his fellow white Republicans refused to acknowledge. Norton's candidacy was not an effort to undermine Republican power on the Virginia Peninsula, but rather a movement to demand that Black constituents receive the representation and rights to which they were entitled. "Their plea of action had been from the beginning to assert the right of the voters of the Radical party to hold, at least, some of the offices," the paper reported in September, "while on the other hand Captain Platt, as the head and front of the carpet-baggers, insists that [Black residents] shall do the voting, and he and his friends will monopolize the offices." Clearly, "The Norton party are in rebellion against this theory and practice." Moreover, the Nortons and their constituents represented the voting majority and by leveraging that majority they were prepared to "demand the rights which belong to that majority."[22] By holding alternative conventions, jollification meetings, and parades, the "Norton party" used their superior numbers to remind their fellow Republicans that in a democracy voting returns should reflect the will of the majority—and they were, and would remain, the majority.

By October, *The Virginian-Pilot* was referring to the election as "a triangular fight" between Platt, Norton, and their Democratic candidate, "Major Lee."[23] Rather than Norton's candidacy drawing voters away from Platt, however, *The Virginian-Pilot* understood the issue to be a matter of Platt drawing voters away from Norton, who they believed was the stronger candidate. "It is sufficient for us to know," they reminded their readers, "that Norton is determined to establish the principle that colored politicians have some rights which white men of the Radical party 'are bound to respect,' and it is because his case is presented in this aspect that we call on our people to rally to our candidate."[24] Failing to prepare and show up to vote, the writer worried, would result in the Democratic candidate losing the election despite the split in the Republican ticket.

The "Norton party" continued to canvass the peninsula in subsequent weeks, holding mass political rallies to gain support and show their strength of force against white Republican rule. Opponents continued their attempts to attack Norton's character in an effort to suggest that he could not be a legitimate candidate and was in the field for personal gain. That white Republicans repeatedly attempted to paint Norton as a fraud disinterested in the good of his constituents revealed the degree to which they were unwilling to acknowledge that a Black candidate could have legitimate qualms with the treatment of Black Southerners after enfranchisement. They consistently failed to acknowledge what even white Democrats conceded: In a democracy, representatives should reflect the will of the people, and the will of the majority on the peninsula was that Black citizens should have an equal opportunity to compete for public office, even at the highest levels of government.

Though Platt successfully gained reelection in 1872, the Nortons and their constituents continued to press the Republican Party for proper recognition in the election of 1874. In voting returns published in *The Virginian-Pilot* on November 8, 1872, only Grant, Platt, Lee, and Greeley were listed as candidates. A note appeared below the returns for Norfolk stating that D. M. Norton had received twenty-two votes at Zion's Church in Norfolk. This framing of the returns suggests that by the time of the election, Norton did not appear as a regular candidate on the ballot. In 1874, however, Robert Norton ran instead of Daniel and presented himself as an independent Republican, indicating his departure from the white Republican establishment on the peninsula. In their political rhetoric both the Nortons and Democratic reporters referred to the Republican establishment on the peninsula as "the customhouse ring," and frequently charged the ring with misusing federal appropriations and leading Black federal employees, especially of the Navy Yard, astray.

On July 4, 1874, the Black community held a mass meeting in Yorktown for the purpose of nominating a candidate for Congress. *The Virginian-Pilot* described this meeting as "one of the largest gatherings of the colored people and leading Republicans that has ever assembled in this section." More than just a political meeting, this event took the form of a mass rally, opening with a march consisting of more than two thousand people who paraded through "the principal streets" before repairing "to a stand which had been erected in a grove."[25] Speaking to the crowd, Robert Norton declared that "the time had come that the Black man in Virginia should demand from the Republican party—a party of which they composed so great a part; the right of representation in the offices." Black voters were "the backbone and the sinew of the Republican party" and he implored them to "demand their rights, and be tools no longer." Daniel Norton and other "well known Republicans" also addressed the crowd, and attendees unanimously nominated Robert Norton as a congressional candidate.[26]

Throughout the election cycle, L. E. Fisher, the president of the Norton Campaign Club, printed editorials in *The Virginian-Pilot* where he articulated the goals and motivations of his peers. He called on Black voters to acknowledge that "the carpet-baggers" had not represented their interests. "They professed friendship for us and pledged us equal civil and political rights," but they had broken those promises. The time had come, he urged his fellow voters, to stop overlooking those broken promises. White Republicans had "given positions to colored men [only] as they found them willing tools, ready to obey them and to do their menial service" but now Black voters would "unite as the colored men have done in North and South Carolina, and send our own men to represent us in Congress, in the Legislature." Black constituents would not consent to the limitations white Republicans imposed. Fisher called on his fellow "true Republicans" to "vote for a colored man to go to Congress to help pass the Civil Rights Bill," and cast out Platt who had "been in Congress six years and who opposes the Civil Rights bill." Time and again, Fisher charged, Platt had shown that he would cultivate Black voters, but he would not appoint Black citizens to public positions. Concluding his remarks, Fisher reminded his readers, "The colored majority in this district is 5,000," suggesting that if they made their voices heard through voting, Norton would carry the field.[27]

In a separate editorial, Fisher responded to charges that his campaign intended to split the Republican ticket. He began by asserting, "It would be better for the negro that he never had been freed than to be put upon political auction blocks and sold to the highest bidder." Freedom without self-determination was not true freedom in Fisher's eyes. Moreover, it was a "standing disgrace to every Black man in the South who has these wrongs inflicted upon him and is yet willing to submit to them." White Republicans, he argued, were only willing for Black people to vote if they would vote for them. Yet, he was "charged with trying to split the Republican party because I am doing what I can to elect Mr. Norton to Congress." White Republicans, he went on, were doing the same thing as Norton was—attempting to run for an office to which they had the right to aspire. Black men would not be free, Fisher concluded, until his votes were also free.[28]

Once again, white Republicans accused the Nortons and their supporters of attempting to split the Republican Party for the sake of white Conservatives, rather than receiving them as equal candidates in the political arena. *The Virginian-Pilot* reprinted an article from the *New York Times* that described Robert Norton as "an independent Republican" who was running against Platt and "industriously egged on by the Conservatives." "Some charge," the article speculated, "that Norton is in the pay of the Conservatives." While it was unclear if this charge was true, reported the *Times,* the correspondent was sure that Norton's "conduct leads many to suspect that he is endangering Republican success in the district in the hope of being bought off." Even if Norton was not actively receiving bribes from the Conservatives, the *New York Times* insisted, he must be so corrupt as to be running for the sake of receiving payoffs in the future.[29] Such rhetoric not only undermined Robert Norton's reputation, but it further undermined the idea of Black men serving in political offices altogether. In the *New York Times'* construction of the situation, Black men could not truly aspire to be political leaders and therefore, if an individual chose to run, it must be because he misunderstood what was in the best interest of his peers or was only concerned about personal gain.

In light of such claims, Fisher continued not only to contradict charges of intentionally splitting the Republican ticket, but further reminded readers on the peninsula that due to popular support, Norton was the rightful Republican candidate. "Ever since the Republican party elected [James] Platt to Congress," he reminded readers, "the party reins have been in the hands of a few bankrupts stationed at the Custom-house and Postoffice in this city, and the people have tried time and time again to oust them." It was not the Norton supporters but rather the majority of "the people" who would defeat Platt in November and, Fisher noted, in recent local meetings the Norton Campaign Club had "routed" Platt supporters.[30]

Despite clear local support for Robert Norton, when the two white candidates met in Yorktown in September for a political rally, Platt apparently refused to share speaking time with Norton. Norton and his supporters, however, met Platt at the wharf in a show of force and "demanded a division of time." Initially refusing this demand, Platt was forced to concede when he saw that "a majority" of the residents present "were in favor of Norton."[31] This show of force at Yorktown included a march with "drum and fife," suggesting that it also involved some level of military display. Military displays of force that had been important in the immediate postwar period in political organizing and action and remained so in the following decades. As Steven Hahn explains, "The rites of democracy had been built on rituals of violence," and no one understood that better than Black Southerners. Paramilitary organization remained "fundamental to the social and political order of freedom."[32] Maintaining self-determination required a willingness to defend it by force, and displaying that willingness was another form of political discourse.

Both Norton brothers spoke to the gathered crowd and contended that "as the Black man had a majority in the district, it was but just that the colored race should be represented in Congress." As Fisher had done, they reminded their listeners of the success of Black political action in North Carolina that had defeated a "carpet-bag" candidate. The reporter for *The Virginian-Pilot* concluded that the "meeting indicated throughout how strong the Nortonites were," and noted that at the close of the Nortons' speeches their delegation paraded through town.[33] At each turn that Platt attempted to deny the legitimacy of Robert Norton's campaign, supporters used displays of their superior numbers and willingness to support their candidate en masse to ensure that their right to choose their own candidate could not be dismissed.

As they had during Daniel Norton's campaign, the Norton Campaign Club widely canvassed the peninsula and held meetings to gain supporters and

share their political message. At each meeting Robert Norton and his supporters—including Thomas Bayne—reminded listeners of white Republicans'
failed promises and patronage politics that were never extended to Black
officeholders.[34] Of particular interest was a meeting in New Kent County
in which Frederick S. Norton spoke as a representative for Robert. Norton
charged that Platt told Black voters that if the Nortons supported him "this
time," then, Platt would "back out for the colored people next time." However,
"that promise had been broken before, and the colored people had lost confidence in such promises."[35] This reference to such a promise having been broken
before suggests that previously Daniel Norton had yielded the political floor
to Platt with the understanding that the white Republicans would support his
candidacy in the next election cycle.[36] But, now that that election cycle had
arrived, Platt continued to reject the legitimacy of a Black candidate.

In October, the nominees met again in Suffolk, Virginia, and again Platt
refused to include Robert Norton in the proceedings. Allies of the Norton
campaign met them at the train station and escorted them "to their headquarters, from whence Robert Norton at once sent forth his challenge to the other
two candidates for a DIVISION OF TIME." According to *The Virginian-Pilot,* John
Goode, the Democratic candidate, consented to this agreement but Platt did
not. Unwilling to "be backed down by Platt," Norton, Bayne, Richard Brooks,
and L. E. Fisher took positions on the speakers' platform along with Goode and
Platt, laying claim, again, to Norton's right to be heard as an equal candidate.[37]
After Robert Norton spoke, Bayne also spoke, noting that Platt and Goode were
"in the same boat, ignoring the claims of the Black men."[38] To elect Platt, Bayne
charged, would be no different than to elect a white Democrat because they
both refused to acknowledge political equality for Black citizens.

Tensions over the election continued to rise, resulting in political violence
at Yorktown on October 30, 1874, just days before the election. Reporting on the
event, the correspondent at Yorktown opened the description of the day by noting "historic old Yorktown was to day the scene of the most disgraceful and out-
rageous riot." Knowing that Yorktown was "Norton's stronghold," the reporter
continued, Platt arrived with "about 250 desperate henchmen, mostly Black."
After arriving in Yorktown, this contingent marched to Norton's headquarters
and "began a quarrel with his men, which resulted in a regular knock down and
drag-out fight." Two men were shot and "the people of Yorktown, particularly
the colored people, [were] very indignant and [would] punish Platt soundly

with their ballots on Tuesday."[39] The display of violence had shown Black residents how far Platt's allies would go to reject their political aspirations.

Immediately after this incident, Robert Norton published an editorial in *The Virginian-Pilot*. He began by noting that he could not have "a hearing in the only Republican paper in the District, because it belongs to the Hon. Jas. H. Platt." Norton then provided an accounting of the events in Yorktown, noting that the day "was fixed for a joint political discussion" and "our citizens assembled as usual to hear and honor the speakers." With this Norton highlighted the fact that Yorktown's Black residents were not rowdy troublemakers, but rather citizens engaged in a regular and orderly political event. Platt arrived, however, with "roughs from the slums of Norfolk and Portsmouth" who "obeying the behest of their master, proceeded to riot through the streets." Platt's followers, Norton charged, "broke open our church, breaking our windows and benches, rushed into private houses insulting and robbing our women, and at last . . . congregated before my store—an organized mob, and with pistols and clubs, created a bloody and shameful riot." Norton made clear his feelings on the matter, declaring, "I have been Ku Kluxed in my own home. Why? Because I'm a colored man, and dare to assert those rights that my own Republican party has endowed me."[40] As Bayne had done in comparing Platt to Goode, Norton likewise reminded readers that white Republicans were capable of exhibiting the same level of violence against Black citizens as the Ku Klux Klan. Moreover, white Republicans were equally intent on denying Black men political equality.

Ultimately, John Goode, the Conservative candidate, carried the 1874 election.[41] Voting returns, however, indicated that Norton remained a strong influence in York County and, *The Virginian-Pilot* asserted, would "again be sent to the [state] Legislature by his colored supporters." This result demonstrated "what the colored people can do for themselves when they have a majority." In particular, *The Virginian-Pilot* looked to Yorktown where they perceived the least amount of voter fraud and where, they believed, the returns best represented the will of Black voters.[42] Indeed, the paper reported later that there had been a "sufficient amount of fraud" and voter intimidation that forced Black voters to side with Platt in many places outside of Yorktown.[43] While their intimidation tactics had not worked in Yorktown where the Black community was large enough to defend itself, the tactics had succeeded elsewhere.

James Platt attempted to contest the results of this election and while there was a congressional investigation into his claims, the election results were not overturned. Many of Platt's allegations in the wake of the election mirrored the accusations he had made before it: That John Goode had paid Robert Norton to split the Republican ticket and that the Norton Campaign Club was not legitimate. Platt also included in his initial accusations a statement that there was a gang called the "Lone Star Society" that operated for no reason other than to promote Robert Norton's interests. Such an accusation rang a familiar tone with Freedmen's Bureau agents who likewise judged the Lone Star Society's actions as against the interest of the Black community when the society opposed bureau policies. Goode responded to the charges by pointing out that Robert Norton had announced his candidacy and was nominated long before Goode had entered the race and pointed out the hypocrisy in Platt's platform. "You seem to be filled with amazement and horror, Goode observed of Platt, "at the bare contemplation of the idea that Robert Norton, who is acknowledged to be an intelligent colored man, could so far acquire the respect and confidence of the members of his own race as to receive 348 votes in the county of his residence, where the colored element largely predominates."[44] Daniel Norton provided a deposition on behalf of Goode, insisting that Platt and his henchmen had orchestrated the pre-election violence in Yorktown and that his brother Robert Norton had not taken any bribes from Goode or his supporters. Despite Platt's accusations, Goode remained in office for the 1875 term.

Platt's assertion that the Lone Star Society operated on behalf of Norton's candidacy reveals the continuity in tactics Black residents of York County employed in postwar politics. Lieutenant Massey, of the Freedmen's Bureau, had likewise bemoaned the existence of the Lone Star Society, insisting that it led Black community members astray and did not represent their best interests. Given the longevity of the club, however, as well as the longevity of the Nortons' political careers, it is clear they held community support for a significant period of time and that Black residents created strong grassroots organizations to advocate for their interests.

As the political landscape shifted in Virginia in the 1880s, so too did the Nortons' political alliances. By the end of the 1870s, historian Nicole Turner explains, Black voters "could no longer clearly identify their political friends."[45] Moreover, the Republican Party was so fractured that in 1877 they failed to produce a candidate for Virginia's governorship. Splinter parties formed made up of alliances between Republicans and Democrats alike. The most notable and successful of these third parties in Virginia was the Readjusters led by former Confederate William Mahone. After officially organizing as a party in 1879, the

Readjusters gained traction and attracted increasing numbers of Black voters.[46] One of the hallmarks of the Readjusters' tactics was their ability to appreciate and then mobilize the networks of Black community activism already extant across the state.[47]

By the early 1880s, newspaper accounts consistently identified Robert and Daniel Norton as allies with the Readjuster Party and its leader, William Mahone. Unlike white Republicans in the state, Mahone understood that Black voters expected a "just biracialism" that consisted of full recognition of their rights and equal political standing in the state.[48] As Nicole Turner has explained, by 1881 the Readjuster movement had gained considerable ground by expanding its platform to include issues that mattered to Black voters such as civil rights and education.[49] Jane Dailey also notes that an ability to capitalize on schisms within the Democratic party enabled the Readjusters to create new political alliances.[50]

In July of 1880, *The Virginian-Pilot* reprinted an article that the Readjusters had run in *the Suffolk Examiner,* proclaiming in all capital letters, "Dr. Norton owes his present position to the action of Dr. R. A. Wise, who withdrew in his favor for the reason that the Peninsula Counties have a large colored majority, and that was recognized as proper by every delegate. The ad continued, "We recognize the Negro as a factor in politics and we propose to give him his civil and political rights. We are not ashamed of Dr. Norton."[51]

That the Readjusters were willing to cede positions to Black representatives was a distinct break from the Nortons' and their followers' experiences with the Republican Party throughout the 1870s. By running this ad, the Readjusters surely hoped to highlight this fact. Furthermore, Black representatives' political strength and viability as candidates was evident in the reaction on the part of the Democratic press. Where *The Virginian-Pilot* had long been willing to acknowledge the hypocrisy of white Republicans, they now found themselves confronted with the threat of Black politicians successfully claiming offices from which their previous allies had barred them. Unsurprisingly, writers for *The Virginian-Pilot* sounded the alarm to their white brethren. "Nothing will stay the [Black man] from obtaining full control of the counties enumerated above," an editorial warned, "unless the white men of the State, in their majesty and strength, resolve to maintain their supremacy by rebuking at the polls in November, the men whose present course is assisting in bringing upon them so terrible a fate."[52] By 1881, the paper identified Daniel Norton as "one of the leading Readjusters in his district," and noted that he represented his constituents in the state senate while his brother, Robert, remained a member of the House of Delegates.[53]

Tensions remained high on the peninsula, and the Nortons and their followers continued to utilize the strategies they had previously crafted to demonstrate their political strength. In August of 1882, *The Virginian-Pilot* reported on a "red hot time" in Yorktown between "the Republican factions." These factions were, in fact, the straight-out Republicans represented by John F. Dezendorf and the Readjusters, represented by Daniel Norton. Dezendorf was to "open the political ball" but in a show of political force, "a colored military company, commanded by a son of Daniel Norton, paraded the town." While Dezendorf gave a speech, "Norton's military company . . . marched and counter-marched through the meeting, attempting to break it up."[54] The article's reference to "a son of Daniel Norton" is especially telling, because according to the 1880 census, Daniel and his wife Sadie had two young sons ages three and five. It seems likely then that the reference to the "son of Daniel Norton" indicated the individual's political allegiances rather than family ties.

Throughout the 1880s, the Nortons and their followers remained a significant "factor in politics" and continued to fight for fair representation within the Republican Party. Again in 1887 *The Virginian-Pilot* reported that the Republican convention in Yorktown was "inharmonious" and that the "Dukes of York— the Nortons—would not succumb to the white element of their organization."[55] Once more, Daniel Norton pursued a congressional seat as an independent candidate and, the reporter expected, would wield great influence over many Black voters.[56] In a subsequent article, the newspaper referred to Norton as the "anti-Mahone" candidate, indicating that he had grown disillusioned with white party leaders and sought to make the voice of Black constituents heard through his candidacy.[57] Though the paper did not elaborate on this distinction, it is clear that the Nortons and their followers constantly adapted to the shifting political landscape of postwar Virginia. Mahone and his party leaders also had a "race ceiling" and the Nortons and their supporters were unwilling to accept an unequal position within the party.[58] Their allegiance could not be taken for granted, and if white leaders did not meet their expectations, they took their strength and their votes elsewhere.

Commemoration as Politics

During this period of political fluctuation, Black residents of the peninsula, and in particular York County, also utilized commemorative events to enact their citizenship within the community. Newspapers frequently noted that while white citizens participated in Confederate Memorial Day events, Black residents were the principal organizers and participants in the federal Memorial Day. Black residents from places such as Hampton and Elizabeth City Counties traveled each year to the Yorktown National Cemetery to participate in ceremonies honoring the Union dead and place flowers on federal soldiers' graves. Grand Army of the Republic (GAR) posts in those locations also consistently sent delegations to Yorktown as well as other national cemeteries on the peninsula.[59]

Though the origins of Memorial Day ceremonies remain uncertain, by the 1870s Black Americans were using the national holiday to advocate for their rights.[60] As Mitch Kachun explains, there was already a long history of Black Americans employing public events and displays of patriotism to demonstrate that they were worthy of being full citizens.[61] Moreover, such events helped foster a "sense of themselves as a people . . . with a significant and positive role to play in the nation's future."[62] Such celebrations existed in dialog with other national holidays that proliferated in the wake of the Civil War. Historian Ellen Litwicki argues that the trauma of the Civil War as well as pressures such as European immigration after the war contributed to the addition of a variety of new civic holidays in the United States. The most important function of these holidays, beyond generating a sense of community identity, was "to reconstruct America, to imagine the nation through the eyes of group members."[63] It is essential to understand postwar Black Memorial Day ceremonies as part of a larger landscape of commemoration in which different groups used public holidays to contest the identity of the nation that had emerged from the Civil War. They were political statements meant to establish a group's belonging in the nation and should be read as such.

In Yorktown, Memorial Day ceremonies had particular resonance in the 1880s as the community prepared for the centennial of Cornwallis's surrender to Washington and the nation collectively considered its shared identity. The centennial of the country "raised mixed feelings among Black Americans," historian William Blair observes, "concerning the national government run by Republicans."[64] As the Nortons' clashes with local Republican representatives demonstrate, Black Southerners' relationship with the party of Lincoln was increasingly strained in this era. Moreover, in the waning decades of the nineteenth century, Mitch Kachun notes, "America's popular imagery defined it more forcefully than ever as a 'white man's country.'"[65] Black Americans, especially in Yorktown where centennial celebrations were elaborate, could not have missed the increasing emphasis on deploying historical commemorations to construct the United States as primarily a white man's country.

On Memorial Day in 1881, John Dezendorf, the Republican congressman from the peninsula and the Nortons' political rival, gave a speech at City Point National Cemetery in Richmond. Dezendorf declared that the struggle of the Civil War had ended, but these dead had not died in vain because "the nation yet lives!" "Is it not then more hospitable for us," he wondered aloud, "to examine the results of their sacrifice, than it would be to recite again the oft told tale of the causes that led to the war; to fight their battles over again?" No, they should not continue to contest the outcomes and meaning of the Civil War, he thought. Rather, they should celebrate the nation that had risen "phoenixlike" from the ashes of war. It was to this nation, he proclaimed, "the down-trodden of all lands turn with longing eyes to this Republic as the one country where the poor are rich—rich in freedom, rich in liberty of conscience and of thought." This nation was "the one country where the poor and the rich are on a political equality, and where each may aspire to all that their natural or acquired talents render them capable of attaining." In these declarations, Dezendorf sought not only to erase the political conflicts that still plagued his party and his state but further to construct a vision of the United States that could be projected throughout the world and could assert itself in global events. "The example of our free institutions," he declared, "is being followed the world over. Freedom is asserting itself."[66] Dezendorf's celebration of the freedom he believed the United States had achieved and was encouraging around the globe erased the ongoing struggle for political equality that still plagued Black residents on the peninsula and throughout the country.

Moreover, Dezendorf called on veterans of the Civil War to end sectional animosities so that the United States could gain additional strength. "Your dead comrades," he implored his audience, "call upon you with a voice from the grave, asking you to do what you can to heal the wounds caused by the war which cost them their lives, they ask you to forget whatever of bitterness may have been caused by that struggle." Instead, they should remember that "we are brethren of a common country, that all our destinies are in common." Turning his attention to Black citizens, he likewise implored them to "enter upon the glorious work of breaking down the bitterness and prejudice engendered by the four years of war."[67] In a sense, Dezendorf was asking Black residents to forget that there was still more work to do to enact political equality and rather be content with acknowledging that if all "destinies were in common" they need not continue to struggle against the white faction of the Republican Party. No doubt Black residents were particularly suspicious of Dezendorf who just a year earlier had threatened to vote with the Democrats in Congress if William Mahone received control of state patronage.[68]

Matters only intensified in the ensuing decades. By the 1890s, federal Memorial Day events in the South were segregated, and it had become clear that Black Americans were not welcome. In speaking at Seven Pines National Cemetery near Richmond in 1888, Pennsylvania-born orator Theodore Bean had made the theme of his speech "the glories and superiorities of the Anglo-Saxon race."[69] Such themes were common as a "growing number of white Americans embraced theories of social Darwinism" at the end of the nineteenth century and "cast 'Anglo-Saxons' as uniquely capable of achieving the qualities of 'progress.'"[70] Speakers echoed such sentiments at federal and Confederate Memorial Days alike.

As men like Dezendorf and Bean used Memorial Day events to construct a vision of the reunited nation in which racial inequality was ignored, Black residents continued to assert their belonging in this phoenixlike nation. In contrast to speeches like Dezendorf's, dedications of a monument to Robert E. Lee in Richmond (the first installment on Monument Avenue) and Confederate memorial activities, Black residents of the peninsula consistently joined together in large numbers on the federal Memorial Day to decorate the graves of Union soldiers. Their leadership in these activities was so conspicuous that white newspapers felt compelled to note each year that "colored people" and "colored G.A.R. posts" were the organizers and principal celebrants. Their patterns of organization and travel for these events reflected the same political realities that had been true in the 1870s and 1880s, as residents of neighboring counties made a point of journeying to different towns and cemeteries to gather together in recognition of their shared political identity.[71] Such organization helped reinforce the existence of a community of Black voters. Moreover, these consistent demonstrations of citizenship and celebrations of Black freedom constructed a narrative that ran counter to those speakers like Dezendorf tried to impose on the postwar South. Black residents knew the work of establishing freedom and equality was not finished, and they used Memorial Day ceremonies as opportunities to remember that and prepare for the struggles yet in front of them.

Documentation of Memorial Day activities in Yorktown is limited, but it is clear that these celebrations persisted from the nineteenth century into the twentieth, and that as they had previously, Black residents adapted their events to meet changing political needs. In 1902, the superintendent of York-town National Cemetery reported that the Grand Army of the Republic had carried on their usual Memorial Day activities and "hundreds of people visited the Cemetery from all parts of the counties and the surrounding cities" and from great distances to attend the event. "Mr Osgood" from the "Nat'l Soldiers Home near Hampton" gave an "eloquent" speech and the "day passed without any disturbance."[72] Though he did not elaborate on Mr. Osgood's status, it is significant that he came as a representative of the national Soldiers' Home at Hampton because that institution specifically served Black veterans. This sug-gests that Black leaders organized the event and selected a speaker who would appeal to Black veterans. "Exercises were held at the colored church opposite the Cemetery" the superintendent noted, and "many good prayers went up to God the giver of all good things."[73] The "colored church" to which he referred was Shiloh Baptist Church, which by that time had relocated to a new building directly across the street from the entrance to the national cemetery.[74]

Ceremonies continued throughout the first decade of the twentieth century, though cemetery superintendents did not always comment on the events. In 1906, however, the superintendent reported that "Decoration Day was a lovely day and well attended." "About 600 attended the grounds" he commented, and "about 1300 . . . visitors at Cemetery and many at the monument that did not reach the cemetery."[75] "The monument" to which the superintendent referred was the *Yorktown Victory Monument* whose care remained under his purview. That he noted some visitors went to the monument but not to the cemetery further suggests that some people chose to pay homage to the legacy of the nation saved by the Union but were less willing to attend Memorial Day events at the national cemetery where the legacy of emancipation and Black freedom was on full display. Additionally, it appears that on Memorial Day sojourners to Yorktown took the opportunity to reflect on the nation's Revolutionary War history as well as its more immediate Civil War past.

Black residents across the peninsula likewise met each year to ensure that Memorial Day was properly observed. Better newspaper coverage of these events provides insight into the concrete ways Black celebrants consti-tuted their vision of the United States through these ceremonies. In 1900, *The Virginian-Pilot* reported that in Suffolk "National Memorial Day was celebrated by a parade of colored G.A.R. Veterans, headed by a brass band." Celebrants "marched through some of the principal streets and visited the cemetery."[76]

Noting the qualifier "National" was an important distinction because during this period white Southerners routinely held elaborate Confederate Memorial Day ceremonies around the same time each year. As had been the case in the previous decade, it appears that on the Virginia Peninsula, it was primarily Black residents who kept the legacy of the federal soldiers' sacrifice alive through Memorial Day events. In 1902, *The Virginian-Pilot* reported that no Memorial Day exercises would be held "except by the colored posts" of the GAR, confirming how Black Peninsula residents had become the keepers of Unionist memory of the Civil War.[77]

These ceremonies were more than memorial events meant to keep the legacy of the Union preserved by the Civil War alive, however. They were also forums in which participants argued for the meanings of race and nation. The same year that *The Virginian-Pilot* noted that only Black GAR posts would actively celebrate Memorial Day, it also published an editorial reflecting on the meaning of Civil War commemoration. "Men say the cause was lost," the author opined, "No so . . . The South, to be sure, was forced back into the Union . . . But in the Union she is destined to become, more and more, as time passes, the conserving force of Anglo-Saxon civilization on this continent."[78] In the eyes of this author, white Southerners, in particular, were doing the necessary work of preserving "Anglo-Saxon civilization" for the sake of the future of the United States. This was not a reflection of a particularly Southern idea of white supremacy, but rather a statement that reflected a contemporary national obsession with the "connection between manhood and racial dominance."[79] As historian Gail Bederman elaborates, references to civilization "denoted a precise stage in human racial evolution."[80] When speakers talked about American "civilization" they meant to signal that the future progress of the American nation belonged to and was dependent upon white men. The fight to suppress Black Americans was not just a Southern fight in the eyes of this author, but rather a contest over the future of the United States.

This author was not the only one anxious about preserving "Anglo-Saxon civilization" during this period. As the twentieth century opened, white Americans generally became increasingly concerned with identifying and preserving key sites related to the nation's history and to a particular history that supported a vision of the United States as an "Anglo-Saxon civilization." In 1906, a year in which President Theodore Roosevelt spoke on Memorial Day in Norfolk, *The Virginian-Pilot* reported that a subcommittee in the House of Representatives had recommended a $410,000 appropriation for the Association for the Preservation of Virginia Antiquities to acquire, police, and develop ground on Jamestown Island.[81] This association would dedicate its time to preserving and interpreting a version of Jamestown's history that focused on the white colonists who "founded" the US nation. In North Carolina, like Virginia, various groups sought to preserve the site that the Roanoke Island Colony had once occupied in an effort to center the story of American "civilization" in the South. As Adam Domby has noted, "Maintaining a historical narrative centered on Anglo-Saxon achievements," that enabled and supported Jim Crow politics encompassed more than just Civil War memory.[82] Again, Black memorial events must be understood not as separate events but as contributors to an ongoing national dialog about both the past and the future of the United States. This was especially true at Yorktown because it had long been acknowledged as a key site in the history of American "civilization" and was quickly becoming a point of interest for national preservation efforts.

Conditions changed briefly at Yorktown's Memorial Day on the eve of World War I. In May of 1914, the national cemetery superintendent reported that "a large number of citizens, school children and Ladies of Yorktown and vicinity graced the Cemetery with their presence." He further noted that "A short but impressive Memorial Day service was held."[83] By the next year, however, Memorial Day services were again the exclusive purview of Yorktown's Black residents and the superintendent noted that "service[s] were conducted by the colored people from the surroundings."[84] In 1919, superintendent A. H. Ackley went on to further specify "the white folks had no service" for Memorial Day. However, as usual, "the colored folks had a service at their church across the way from Cemetery." After the service they "formed a parade and marched from church to the N.E. section where the colored soldiers are interred and held a service there which was very impressive and harmonious."[85] That Ackley specifically noted that the marchers held their service "where the colored soldiers were interred" illuminates an important reality. Yorktown's national cemetery was not formally segregated, but in the postwar years it quickly ran out of space. As a consequence, as noted earlier, superintendents began burying veterans who died after the war and wished to be buried their on top of the graves of other soldiers—usually unknown. Thus, Ackley could likely specify "where the colored soldiers were interred" because a significant portion of postwar burials at Yorktown were veterans of the United States Colored Troops.

Moreover, it also suggests a specific community tie to the memory of Black soldiers, many of whom lived in the area after the war.[86] By drawing attention specifically to Black veterans, celebrants sought to ensure that the crucial role Black men had played in saving the Union and securing the legacy of US "progress" would be remembered. Ellen Litwicki asserts that organizers of public celebrations during this era intended to "sustain their own claims to be exemplars of Americanism."[87] By emphasizing the memory of Black soldiers who had died in service to the federal government, organizers of Yorktown's Memorial Day event reminded participants that Black men too had been exemplary Americans. Further, they highlighted the fact that Black soldiers had played a significant role in preserving American "civilization." Black celebrants frequently drew a direct line between the Declaration of Independence and the Emancipation Proclamation—which had allowed for the enlistment of Black soldiers—envisioning Black freedom as an integral part of the history of American independence and the progressive march towards fully embodying ideals of freedom.[88]

Elsewhere on the peninsula, Memorial Day likewise took on new significance as the United States' entrance into other wars resulted in the creation of a larger population of white US veterans residing in the South than had existed immediately after the Civil War. It appears that as a result, white residents began holding Memorial Day ceremonies in larger numbers. They did not, however, join their Black neighbors in existing celebrations. In 1915, *The Virginian-Pilot* took care to note that "National Decoration Day will be fittingly observed by both the white and colored members of the Grand Army of the Republic, and the Spanish War veterans." However, the white soldiers would decorate graves in the morning, "holding exercises in Elmwood cemetery" and the "colored exercises" would take place in the afternoon at West Point Cemetery "preceded by a parade."[89] This parade included the GAR, Spanish War veterans, US sailors, the Knights of Pythias, and a variety of other civic organizations. Such an accumulation of civic organizations was common for Black Memorial Day ceremonies, which frequently used the event as an opportunity to display the progress Black Americans had made and the contributions they were making to society. Describing the same event in 1917, *The Virginian-Pilot* reported that more than a thousand people participated in the parade alone, including several hundred school children.[90]

As historians Mitch Kachun and Patricia Clark have noted, such events were important not just for enacting citizenship in physical and visible ways, but also for constructing a usable past for Black Americans in a period when national history consistently ignored their existence. In 1920, John Cromwell

wrote an editorial for *The Richmond Planet* seeking to alleviate this very problem. Cromwell noted, "It has been repeatedly charged that we have no racial
history." The previous year, Cromwell explained, the *Journal of Negro History*
had published a list of Black representatives who had served in the legislature
since the Civil War. But somehow, the service of Black representatives in Virginia had already been lost because they were not included. "When it came to
Virginia," Cromwell pointed out, "the contrast was most painful. . . . For a time
I felt like disowning that Virginia was my native State." Rather than disown his
home state, however, Cromwell determined to reconstruct a list of Black representatives from Virginia, which he submitted to the *Richmond Planet* for publication.[91] Cromwell's effort to restore the history of Virginia's Black politicians
reflected a growing effort to combat historians' renderings of Black Americans'
identity as "childlike under slavery [and] animal-like and barbaric in freedom."
Such renderings of Black identity "complemented the scientific theories of
racial hierarchies" that were also gaining ground during this period.[92] Thus,
Cromwell and others were doing more than correcting the historical record.
As the Norton brothers and their supporters had earlier, they were participating in a national dialog about the fitness of Black Americans for a full range of
citizenship rights.

In the early 1920s, Norfolk's *New Journal and Guide,* a leading Black newspaper on the peninsula, took aim at segregated ceremonies and what they
meant for the unity of the American nation. In June of 1922, an editorial pointed
out that "two separate Memorial Day celebrations were held here May 30th—
one white, one colored." Yet, "under the new order the day is supposed to be
observed for the men who have died for the nation in all its wars." "Blacks and
whites died on the same battlefields," the author pointed out, "They fought and
died together for one common country." Could a segregated Memorial Day be
a real Memorial Day, the author wondered?[93] Two years later another article in
the *New Journal and Guide* elaborated on a similar theme. The author insisted
that when Black soldiers fought in the Spanish-American War "they fought for
this whole country . . . they didn't fight for any colored sections of it, or for any
particular racial group. They laid their lives upon the altar for their country,
unqualifiedly and without reserve." Still, Norfolk's city council had issued a
permit for Black Spanish-American War veterans to sell poppies only in "the
colored section" on Memorial Day. If these soldiers had been good enough to
"fight for their country in the hour of its need" the author insisted, "they should
be good enough to sell poppies anywhere in their country in time of peace."[94]

Maintaining segregation in the very ceremonies meant to honor the service of fallen soldiers, this author pointed out, was antithetical to the principles for which they had supposedly died. Moreover, it was a direct contradiction of the ideals of equality and freedom the United States was supposedly helping to spread around the world.

Though the *New Journal and Guide*'s reports did not originate in Yorktown, the long history of Black residents of the peninsula traveling to organize politically and celebrate Memorial Day suggests that these details provide insight into the meaning of such ceremonies wherever they occurred during this period. Memorial Day ceremonies often featured similar themes, imagery, and speakers throughout the area. In 1926, the *New Journal and Guide* made a point of acknowledging this fact and highlighting that Black residents of the peninsula had always been loyal in their efforts to honor the country in which they belonged. "It was Decoration Day," the *New Journal and Guide* noted, "and the colored citizens of this city on that day never fail to honor their dead."[95] In other words, Black citizens never failed to do justice to the memory of those who had died for their nation. They never failed in their responsibilities as members of the body politic.

That same year, Reverend L. L. Berry, the orator for Memorial Day in Norfolk, used the occasion once again to highlight current political struggles and tie the heritage of Black Americans to the heritage of the US nation. "Dr. Berry reviewed the history of the country briefly," the *New Journal and Guide* noted, "pointing out its contribution to the well being of the nations of the earth." He referred to the "spirit of independence" that drove the "Fathers of '76 to strike for their liberty" and "reviewed the wars in which the Negro has taken prominent parts." Berry especially reviewed the efforts of Crispus Attucks, the Black sailor killed during the Boston Massacre, and "told of the Negro sailors who distinguished themselves with Commodore Perry, of the bravery and daring of the soldiers of the Civil, Spanish and World Wars." Such commentary was more than just a reminder. In his review of Black Americans' contributions to US history, Berry constructed a usable past from which they could continue to make claims on the nation that had yet to fully grant them their constitutionally guaranteed equality.[96] "There are greater battles to be fought this day than were fought in those periods just mentioned," Berry continued. He then went on to explain how Black Americans must maintain their fight "through the church, the school and the home," against "the great monster ignorance [and] the social evils that stand out against the progress of our people of today."[97] This moment was about remembering and about planning a course for the future.

Berry gave this speech the same year that the Ku Klux Klan held open-air ceremonies on Memorial Day weekend in the Wythe Street playground in Norfolk. *The Virginian-Pilot* reported this event on the same page that it announced Memorial Day parade plans and anticipated that approximately one thousand Klansmen and a "large number" of new members would march "through High and Court streets to the playgrounds."[98] Throughout the 1920s, articles describing Black Memorial Day events appeared alongside articles in the *New Journal and Guide* reporting on lynchings, race riots, and ongoing violence perpetuated against Black Americans and intended to suppress their impact on politics. Thus, such Memorial Day ceremonies stood as direct testimonies against the continued unjust treatment of Black Americans and insisted on their equal citizenship despite violent white neighbors' attempts to deny it.

Black residents of the peninsula continued to use Memorial Day activities to contest political issues into the 1930s. In 1931, Reverend R. H. Bowling spoke at Memorial Day ceremonies in Norfolk and once again reminded his audience of Black soldiers' contributions to the United States' goals in its various wars. "In the Revolution we were fighting to free [ourselves] from tyranny," he explained, "In the Civil War we were fighting to perpetuate national unity and to bring freedom to the slave." Moreover, "In 1898 our aim was freedom to Cuba . . . In 1918 we strove in war to end war and to insure freedom for world-wide application of democratic ideals." Still, they needed also to pursue peacetime objectives. Bowling insisted that "it is not enough that we pause to take note of what has been brought to pass." They could not just remember, they also had to look ahead. "God hasten the day," he proclaimed, "when Negro America, catching the spirit of her wartime volunteers, shall set herself to the hard work of establishing her right to the ballot, of proving that Negroes can work together in large and cooperative enterprises."[99] The work of the dead on behalf of the nation, Bowling hoped, would inspire current generations to continue the effort to secure the rights of citizenship for Black Americans.

Reverend J. A. Hunter echoed similar themes in his Memorial Day speech in Norfolk in 1933. "As we gather here to pay respect to our heroes," Hunter declared, "let us not be unmindful of the fact that we, the living, create here and now a memorial in the lives of our sons and daughters." Their work of memory was not for the sake of the past, but for the sake of delineating a particular future for their children. This memorial would remind Black children of "the belief that the Negro feels he has a right to live wherever he is able to purchase a home . . . to have a right to use the ballot, and to protect himself and family from discrimination and violence from mobs and cowardly officials of the law." Paying tribute to soldiers from all of the United States' wars through a reading of the Gettysburg Address and Thaddeus Smith's poem "Flanders Field," Hunter continued his oration. "We come here to reconsecrate ourselves to the preservation of what they achieved," but they were also there to remember that they were involved in still another battle. "We are paying our tribute and yet there is a memorial in which all of us make take part," Hunter proclaimed, "and that is the memorial of the battle of the ballot." As long as there were "miscarriages of justice in our land," he reminded the crowd, "we will have a memorial to observe." Social equality had yet to be achieved, and Black Americans still wanted "economic, industrial, and educational equality, and equality before the law." It was hypocritical to ask Black soldiers to fight "to make the world safe for Democracy" and not expect equality for Black soldiers when they returned home. He further pleaded that lynching of Black men and women cease and that unjust trials of Black citizens "be transferred from the pine thickets back to court houses and orderly procession of the law."[100] Hunter rejected a newly constituted United States in which Black Americans could not operate as equal citizens. In drawing attention to the problem of lynching and backwoods "justice," he further highlighted how far the United States was from the ideals it claimed to embody. Still, Hunter did not just call on white Americans to end the violence to solve the problem. He insisted that Black Americans had an integral role to play in the country's efforts to secure justice and a sound democracy, just as they always had.

Jane Dailey has argued that the establishment of Jim Crow should not be seen as inevitable, but rather as a reaction to Black Americans' success in post–Civil War politics. The same is true of the ascendancy of Lost Cause narratives of the Civil War that eliminated histories of emancipation and Black citizenship. White Americans had to work to construct a history of the United States that was exclusively white because in the decades after the Civil War they were constantly confronted with the reality that American politics were no longer the exclusive domain of elite white men. As the Norton brothers' political careers illustrate, Black Southerners knew how to make their voices heard, and they navigated the postwar landscape with skill and determination to make their influence matter. Efforts on the part of those same constituents in Yorktown and the Virginia Peninsula after disenfranchisement reflected that same awareness and skill and demonstrate continuity in message and vision for Black Southerners. These memorial events likewise provide an important window into the ways Black Southerners navigated shifting political waters and continued their efforts to construct a meaningful freedom for themselves. They represent echoes of a political voice that endured even in the darkest days of Jim Crow.

Conclusion

The Coming of the National Park Service

By the 1940s, Memorial Day celebrations in the Yorktown National Cemetery had ended. In 1946, superintendent J. C. Harrington reported to a representative for the Grand Army of the Republic, "The Cemetery presented a very impressive and attractive appearance on Memorial Day this year." A wreath sent by the GAR had arrived in good condition, Harrington noted, and "again this year, no special exercises were held here on Memorial Day."[1] It is unclear when exactly Memorial Day exercises ceased in the Yorktown National Cemetery, but by the 1940s, regular events no longer occurred.[2] Ten years prior, the federal government had incorporated Yorktown into the newly established Colonial National Historical Park. National Park Service (NPS) administrators believed that the most important story the landscape at Yorktown could tell was the history of the Revolutionary War siege in 1781, a moment, they believed, that sealed the future of the United States as an independent nation. As the NPS acquired land, made decisions about "restoring" the landscape, and defined its interpretive priorities, the belief that the siege was their "most capital story" led administrators to view any physical aspects of the area that could obscure visitors' understanding of this narrative as a problem.[3] Visitors, park planners believed, would be best served if they could view a unified landscape that spoke of only one story. By necessity then, all other visual and physical "intrusions" needed to be removed from the new national park.[4]

Such a belief was not specific to Yorktown, but rather reflected trends in historical preservation and interpretation that swept the nation during this era. As one of the first historical parks incorporated into the National Park Service, the agency's desire to create a nationwide network of historic sites guided the development of the Colonial National Historical Park. Leaders in this process, and especially early NPS directors Horace Albright and Arno Cammerer, believed that they were creating a vast narrative landscape that would teach Americans about the progressive unfolding of the United States.[5] As visitors encountered each park sequentially, they could learn a piece of the fundamental story of the United States' birth and evolutionary growth. Each site, then, needed to tell only one part of the story. Eventually, this devotion to creating a unified landscape as well as a focus on specifically "Anglo-Saxon" America would mean removing the Black community from the memorial landscape at Yorktown.[6]

On December 30, 1930, President Herbert Hoover established Colonial National Monument, later redesignated Colonial National Historical Park, by presidential proclamation.[7] This was the National Park Service's first foray into historical work, and the agency's decisions at Colonial NHP as well as the George Washington Birthplace National Monument on the Northern Neck of Virginia would lay the groundwork for a rapid expansion of historical acquisitions. In establishing these first national historical parks, NPS administrators prioritized sites they thought would speak to the foundational history of the United States. These were more than tourist destinations; they were tools through which the federal government could communicate a particular vision of the United States that defined national ideals and a single national identity.[8]

Early efforts to convey Yorktown's historical significance to the public stressed the importance of the Revolutionary War siege to the founding and future of the young United States. Initial commemorative events not only emphasized the significance of the siege for the United States' birth, but further highlighted the role modern day Americans hoped the country would play on a world stage. Their message was not just about the past, but about the future of a country they believed was destined to spread democracy and freedom around the globe. Moreover, their efforts constructed a distinct culture for the United States which, as historian John Gilkeson has explained, was supposed to be a marker of an independent nation-state in the early twentieth century.[9]

In 1931, the NPS and its partners celebrated the creation of the national park along with the sesquicentennial of George Washington's victory at Yorktown. While dedicating the park, founders articulated the meaning they hoped it would have and the messages the park should impart.[10] The official program of the sesquicentennial dedicated the event "to the Revolutionary Armies and Navies . . . in memory of their glorious valor and sacrifice, which, through the victory at Yorktown in 1781, made secure the American national structure [and] whose strength has ever been a symbol for peoples oppressed throughout the world, a vision of hope and a light-house of faith." The program also featured a copy of President Hoover's proclamation establishing Yorktown as a part of Colonial National Monument. "It is fitting that this momentous event in the history of the nation be commemorated," Hoover declared, "in such a manner as to inspire love of our country and devotion to its ideals by recalling to this generation the struggles of the past." It was not important, in Hoover's estimation, simply to remember what happened at Yorktown. Rather, commemorations should inspire continued loyalty and commitment to the United States.[11]

W. A. R. Goodwin, president of the Yorktown Sesquicentennial Association and the "father" of the restoration movement at nearby Colonial Williamsburg, elaborated on these themes in his dedication speech, which was also printed in the official program. The United States needed "to be reminded of the richness of its heritage," Goodwin insisted, because "it bequeaths what it has created." Yorktown was a symbol for the world, and the celebration would be a fitting acknowledgement of that. "Yorktown eloquently speaks of the nation's past, and is a national memory and responsibility," he explained. Remembering Yorktown the right way would remind Americans of their continued responsibility to the nation. Not only did Yorktown speak of the past, but it had "much to say to the future." Yorktown—and by extension American success in the Revolution—was "the justifying reason for a worldwide hope for liberty founded in justice." As a symbol, Yorktown reminded Americans of their responsibilities and served as a beacon for nations around the world who Goodwin insisted longed for liberty and self-determination. For these reasons, Yorktown would become a permanent part of the national park system. But in dedicating the park correctly, participants in the celebration would "enrich the national memory" by being careful to articulate just what Yorktown should mean to people. This was necessary, according to Goodwin, because "the nation, like the individual, forgets." The sesquicentennial would remind Americans to "pause and take inventory" and would leave Yorktown "more deeply enshrined in the heart of the nation" while also ensuring that those outside of the United States would view it as a "gift of hope and inspiration to the world."[12] Yorktown belonged in the national park system not just because Americans needed to remember what happened there, but so that all people of the world could have the opportunity to learn lessons of independence and freedom from encounters with the memory the sesquicentennial celebration constructed and the park would perpetuate.

In an additional speech, Lyon G. Tyler, president emeritus of the College of William and Mary, located in nearby Williamsburg, elaborated on the principles of the Revolution and their application to the more recent Civil War.[13] "Not always has the current run smoothly in America itself," he noted. "There were men and parties in the United States who thought that democracy was dangerous . . . When the Southern States, composing a country half the size of Europe and capable of waging one of the greatest wars on record, tested the doctrine of self-government by secession," he complained, "the Northern States . . . were unwilling to recognize it." "Perhaps even today," Tyler thought, "there may be cause for thinking this country is no nearer the principle of the Declaration of Independence than Great Britain or France." A greater commitment to ideals of "self-government" was necessary, in Tyler's estimation, and a new historical park at Yorktown could remind Americans to rededicate themselves to the right interpretation of Revolutionary principles.[14]

The events featured in the sesquicentennial depicted a colonial United States composed entirely of white gentry. Each day had a theme, including "Colonial Day," "Revolutionary Day," "Religious Day," and "Anniversary Day." Different days featured official luncheons—open only to those with invitations—various exhibits, pageants, and a grand military review. On Anniversary Day, the main pageant depicted "the historical scene representing the Surrender of the British forces" followed by a "scene of the dinner given to Lord Cornwallis and General Rochambeau by General Washington." A "masque dealing in symbolic or allegorical form with the great developments after the events of Yorktown," followed, elaborating on the principles that event organizers believed the surrender at Yorktown had established. These included the "main motifs of Peace, Liberty, and Democracy."[15] With each element of the celebration, organizers hoped to articulate Yorktown's meaning for future generations.

A colonial fair and harvest festival featured "descendants of the Pamunkey and Mattaponi Tribes" who had "inhabited the Colonial Tidewater section of Virginia in the earliest days." Such a depiction of particular Indigenous cultures was not uncommon during this era of NPS interpretation. At the Grand Canyon, the NPS had selectively allowed members of Indigenous nations to demonstrate and market traditional crafts while excluding others. As historian Hal Rothman explains, these depictions of Indigenous groups served to reinforce the narrative of the United States drawing greatness from its physical landscape and precolonial history. Administrators excluded Indigenous tribes whose histories, they believed, were "incidental" to their efforts to mythologize the landscape.[16] Thus Indigenous participation was not for the sake of cultural understanding but because their history contributed to the overall narrative the NPS wanted to display.

President Hoover likewise offered his thoughts on Yorktown's significance in a sesquicentennial address in which he tied its history to the present through a theme of the progressive evolution of the United States as a free nation. "The national shrine stands for more than a glorious battle," Hoover remarked, "It is a shrine which symbolizes things of the spirit." This was a place that demonstrated essentially American ideals and its creation would help perpetuate those ideals into the future. The victory at Yorktown was "a victory of the spirit . . . another blaze in the great trail of human freedom." More than a military victory, "Through these ideas and ideals the minds of a people were liberated." If Americans would take the opportunity presented by these new historic sites to look back and remember, they would "see our Nation making progress with every decade." They would see a nation that had "attained a wider diffusion of liberty and happiness and more of material things than humanity has ever known before." Despite the obstacles the founders had faced, the nation had "swept forward to ever-increasing strength."[17] Again, Hoover's declarations mirrored themes that colored representations of US history throughout this period. Marguerite Shaffer has demonstrated that park developers in the decade prior had invented "an American tradition that reinforced the Progressive era's ideals of progress and obscured the racial and ethnic conflict that marred the nation's past."[18] With his words, Hoover helped construct a myth of a strong United States that had moved forward through history committed to ideals of liberty and freedom without acknowledging that those ideals extended only to select portions of the population.[19]

Each subsequent year, Colonial National Historical Park continued to host annual pageants to commemorate the anniversary of Washington's victory and ensure they consciously articulated these ideas. As historian John Bodnar notes, by the 1930s such pageants and similarly "elaborate commemorative ceremonies were plentiful as the United States appeared to turn to its past for entertainment, consolation, patriotic renewal, education, and inspiration from the deeds of ancestors."[20] While these pageants seemed to serve the immediate needs of dominant members of the nation in ensuring group cohesion and loyalty, they also consistently left others out.

Beyond the initial sesquicentennial celebration, park administrators sought to ensure that visitors to Yorktown would learn the messages they intended the park to communicate whenever they visited. To this end, park employees engaged in outreach throughout eastern Virginia, seeking to familiarize the public with their park and its purpose.[21] In August of 1931, B. Floyd Flickinger, park historian and later superintendent, recommended that "lectures before schools and civic organizations would enlighten the people here in the East where the National Park Service is not as well known as in the West."[22] He further recommended that the park have "more detailed publicity in magazines and papers."[23] As Marguerite Shaffer has elaborated, during these early years of the park service's founding, the federal government printed a plethora of reading materials meant to teach the visiting public how to view the landscapes they encountered. In particular, an early series publicizing new national parks, *Picturesque America,* "taught readers or potential tourists how to frame the view, creating a well-composed image in which anomalous surroundings could be edited out."[24] Such guides "defined a very particular narrative of American history by deliberately selecting and presenting certain historical facts."[25] Moreover, by crafting this view, guides could teach visitors how to filter out conflicting narratives on the same landscapes. They taught people what to focus on in viewing a physical space. This was especially important at Yorktown in its early years, where the national cemetery, Uniontown, and other features of the postwar community presented obstacles to visual unity in the eyes of park planners. Visitors to Yorktown would need to know not just what they were looking at, but where they should focus their gaze in order to discern the narrative the NPS wished to convey.

That same month park superintendent William Robinson wrote to Flickinger noting that "Mr. [Arthur] Demaray is very anxious that we should institute public guide service[s] as soon as possible."[26] Robinson directed that these guided services include caravans of visitors in their own cars moving from station to station on the battlefield with "two or three minute talks at each stopping point." Anticipating a wide reach, Robinson also noted that he would give press releases to newspapers in Virginia, Washington, DC, and New York and that these tours would commence immediately.[27] Unfortunately for Flickinger, his initial efforts to organize a guided tour met with no success. After his first attempts he reported to Robinson that "I can readily understand the feelings of the bride deserted at the altar." While many cars had passed by, none had stopped to take advantage of the service.[28]

As staff members continued to establish the park's interpretive program, they presented summer lectures on a variety of topics. These programs included,

"Jamestown, the Birthplace of Anglo-Saxon America," and "How American Independence was Won at Yorktown, 1781."[29] Such an emphasis on specifically
"Anglo-Saxon" America suggested that while Colonial National Historical Park
preserved spaces fundamental to US history, only white Americans could lay
claim to the heritage it represented. By extension, white Americans were the
true inheritors of American independence.[30] Newly developed tourist destinations across the United States represented similar ideas. Marguerite Shaffer
notes that tourist attractions "manifested a distinct national identity" that
encouraged "white, native-born middle-and-upper class Americans to reaffirm
their American-ness by following the footsteps of American history and seeing
the nation firsthand."[31] By traveling to these sites, white Americans could so-
lidify their belonging and, by extension, confirm their unique claim to the rights
of citizenship in an increasingly diverse United States.

From the outset, NPS administrators recognized that the landscape at Yorktown had multiple histories. They understood that the 1862 siege during the
Civil War was important, but they did not believe it was as important as the
Revolutionary siege. This historical conflict presented a problem they spent
years trying to resolve. In 1934, Clarke Venable, a historical technician, reported
to NPS Chief Historian Verne E. Chatelain, on the state of interpretation at the
newly created historical parks in Virginia. In particular, Venable was concerned
about the "Civil War problem on the Yorktown field." As the NPS considered
how best to interpret the site to visitors, Venable believed that marking both
Civil War and Revolutionary War sites at Yorktown would be a mistake. "To the
average visitor," he insisted, "Yorktown is a colonial and Revolutionary field.
To ask the average visitor to be continually jumping from the Revolutionary to
the Civil War is to ask a mental transition too swift and too sharp." Moreover,

This focus fit with a trend reflected in other sites under construction during this same era. Park employees at Colonial NHP contributed to studies of
another restoration project, this time at Roanoke Island in North Carolina that
emphasized the site as another important "birthplace."[32] The site from which
the English Roanoke Colony disappeared, Roanoke Island was also the former
site of a Civil War refugee community. Still today, signs directing tourists to
the national park site declare it the "Birthplace of the First English Child in
America." Likewise, as historian Seth Bruggeman has detailed, development at
the George Washington Birthplace centered on ideas of authenticity and restoration and emphasized the ability of the public to envision Washington in the
space two hundred years later.[33]

the NPS was already at work establishing Civil War battlefield parks whose histories were "infinitely more significant than the Yorktown field." To mark the Civil War history at Yorktown would be a mistake and would "accomplish nothing by example, little by way of education," and would, most importantly, "destroy Yorktown as a pure Colonial field—in which it stands alone."[34] Such conclusions reflected prevailing interpretive philosophies in the NPS as a whole during this era. John Bodnar explains that NPS administrators assumed that "the public could comprehend neither all the historical detail at a given site nor the entire mass of American history." Consequently, representations would need to be both selective and symbolic.[35] Such an emphasis on ensuring that visitors did not have to do too much interpretive work on their own—that the landscape they viewed reflected only one story—also spoke to a desire to control how tourists thought about the past. If the scene was uniform, there was less chance that visitors might come to their own conclusions, rather than those NPS administrators desired.

In response to Venable's report, members of Colonial NHP's historical staff weighed in on the issue. Malcolm Gardner, another historical technician, agreed that the Civil War story was best told elsewhere. "The ordinary visitor can get visual impressions of Civil War movements and works at Fredericksburg, Petersburg, and Richmond," he concluded. Gardner recommended that "the Yorktown battlefield area be exclusively Revolutionary in its markers."[36] Joseph C. Robert, another historical technician, also agreed, but believed that the Civil War story should at least be acknowledged. The presence of the national cemetery, the existence of Civil War fortifications, and the ties visitors felt to Civil War ancestors demanded that the story be mentioned at least in passing. However, "To exaggerate the Civil War at Yorktown," Robert believed, "would be to confuse the visitor and distort the truth." The Peninsula Campaign was important, he acknowledged, but did "not compare in significance with the events of 1781."[37] Again, park administrators made clear determinations about which stories belonged at Yorktown, based on an idea of significance in historical information that skewed towards elite white Americans' actions.

The question of how best to organize the narrative landscape to make it legible to park visitors preoccupied early park staff. Administrators believed that intrusions on the physical appearance of the park, as the various historical technicians' comments reflected, would confuse visitors. Instead, Arno B. Cammerer, director of the National Park Service, instructed B. Floyd Flickinger to ensure that as visitors traveled from Jamestown to Yorktown, the landscape should "form a unified and connected story."[38] Again, the entire design of the park and decisions about what to preserve and what to remove, had to reflect a commitment to this single Revolutionary story.

This insistence reflected NPS policies that were transforming the national commemorative landscape nationwide. In a speech announcing the development of Richmond National Battlefield, B. Floyd Flickinger explained to his audience that "the orderly sequence" of "contacting historical places" was "fundamental to the proper presentation of historical information." To that end, "The National Park Service is giving in its study of historical educational methods a good deal of attention to the development of the nation [and] of the progressive unfolding of history through contact with the physical sites where history has occurred."[39] Collectively the sites the NPS was developing, Flickinger noted, "represent [a] more or less complete narrative and from them we can watch American history go by."[40] Visitors need not understand more than a single event at one place because as they traveled from park to park the NPS would knit together a comprehensive story for them.

Flickinger's assertion highlighted another reason park administrators felt they did not need to interpret the Civil War story at Yorktown. Not only did they think the Revolutionary War history of the town was most important, but they also believed that visitors would learn what they needed to know about the Civil War somewhere else. Administrators were not interested in telling a complicated or conflicted story of the past, and the other battlefield parks then in development in Virginia would allow them to represent a straightforward narrative of the eastern Civil War campaigns.

Park administrators were so concerned about creating a unified narrative landscape that they advocated for the removal of the national cemetery. In 1932, while the national cemetery was still under the jurisdiction of the War Department, the National Park Service undertook negotiations to relocate the cemetery to another place within the park.[41] While the War Department did agree not to enlarge the cemetery, conversations about its relocation waned.[42] In 1936, as superintendent, Flickinger reopened the matter with the Secretary of the Interior. "As one of the objectives in the physical development of the area and the interpretation of its story by our guides is that of showing how the Siege was conducted," Flickinger reasoned, "it is necessary that we have an uninterrupted view from one parallel to another, and from the parallels to the

British trenches around town."[43] To that end, Flickinger advised that his staff would undertake a study of the issue to make further suggestions regarding the cemetery's proper location.

Bingham Duncan, acting park historian, advised Flickinger that a "number of historical considerations" were involved in the issue.[44] First, Duncan explained, the cemetery rested "on the site of a zig-zag approach or covering trench between the first parallel at the French Grand Battery and the second parallel." This "prominent central position" during the final days of the siege would be best interpreted if it were "unobstructed." In other words, visitors would understand this location on the battlefield better if they could see it better. Second, the cemetery was located "directly between the restored French Battery and the British Hornwork, two of the most important works on the battlefield." Moreover, it stood "on a site important to the surrender ceremonies." Collectively, Duncan concluded "these considerations make difficult the clear interpretation and explanation of the battlefield area to visitors," and thus the cemetery should be removed because its present location was "unfortunate with respect to the battlefield." Duncan further advised that the cemetery's soldiers should be relocated to Hampton National Cemetery, Poplar Grove National Cemetery in Petersburg, VA, or the Naval Mine Depot in Yorktown.[45]

Flickinger also consulted with A. Wilhelm, the resident landscape architect in Williamsburg. Wilhelm concurred that the cemetery should be moved and went so far as to suggest that its location was entirely inappropriate because it had no ties to the history of its location. He noted that "a large proportion" of the bodies in the cemetery were from the Civil War and "none or very few" were dead "from the Revolutionary period." It would not be appropriate to move the cemetery anywhere within the park's boundary, Wilhelm believed, because it should be located on a site "more in connection with events connected with the time of the burials or lives of those buried." While Duncan had not commented on the matter, Wilhelm further pointed out that the Black cemetery "to the east of the national Cemetery . . . would probably have to be moved."[46] Wilhelm's comments suggested how quickly the significance of the national cemetery and the Civil War history of Yorktown had been lost. Based on his comments, it appears that Wilhelm was unaware that the national cemetery and Black cemetery dated from the Civil War or that Civil War operations had occurred in Yorktown.

Elbert Cox, who succeeded Flickinger as park superintendent, revived the matter yet again in 1940. Writing to the NPS director, Cox noted that the last word from the Washington office indicated that the matter was still open for consideration. It should be reconsidered, Cox explained, because the cemetery superintendent's home was "near the point of condemnation, and, if there is a likelihood of the cemetery being moved, a new building should not be placed within the existing location." He hoped the director would look favorably on the issue because, Cox believed, relocation of the cemetery was "highly desirable" and "the sooner it [could] be done, the better."[47] The sooner the national cemetery and Black cemetery were removed, the sooner the Park Service could "restore" the Revolutionary landscape around it and make this portion of the battlefield physically uniform.[48]

Evidently familiar with the issue, Director Arno Cammerer agreed that it was "desirable that the battle zone be cleared of all structures and trees in order to give a clear view of Yorktown and the English works as seen from the Grand French Battery." However, given the likelihood of "local opposition and other difficulties attendant upon such a delicate situation as the removal of a cemetery," he suggested instead that efforts "be made to obtain the desired vista by other methods." Even if the cemetery were removed, Cammerer continued, "the view from the Grand French Battery would be particularly obstructed by the Masonic Cemetery (colored) and by Shiloh Church."[49] This was not the final word on the matter, however, and the issue would continue to recur. [50]

Concern over the restoration of the Revolutionary War landscape and the need to create a unified narrative landscape also led park administrators to set their sights on the landscape around the national cemetery, including Uniontown, Shiloh Baptist Church, and the Masonic cemetery behind the national cemetery. In 1934, historical assistants Bingham Duncan and C. L. Coston reported to B. Floyd Flickinger that they believed that a French battery located 150 yards from the national cemetery was "ideally situated" for restoration of a representative fortification. They reasoned that its "proximity to the York-Hampton road" made it "easily visible to tourists either entering or leaving the town by this road."[51] By 1935 park administrators had already collected the history of land ownership for lots in Uniontown as well as names of families who had outstanding taxes due and liens on their property.[52] In detailing the history of the park's land acquisition program later, superintendent George F. Emery would describe this phase as a "buyer's market."[53] His veiled phrase, as well as the earlier references to unpaid taxes, skirted the heart of the issue. The Great Depression had gained a substantial foothold in the United States and families desperate to make ends meet were more likely to sell to the park at low prices.

As a result, the NPS had an opportunity to dislocate families—many of whom had passed their land down in the previous decades rather than sell—at relatively low cost to the federal government. That park employees saw this as an opportunity rather than a tragedy highlights the extent to which they believed their work was critical to the nation and that the goal of restoration was inherently good.

Despite this reality, Emery later explained, the park ran out of money in their land acquisition program. Initial efforts had focused on the purchasing of land on Jamestown Island, rights-of-way for the Colonial Parkway, and sections of the Yorktown Battlefield. In the 1940s, federal attention shifted to waging World War II and funding for the National Park Service remained low. Circumstances for the park's acquisition program did not improve until the mid-1950s when the federal government made more funds available for the purchasing of land. In December of 1964, Emery wrote to the director of the southeast region detailing the park's plans for "future acquisitions." By this time, Colonial National Historical Park had already received a substantial amount of special funding and had utilized it to, among other things, build new visitor centers at Jamestown and Yorktown in anticipation of the 350th celebration of Jamestown.[54] Still, the park wanted the area around the French earthworks they had coveted since the park's founding. "We are trying to get all of the properties in the Grand French Battery area," Emery noted, "so that reconstruction may go forward." Moreover, the matter was pressing. "As acquisitions [are] delayed," Emery noted, "heirs multiply." "A number of Yorktown Battlefield properties show ownership dates in the 19th century," he explained, "the many heirs involved in claims to these estates will make it necessary to institute condemnation suits to clear title."[55] One hundred years later, Colonial National Historical Park's superintendent ignored the dynamic history that "ownership dates in the 19th century" represented—families who had clung tightly to their footholds in freedom, gained ownership of land, and passed that land and its legacy on to their heirs.[56]

Ultimately, Colonial National Historical Park succeeded in removing what was left of the former Slabtown, later Uniontown, community by buying all of the property from descendants of the Civil War-era Black community. Those who were unwilling to sell were ultimately forced to do so. In 2015, Floyd Hill remembered the loss of Uniontown to the park's expansion. Hill recalled that the "only thing we were able to keep was the cemetery."[57] Indeed, the physical landscape of the park testifies to Hill's assertion. The National Park Service

Figure 13. Robert
Norton's headstone.
Author photograph, 2021.

demolished all of the houses—both historic and modern—in the neighborhood. While the national cemetery remained in place, Uniontown met an entirely different fate. Where a bustling community once stood, only road traces, debris, and woods linger. The Masonic cemetery behind the national cemetery and Shiloh Church's original cemetery—where Robert Norton and Godfrey Harrod are buried—remain behind. But even these monuments to the Black community at Yorktown testify to the neglect the story has received at the hands of those tasked with preserving this mythic heart of the American nation. While once a prominent leader in Yorktown, Robert Norton's headstone sits toppled over and broken in half. Godfrey Harrod's headstone, despite his many years of service tending the graves in the national cemetery, sits in a similarly broken state.

It would be an injustice, however, to suggest that this story has been forgotten or lost. It was never lost, and these remaining monuments testify to that reality. Flowers still adorn the graves of loved ones buried in the Masonic cemetery, including veterans of later US wars. Shiloh Baptist Church remains a vibrant community institution, though it no longer stands across from the national cemetery. Two interpretive markers placed in the twenty-first century

Figure 14. Modern view of road entering Uniontown along the side
of the Yorktown National Cemetery. Author photograph, 2021.

mention Uniontown's existence but give little impression to modern-day visitors that this community had a history that lasted well beyond the Civil War.
These markers do not speak to the people who fought mightily to make Black
freedom meaningful—to hang on to the land despite repeated efforts of white
landowners to evict them and to retain a political voice through the era of Jim
Crow.

Understanding that this history exists is a first step towards a better reckon-
ing with the past Yorktown Battlefield represents. While Yorktown's history
is in some ways unique, in its history of NPS removal and whitewashing, it is
part of a much bigger story. These spaces, constructed as national spaces where
Americans could and should go to understand their collective past, present, and
future, have long been exclusionary spaces. Beyond the history of segregation,
the stories these places have told have been limited by narrow definitions of
what stories belong in public spaces. All too often, we continue to reproduce
that exclusion under the guise of preservation. If such places are meant to represent the United States, then they should likewise represent all of the people

who call and have called this place home. They should acknowledge that preservation does not mean a place has not changed over time, but rather that in the decades since the National Park Service's founding, preservation has often meant destruction and reconstruction. To tell a fuller story at these sites is not to erase the past but rather do justice to stories that we have excluded from commemorative landscapes for far too long.

ACKNOWLEDGMENTS

I thank, first and foremost, my dissertation advisor at William & Mary, Dr. Hannah Rosen, and the members of my committee, Dr. Adrienne Petty, Dr. Frederick Corney, and Dr. Chandra Manning. Another faculty member once commented that I had selected the kindest members of the department to sit on my committee, and the statement has held true. At various points in the process of researching this project I encountered roadblocks in accessing sources and my committee members have been tireless advocates for my work. I am extremely grateful for their efforts to help solve problems, offer solutions, and of course provide feedback throughout both the researching and writing phases.

I was also privileged to be a part of (what I consider) the best possible cohort of fellow PhD students. Dr. Holly Gruntner, Dr. James Rick, Dr. Frances Bell, Mitch Oxford, Kaila Schwartz, and Emily Wells have been wonderful coworkers and even better friends. I also want to thank friends and coworkers in the American Studies Department at William & Mary, Chris Slaby, Dr. Ravynn Stringfield, and Kelsey Smoot, especially. I learned lessons from our colleagues in American Studies that have framed the way I thought about this project and changed the way I think about the work of history.

Throughout the research process I have also incurred plenty of debts. Most important to note I thank the staff at the Earl G. Swem Special Collections Research Center at William & Mary. They pointed me to a collection of resources in the earliest stages of this project that gave me hope that I could tell this story and have remained strong advocates for the work their researchers do. We are, again, privileged to get to call such a supportive institution home.

I also want to thank former National Park Service (NPS) employee Diane Depew and current NPS employee Robbie Smith for being allies in this work all along the way. Diane compiled wonderful resources on the history of the Slabtown community while working for the park, and though she retired before I began this project, Robbie has helped make those resources available to me. Diane also generously shared her own personal research with me, much of which would have taken me years to track down myself. It has been a joy to get to visit Robbie regularly to borrow research and talk to her about this project as well as her own research projects at Yorktown.

John Hennessy hired me into my first permanent position with the National Park Service, but more importantly set an example for moving our historical interpretation program forward. John also generously shared his personal archive of soldier correspondence with me to support this project.

My friends Ryan Quint, Joanna Jourdan, and Dr. Holly Grunter also deserve special thanks. They rallied to my aid when staff members from Colonial National Historical Park came to take the Flickinger Collection from Swem Library and spent a series of harried days in the archive, helping me photograph everything before the files became inaccessible. Those files have been integral to this project and have informed the way I approach my work as an NPS interpreter.

Prior to attending William & Mary, I received a master's degree from Villanova University and had the opportunity to work with a wonderful group of people who I must also thank. If it were not for the support of my Villanova crew—Dr. Judith Giesberg, Ruby Johnson, Dr. Jackie Beatty, and Dr. Tom Foley—I probably would not have returned to graduate school. Throughout this project they have encouraged me and remained sounding boards and cheerleaders. The most credit goes to Dr. Giesberg, however, who looked at me in Fall 2015 and said, "so you're going to get your PhD now, right?" And then, as she always does, remained my number one coach and supporter throughout the application process—carefully (and ruthlessly) editing more drafts of research statements than I care to think about.

I also owe great thanks to Park Service colleagues and conspirators whose commitment to good work and inclusive stories reminds me that if we work together, we can create more representative spaces to contemplate our shared past, present, and future. Beth Parnizca, Peter Maugle, Ryan Quint, Maddie Hollis, Mary O'Neill, John Launius, Hilary Grabowska, and many others work tirelessly to tell better stories. I'm very proud to call them my friends.

Most of all though I want to thank my husband, Ethan Toy, who has weathered the journey of graduate school and entering the post-PhD job market right along with me—from traipsing through tick-infested woods looking for road traces in Uniontown, to commuting 170 miles a day while we waited to move until I could finish my research, to taking extra shifts watching our daughter so I could edit this manuscript—his support has been unwavering.

NOTES

Introduction

1. "War Memorial Monument," https://www.yorkcounty.gov/1478/War-Memorial-Monument.

2. A brief search of the National Park Service's soldiers and sailors database pulls the service information for individuals listed who enlisted in York County's various Confederate units.

3. These men and others were identified by Jordan Smiley and Ryan Brookens who worked as interns for the Interpretive Branch at Colonial National Historical Park. Their research is preserved in a document entitled, "Slabtown Genesis," held by the Interpretive Branch at Colonial National Historical Park (COLO). Smiley and Brookens identified other USCT soldiers originally from Yorktown including Joseph Saunders, Co. K, 36th USCT; John Tolliver, Co. F, 36th USCT; Washington Whitish, Co. K, 36th USCT; Charles Gordon, Co. G, 36th, USCT; W. L. Peterson, Co. F, 1 US Colored Cavalry; and Edward Robinson, Co. K, 36th USCT. They also identified additional individuals who were born in Gloucester and enlisted in York County, and who, based on the identifying information available for men listed on the current monument, would also be eligible for inclusion.

4. It also bears noting that this monument likewise does not include Black servicemembers from later wars who are buried outside of the Yorktown National Cemetery and clearly identified as veterans by their headstones.

5. When the story of Black freedom in Yorktown has been told, it has focused exclusively on one community, known originally as Slabtown and later renamed Uniontown by residents. This is likely because Uniontown endured on the landscape until the 1960s, and its dislocation was highly visible. However, Uniontown was only part of a much broader Black community during and after the Civil War. For examples, see Erikson, "Lost Black Township Lives," https://www.dailypress .com/2016/02/22/lost-black-township-in-york-county-lives-on-in-memory/; Deetz, "Slabtown"; and Torkelson, "Where Shall We Go?"

6. Hahn, *Nation Under Our Feet,* 165.

7. Hahn, *Nation Under Our Feet,* 166.

8. Other historians have written studies that examined individual refugee communities. Willie Lee Rose's seminal study, *The Port Royal Experiment,* focused on Port Royal, SC, and argued that the rise and fall of efforts to aid formerly enslaved people at the fort foreshadowed the failures of Reconstruction. Rose's focus, however, was not on the refugees themselves but on the federal agents who sought to construct policies that could be implemented across the South in the wake of slavery's demise. As a result, the work of refugees from slavery in constructing freedom is glimpsed primarily through anecdotal stories. More recently, Patricia Click published a study on the Roanoke Island refugee colony in North Carolina. However, Click is also nearly exclusively focused on the work of white missionaries, whose accounts she relies on, rather than refugees themselves. Other studies such as Cimbala's *Under the Guardianship of the nation;* Nieman's *To Set the Law in Motion;* and Louis S. Gerteis's *From Contraband to Freedman: Federal Policy Toward Southern Blacks, 1861–1865* (Westport,

CT: Greenwood Press, 1973) similarly focus on the Freedmen's Bureau's efforts in the postwar South. Much like Willie Lee Rose, these authors look ahead to Reconstruction and detail how federal policies implemented by the bureau reflected and foreshadowed the prevailing Republican ideologies that would ultimately undermine Black Southerners' independence. Scholars of the Freedmen's Bureau agree that the agency itself had generally benevolent intentions but failed to create lasting change because of a lack of resources, overextended agents, and not enough military force. Again, however, the central actors in this story are white bureau agents and federal policymakers, not Black Southerners.

9. H. A. Williams, *Self-Taught,* Introduction.

10. Ronald E. Butchart's *Schooling the Freed People* similarly notes that Black teachers are underrepresented in these histories.

11. H. A. Williams, *Self-Taught,* Introduction.

12. Du Bois, *Black Reconstruction,* 49.

13. Dailey, *Before Jim Crow,* 2.

14. Kachun, *Festivals of Freedom.*

15. Kachun, *Festivals of Freedom,* 4.

16. Blair, *Cities of the Dead,* 1.

17. Blight, *Race and Reunion,* 386.

18. Janney, *Remembering the Civil War,* 4.

19. Domby, *The False Cause.*

20. Oakes, *Freedom National.* For a review of this earlier debate see Berlin, "Who Freed the Slaves? Emancipation and Its Meaning," and McPherson, "Who Freed the Slaves?"

21. Rosen, *Terror in the Heart of Freedom* and Masur, *Example for All the Land.*

22. Joseph Reidy elaborates on these new geographies in his book *Illusions of Emancipation.*

23. Additional scholars have traced communities on the Virginia Peninsula who were displaced by the federal government in the twentieth century. For examples see, Mahoney, "Community Building After Emancipation"; Harris, "Lost Tribe of Magruder"; and Bragdon, McDonald, and Struck, "Cast Down Your Bucket Where You Are."

24. As historians such as Richard White have detailed, it is often the case that the historical record does not always line up with individuals' memories and the histories that are passed down from person to person. The lack of historical documentation to confirm such memories does not negate the process of passing down memories through an oral record as a way of knowing the history of a place. Richard White, *Remembering Ahanagran: A History of Stories* (University of Washington Press, 2003).

Chapter 1: "They Appear like Freemen"

1. Quoted in Brasher, *Peninsula Campaign,* 93.

2. Manning, *Troubled Refuge;* Taylor, *Embattled Freedom.* Both Manning and Taylor take wide-view perspectives of the unfolding of emancipation in the Union army's numerous refugee camps located throughout the South. And overwhelming theme in both works is the inherent danger and uncertainty for refugees from slavery in the war-torn South that resulted from the Union army's lack of preparedness for the humanitarian crisis presented by wartime freedom and the changeable nature of Union policy towards refugees.

3. It bears repeating that security when applied to refugee communities, even in forts the Union army held for the duration of the war such as Fort Monroe, is a relative term. Military security did not translate directly into physical security for refugees who faced, as Chandra Manning had

poignantly demonstrated, simple insecurities such as lack of clean water as well as forced relocation by Union soldiers. Manning, *Troubled Refuge,* 52.

4. Berlin, Fields, Glymph, Reidy, and Rowland, "Destruction of Slavery," 6. This study largely relies on digitized Freedmen's Bureau sources because they are organized geographically. However, my first introduction to these records came through the pioneering work of the Freedmen and Southern Society Project's published volumes, especially *Wartime Genesis of Free Labor* edited by Berlin, Miller, Reidy, and Rowland.

5. As Kate Masur has noted, by the spring of 1862 both the Union military and press utilized the term "intelligent" to modify descriptions of Black individuals who provided military intelligence. Such use of the term, Masur explains, conferred "intellectual authority on people who otherwise" white Unionist considered to be lacking. Masur, "A Rare Phenomenon" 1050–84: 1059.

6. E. J. Allen [Allen Pinkerton] to HDQRS. Provost-Marshal-General, *Official Records of the War of Rebellion,* Army of the Potomac, March 29, 1862.

7. Official Records of the War of Rebellion, Major General George B. McClellan, Headquarters Army of the Potomac, Camp at Yorktown, May 3, 1862. As Kate Masur also notes, the term "contraband" came into popular use among the white public and Union military after Benjamin Butler admitted refugees from enslavement into Fort Monroe. By using the term initially, Butler created a rationale for retaining the refugees but did not challenge the concept of human bondage. The term, Masur explains, "had long been used to describe property," but it further "implied the transitional status of the people to whom it referred." Moreover, it implied a state of need and dependence. Masur, "Rare Phenomenon," 1050–53. While the term received widespread usage at the time, it is not reproduced here except when citing original sources.

8. Brasher, *Peninsula Campaign,* 104.

9. Brasher, *Peninsula Campaign,* 215–28.

10. "Army Correspondence," *Columbia Democrat,* May 10, 1862.

11. *Concord Independent Democrat,* May 22, 1862.

12. John A. Dix to Abraham Lincoln, January 15, 1863, Abraham Lincoln Papers, Library of Congress. Quoted in Depew, "They Had Bidden," 3.

13. Such an understanding of the war among enslaved people was not unique to the Virginia Peninsula. As the editors of *Freedom: A Documentary History* have noted, the "general politicization of Southern society" registered in enslaved communities, and individuals imparted "momentous significance to Lincoln's election, Southern secession, and military mobilization." "Destruction of Slavery," 8–9.

14. Brasher, *Peninsula Campaign,* 27.

15. Brasher, *Peninsula Campaign,* 35.

16. Oakes, *Freedom National,* 111.

17. Brasher, in particular, provides a wealth of examples of the Northern press, and at times Union generals, commenting on enslaved people's willingness to side with the Union army and that the only "loyal" people in the South were people of color.

18. Brasher, *Peninsula Campaign,* 104.

19. Taylor recounts numerous instances in which Black individuals accumulated significant profits, invested them in securing more retail goods to sell in their shops, and lost those goods to marauding soldiers. In other instances, refugees from slavery invested in building homes and businesses in camps only to have to relocate when the Union army necessarily had to move due to the pressures of war. Taylor, *Embattled Freedom,* 83–100.

20. Testimony of Robert Ruffin, Southern Claims Commission, July 25, 1871. Ruffin's enterprise becomes visible in the archive because he submitted a claim to the Southern Claims Commission seeking restitution goods from his shop stolen by soldiers from the US Army. While he did not receive full restitution for what he lost during the war, this does not detract from the significant and successful efforts he made in a short period of time to turn a profit and expand the business. Similar cases abound in the Southern Claims Commission files, even in places the Union army inconsistently occupied. George Madowney and Patterson Barksley lived in Fredericksburg, VA, which changed hands numerous times during the war. Both men managed to purchase their freedom in 1861 and remained in the city working for themselves. When the Union army occupied Fredericksburg in 1864, soldiers appropriated horses, carts, and equipment the two men owned. While they subsequently lost some of their property, it is also clear from their claims that they had accumulated considerable resources to labor for themselves in a short period of time. Testimony of George Madowney, Disallowed and Barred Claims, Southern Claims Commission, No. 15212; Testimony of Patterson Barksley, Southern Claims Commission, December 20, 1875.

21. "Letter from the 49th Regiment, May 7, 1862" *Lockport Daily Journal Courier,* May 21, 1862.

22. "From the Seat of War," *Cambridge Chronicle,* May 17, 1862. It is important to note that it is impossible to know the true status of the presumably Black people Union soldiers described as "contraband." York County did have a free Black population prior to the Civil War and given the prevalence with which Union soldiers used the term, it is unclear if they knew the people with whom they conversed were refugees from enslavement, or simply Black people in the South. I have chosen to leave the term in quotes rather than rephrase it to reflect the lack of certainty with which I can identify these individuals based on the information provided.

23. "From the Connecticut Artillery, May 6, 1862," *Waterbury American,* May 30, 1862.

24. Brasher, *Peninsula Campaign,* 171.

25. Oakes, *Freedom National,* 138.

26. "Letter from Harrison DeLong," *Yates County Chronicle,* May 15, 1862.

27. "Letter from the 19th Regiment," *Waltham Sentinel,* May 2, 1862.

28. Brasher, *Peninsula Campaign,* 12–13.

29. Taylor notes numerous examples of ground lost not only to the Confederate army, but to natural disasters such as floods. Aligning one's freedom with the Union army held no guarantees that freedom could be retained throughout the war. For example, when Union command in Helena, AR, changed in the fall of 1862, Brigadier General Frederick Steele, a conservative Democrat, expelled more than five hundred women and children who the previous commander, General Samuel R. Curtis, had protected within his lines. Taylor, *Embattled Freedom,* 108.

30. *Geneva Gazette,* May 20, 1862.

31. *Orleans Independent Standard,* May 15, 1862. Brasher notes that such rumors were not only widespread, but extremely consistent. Other than bodily harm, white Southerners also routinely assured enslaved people that should they fall into Union hands, the federal government would ship them to Cuba.

32. "The Advance on Richmond," *Oneida Sachem,* May 23, 1862.

33. "The Advance on Richmond," *Oneida Sachem,* May 23, 1862.

34. "From the Fifth Regiment," *Orleans Independent Standard,* May 23, 1862.

35. Oakes, *Freedom National,* 255.

36. Oakes, *Freedom National,* 254.

37. Both Brasher and Oakes note that the interactions with enslaved people in Virginia, especially during the Peninsula Campaign, carried significant weight in the Northern press and contributed to the ultimate success of the Second Confiscation Act and Emancipation Proclamation.

38. Nash, *History of the Forty-Fourth*, 72. Quoted in Depew, "They Had Bidden."

39. "RATS," *The Cavalier*, March 24, 1863.

40. *The Friend*, February 20, 1864.

41. Amy Murrell Taylor mentions the limitations of the Emancipation Proclamation in relation to the refugees at Fort Monroe to the same effect. The Colonial National Historical Park, which interprets the history of Slabtown to a limited degree, also maintains that refugees were not free because of this exemption. However, as James Oakes has argued, while the Emancipation Proclamation did exclude large portions of eastern Virginia, those who had already come into Union lines were already free. Regardless of their official legal status though, refugees from enslavement behaved as free people and conducted their affairs accordingly.

42. Oakes, *Freedom National*, 267.

43. W. Davis, *History of the 104th*, 162. Quoted in Depew, "They Had Bidden," 5.

44. Taylor, *Embattled Freedom*, 37.

45. Sergeant Stephen T. Buckson to Harriet Buckson, January 11, 1863. Letters of Stephen T. Buckson, 4th Delaware Regiment. Quoted in Depew, "They Had Bidden," 5.

46. "The Coloured Freemen of Yorktown, Norfolk, and Hampton," *The Friend*, December 26, 1863.

47. "Our Motto," *The Cavalier*, June 25, 1862.

48. Official Records of the War of Rebellion, Report of Major Jacob P. Wilson, Fifth Pennsylvania Cavalry, July 10, 1862.

49. Official Records of the War of Rebellion, I. J. Wistar to Colonel J. W. Shaffer, February 15, 1864.

50. "Departure of Maj. Gen. Keyes," *The Cavalier*, July 14, 1863.

51. Wistar, *Autobiography*, 417. Wistar's description of the situation at Yorktown leaves some room for questioning, because at no other point in the war did the refugee population come close to numbering twelve thousand. If Wistar did encounter a population this large, it is possible that the refugees were not all original inhabitants of the fort, but others who had taken shelter from enslavement elsewhere and fled to the fort in the wake of the Suffolk campaign. In April 1863, thirteen hundred refugees fled Uniontown, a planned settlement in Suffolk (Taylor, *Embattled Freedom*, 93–4). Given the fact that in March of 1863, *The Cavalier* had reported only two thousand refugees inside the fort, it is possible that the population of the fort swelled while conditions in the surrounding area remained threatened by Longstreet's Confederate forces. It is also possible that Wistar simply misremembered the population statistics and conflated the entire refugee population of the peninsula with Yorktown's population in his postwar recollections. Wistar wrote his memoir in 1892 and admitted that "these notes have been written almost entirely from recollection" (Preface, Wistar, *Autobiography*, ix). Whether or not there were twelve thousand refugees in the fort in May, by late summer the refugee population had returned to a more reasonable number. The "Census Return of Colored Population within the Lines at Yorktown and Vicinity . . . taken between July 1st 1863 and August 20th 1863" recorded 2,316 people. Of that numbed, 1,761 were identified as "contraband" and 252 were identified as free. Census Return, National Archives, Record Group 393, 5063, Letters Received, Department of Virginia. Reproduced in Depew, "They Had Bidden," 9.

52. 1850 Census Free Population and 1850 Slave Schedule, York County, VA.

53. Descriptions of Fort Yorktown indicate that the fortified area included the city of Yorktown,

which was fairly small. Union soldiers and Northern visitors routinely described themselves as disappointed by the small size and undeveloped nature of Yorktown's city.

54. 1850 Census Free Population of York County.

55. Wistar, *Autobiography*, 418.

56. Roll 200, Endorsements Sent and Received, E. W. Coffin to Capt. A. S. Flagg, August 17, 1865. Interestingly, F. W. Powers's brother, Robert Powers, served as justice of the peace in York County after the war and would play a significant role in conversations about the future of the refugee population, frequently advocating for their dispersal.

57. James Oakes notes that abandonment of property by white residents in the face of the Union army was enough for the Union army to consider a person rebellious and their property thus available for confiscation. Thus, even though federal agents determined that Powers had not aided the rebellion, the fact that he left his property was enough to shift its status during the war.

58. Wistar, *Autobiography*, 418, 438.

59. Wistar, *Autobiography*, 419.

60. Wistar, *Autobiography*, 438.

61. Wistar, *Autobiography*, 438. Placing refugees on "government farms" would become common practice on the Virginia Peninsula.

62. Captain C. B. Wilder to Major General John A. Dix, May 5, 1863. National Archives, Record Group 393, 5063, Letters Received, Department of Virginia. Quoted in Depew, "They Had Bidden," 7.

63. Oakes, *Freedom National*, 269.

64. Wistar, *Autobiography*, 438.

65. Wistar, *Autobiography*, 438.

66. Roll 200, Endorsements Sent and Received, E. W. Coffin to Capt. A. S. Flagg, August 17, 1865. In his postwar recollections, Wistar does not mention this second settlement, but Freedmen's Bureau records specify that Newtown was originally established by Wistar. It is possible that Wistar misremembered this fact, or that he considered everything he established to be a single unit and over time, because the two settlements existed on different landowners' properties, they took on unique identification.

67. "The Coloured Freemen of Yorktown, Norfolk, and Hampton," *The Friend*, December 26, 1863.

68. 1850 Slave Schedule, York County, VA.

69. Roll 200, Endorsements Sent and Received, E. W. Coffin to Capt A. S. Flagg, August 15, 1865.

70. Two key locations that also experienced a state of semipermanence, and have been the subject of their own studies, are the refugee settlement at Roanoke Island, NC, and the settlement at Port Royal, SC.

71. Wistar would describe Slabtown as "if not exactly metropolitan . . . large and populous." However, as these communities developed they most certainly could be described as metropolitan, especially when compared with nearby Yorktown.

72. "A Place of Safety," *The Cavalier*, June 23, 1863.

73. "An Attack on Fort Magruder," *The Cavalier*, April 14, 1863. For more on the military situation and security of Williamsburg see Dubbs, *Defend This Old Town*.

74. "Successful Raid into Matthews County, Va," *The Cavalier*, October 12, 1863.

75. *Official Records of the War of Rebellion*, I. J. Wistar, "Expedition to Matthews [*sic*] County, VA, October 10, 1863.

76. "Another Rebel Raid," *The Cavalier*, March 17, 1863. The reference to "that well-known person"

likely did not suggest that readers knew the identity of this individual. Rather, as Kate Masur has noted, the trope of the "intelligent contraband" had achieved widespread usage in the US press by this point in the war. Masur, 1059.

77. *The Cavalier,* September 28, 1863.

78. James Oakes notes that Republicans in Congress, as well as President Lincoln, were keenly aware that military emancipation could not guarantee perpetual freedom once the war ended. While they actively debated a method by which to accomplish this, the path was not clear until they began pursuing the Thirteenth Amendment in the final years of the war.

79. *Official Records of the War of Rebellion,* Report of Lieutenant Colonel George Rogers, Fourth US Colored Troops, Yorktown, April 1, 1864.

80. Roll 199, Letters Sent Volume 1, March 30, 1866.

81. Roll 199, Letters Sent Volume 1, March 30, 1866.

82. Roll 200, Letters and Orders Received, July 12, 1865.

83. Roll 199, Letters Sent Volume 1, May 23, 1866.

Chapter 2: "How Much We Can Do Ourselves"

1. Cadbury, *Letters from Slabtown.*

2. For example, see Rose, *Rehearsal for Reconstruction;* and Click, *Time Full of Trials.* Both books focus on educational initiatives from the perspective of white Northerners and the visions of Black freedom they hoped to construct in their respective refugee communities.

3. As Ronald Butchart has carefully chronicled, earlier studies of wartime educational efforts centered on white teachers and painted them as benevolent "civilizing" agents. Such depictions appear in the work of historians such as Henry Swint and Jacqueline Jones. Butchart, *Schooling the Freed People,* x. Swint, *Northern Teacher.* J. Jones, *Soldiers of Light.*

4. H. A. Williams, *Self-Taught.* Ronald Butchart also notes that there was "no historical precedent to African American demand for access to knowledge or historical equivalent to the Black effort to assure that access." Butchart, *Schooling the Freed People,* xvi.

5. H. A. Williams, *Self-Taught: African American Education in Slavery and Freedom.*

6. Taylor, *Embattled Freedom,* 4, 8.

7. Taylor, 195. Butchart further explains that Black individuals understood that literacy was a "means to self-protection." Butchart, *Schooling the Freed People,* 11–12.

8. H. A. Williams, *Self-Taught.*

9. Unfortunately, as Ronald Butchart has detailed, historians in the twentieth century reproduced this discrepancy, focusing on white teachers and ignoring Black teachers. However, in identifying as many teachers as possible, Butchart found that "one-third of all teachers in the southern Black schools between 1861 and 1876 were African Americans." This statistic includes Black Northern teachers who traveled south to teach. Butchart, *Schooling the Freed People,* xii.

10. H. A. Williams, *Self-Taught.*

11. Lockwood to Brethren, October 6, 1862. Quoted in H. A. Williams, *Self-Taught.* The 1865 Freedmen's Bureau census recorded two men living in York County named Peter Cook. One, aged forty, lived at Slabtown with his wife Chloe. His occupation was not recorded. Another Peter Cook, aged thirty, lived at Wormley Creek with his wife Sally and was identified in the census as a "laborer." Roll 203, Census Returns, March 1865.

12. Lockwood to Brethren, March 6, 1862. Quoted in H. A. Williams, *Self-Taught.*

13. Lockwood to Brethren, July 17, 1862. Quoted in H. A. Williams, *Self-Taught.*

14. Roll 202, Monthly Reports, "Report of a 'Personal Inspection' of all Freedmens Schools in the 3 and 4 Div. 5th Sub Dist. Va. For the month of February 1868."

15. "Report of the Women's Aid Association of Friends for the Relief of Coloured Refugees," *The Friend,* October 24, 1863.

16. "The Freedpeople of Eastern Virginia," *Friends' Review,* December 12, 1863.

17. "The Freedpeople of Eastern Virginia," *Friends' Review,* December 12, 1863. Again, it is difficult to know if this report referred to Peter Cook or another Black teacher. A Black teacher, Elijah Billups, appears on the 1865 census living at Tinsley Farm with his occupation described as "school teacher." Roll 203, Census Returns of the Black Population of York County, March 1865.

18. "The Instruction Committee Report," *The Friend,* June 25, 1864.

19. Manning, *Troubled Refuge,* 117.

20. Click, *Time Full of Trial,* 15.

21. H. A. Williams, *Self-Taught.*

22. Today, Brown Cottage is known as the first educational building of the Hampton Institute, modern-day Hampton University.

23. Newby-Alexander, *African American History,* 34.

24. H. A. Williams, *Self-Taught.*

25. Quoted in H. A. Williams, *Self-Taught.*

26. H. A. Williams, *Self-Taught.*

27. H. A. Williams, *Self-Taught.*

28. Nancy Battey, December 30, 1864, Letters of Nancy S. Battey, Haverford College Quaker and Special Collections.

29. Nancy Battey, December 30, 1864, Letters of Nancy S. Battey.

30. "Report of the Women's Aid Association of Friends," *Friends' Review,* May 28, 1864. It is possible that this teacher was Elijah Billups, the only person in the 1865 census recorded as working as a schoolteacher. The census taker noted in his remarks that Billups was a "cripple," suggesting that he could have been the same teacher who only had one leg.

31. Darlington Farm bore the name of its owner, E. C. Darlington, a prominent resident of York County, VA. Newtown/Acretown was located on Stafford G. Cooke's land. Most records use the name Newtown or Acretown, but a handful of early articles from *The Friend* and *Friends' Review* use the name Acreville. Such inconsistencies in naming plague records from this period.

32. "Report of the Women's Aid Association of Friends," *Friends' Review,* May 28, 1864.

33. *Friends' Review,* December 24, 1864.

34. Nancy Battey letters, November 19, 1864. This reflected trends in other refugee communities that existed during the Civil War. As Ronald Butchart explains, adults frequently attended night school so that they could work during the daytime. As a result, "the Black day school began to look more like traditional schools, filled with school-age children." Butchart, *Schooling the Freed People,* 7.

35. "Second Report of the Executive Board of the Friends' Association of Philadelphia and its Vicinity, for the Relief of Colored Freedmen," *Friends' Review,* July 1, 1865.

36. "Second Report of the Executive Board of the Friends' Association of Philadelphia and its Vicinity, for the Relief of Colored Freedmen," *Friends' Review,* July 1, 1865.

37. "Second Report of the Executive Board of the Friends' Association of Philadelphia and its Vicinity, for the Relief of Colored Freedmen," *Friends' Review,* July 1, 1865.

38. Roll 200, Letters and Orders Received, "Slabtown 4 mo. 4 1865."

39. Roll 200, Letters and Orders Received, "Slabtown 4 mo. 4 1865."

40. "Marriages," *The Cavalier,* March 17, 1863.

41. Levi and Harriet Washington appear on the 1865 Freedmen's Bureau census living at Newtown. By 1865 Levi was working as a grocer.

42. As Edna Greene Medford has documented, overdependence on tobacco production had necessitated a switch to a "program diversification," including the production of cereal grains and livestock, with the "virtual abandonment of tobacco as a principal crop." Peninsula planters had successfully converted their enslaved labor system over to mixed farming prior to the Civil War. Medford, "Land and Labor," 568.

43. "Report of the Industrial Committee of Friends' Association of Philadelphia, for the Relief of Freedmen," *Friends' Review,* May 13, 1865.

44. Roll 200, Letters and Orders Received, "Slabtown 4 mo. 4 1865."

45. Click, *Time Full of Trials.*

46. Taylor, *Embattled Freedom,* 197.

47. Click, *Time Full of Trials,* 106.

48. Click, *Time Full of Trials,* 112.

49. Census of Colored Population in York County, 11 March 1865.

50. Thorpe, *Life in Virginia by a Yankee Teacher.* Earl G. Swem Special Collections Research Center, William & Mary, Williamsburg, VA. Richard L. Morton published an edited version of Thorpe's memoirs in the *Virginia Magazine of History and Biography* in 1956. All citations that follow, however, are from the original manuscript.

51. Thorpe, *Life in Virginia.*

52. Butchart argues that the ability to read the Bible was one of the most commonly expressed goals among Black students. To do so was more than an "expression of Black piety." It was also a declaration, Butchart maintains, of "emancipation from white churches and from decades . . . of being told by white preachers what to believe." Butchart, *Schooling the Freed People,* 10.

53. Thorpe, *Life in Virginia.* Thorpe appears to have first referenced the presence of the Ku Klux Klan in the area in 1867. She recorded her memoirs for her daughter in 1907.

54. Thorpe, *Life in Virginia.*

55. Thorpe, *Life in Virginia.*

56. "Report of the Instruction Committee," *Friends' Review,* April 29, 1865.

57. Roll 199, Letters Sent, Volume 1, May 23, 1866.

58. Roll 199, Letters Sent, Volume 1, April 7, 1866.

59. Engs, *Freedom's First Generation,* 69.

60. Williams. Butchart further elaborates that white Southerners' opposition specifically to Black literacy "betrayed an uneasiness about white racial superiority," which had been the bedrock of slavery. Butchart, *Schooling the Freed People,* 15.

61. "The Freed-People in Virginia," *Friends' Review,* November 24, 1866. Patricia Click notes that Black residents of Roanoke Island similarly requested that their teachers remain for the summer or extend their school year to allow for more access to instruction.

62. "The Freed-People in Virginia," *Friends' Review,* November 24, 1866. Two William Fields appear on the 1865 census. One, fifteen years old in 1865, lived at Slabtown and worked as an oysterman. The other, seven years old in 1865, lived at Stumptown. Given his reference to the schoolhouse and church, it seems likely that the William Fields in question was the fifteen-year-old oysterman.

63. Thorpe, *Life in Virginia*.

64. "Extract of a letter from Jacob H. Vining," *The Friend*, December 8, 1866. Heather Andrea Williams notes that this pattern was commonplace. Often, Black Southerners built schools before teachers had even committed to utilize them, beginning the work ahead of white benevolent organizations' direction.

65. *The Friend*, December 22, 1866. Vining apparently thought that local white residents had begun to support the educational system for Black residents. Perhaps white local leaders did so in conversation with Vining, but as the schoolhouse fires indicate, Vining was likely mistaken in his judgment that public sentiment had truly shifted.

66. Cadbury, *Letters from Slabtown*, 109.

67. H.A. Williams, *Self Taught*.

68. Massey to Armstrong, Roll 199, Letters Sent, Volume 1, September 1, 1866.

69. *The Friend*, March 9, 1867.

70. *The Friend*, April 20, 1867.

71. By 1868 the Freedmen's Bureau office in Yorktown was in the process of shuttering most of its services. In fact, Ayres took over for Massey after Massey resigned his commission, feeling that there was little work left for him to do.

72. Roll 200, Letters Received, S. C. Armstrong to H. K. Ayres, September 14, 1868.

73. 1868 Report, Roll 202, Monthly Reports, April 1866–December 1868.

74. Roll 200, Letters Received, Armstrong to Ayres, November 17, 1868.

75. Roll 200, Letters Received, Armstrong to Ayres, November 17, 1868.

76. H. A. Williams, *Self Taught*.

77. Heather Andrea Williams further argues that the success of Black educational efforts during the emancipation period led ultimately to the creation of a public education system in the postwar South.

78. Nancy Battey Letters, November 19, 1864.

79. Nancy Battey Letters, November 19, 1864.

80. Saville, *Work of Reconstruction*, 146.

81. Saville, *Work of Reconstruction*, 147.

82. Saville, *Work of Reconstruction*, 147.

83. Thorpe, *Life in Virginia*, 18.

84. Thorpe, *Life in Virginia*.

85. Harper, *The End of Days*, 13. Harper further argues that it is in the ground-level study of Black people's political work that the significance of their religious life becomes clear.

86. Harper, *The End of Days*, 20.

87. Harper, *The End of Days*, 41.

88. Roll 199, Letters Sent, April 24, 1866.

89. Engs, *Freedom's First Generation*, 70. According to historian Robert Engs, tensions between white and Black members of the community had been building in the months prior to the April 1866 parade. That Black residents' determination to hold the parade at all after threats of white retaliation against any "disturbances" was a further rejection of white neighbors' attempts to control and limit Black people's participation in the public sphere.

90. Cadbury, *Letters from Slabtown*, 108.

91. Cadbury Correspondence, April 19, 1866, Sarah Cadbury Papers, Haverford College Quaker and Special Collections.

92. Visitors to modern-day Yorktown may note that the historic Shiloh Baptist Church is more closely associated with Slabtown. Indeed, the church building moved locations multiple times during the postwar period. However, Cadbury spent a considerable amount of time describing the two churches mentioned here and visited them both on a regular basis, suggesting that her description of the churches' locations is fairly reliable.

93. The only John Carey who appears on the 1865 census was listed as two months old.

94. Shiloh Baptist Church currently dates its founding to 1863 and identifies Carey as its first pastor. "History of Shiloh Baptist Church," http://03bd6a2.netsolhost.com/wpshiloh2015/about-shiloh/history/. It is unclear why this discrepancy exists, as Cadbury definitively identified Napper as Shiloh's pastor and Carey as the pastor of the Slabtown church in her letters home. Moreover, Cadbury and her peers frequently met with Napper and his elders, ensuring that her identification of the men is reliable. Perhaps the frequent mixing of the congregations produced a single congregation in the postwar years. Adding confusion to the story is the existence of Rising Sun Baptist Church, located in modern-day Lackey—the former site of Acretown—with oral history that also dates from the Civil War era. Interview with Diane Depew, former supervisory ranger, Colonial National Historical Park, April 2019.

95. Thomas and Lucy Napper appear on the 1865 census living at Fort Yorktown. Thomas' occupation was listed as "carter." Interestingly, the only individual listed on this census specifically as a "minister" was a man named William Thomas who lived at Newtown and worked as a farmer. William Thomas does not appear in any of Cadbury or others' descriptions of church services.

96. Cadbury Correspondence, April 25, 1866. As Elsa Barkley Brown explains, the church was the foundation of the Black public sphere in the post-emancipation South. The church was a political space that men, women, and children could occupy and allowed for the construction of "political concerns in democratic space." Brown, "Negotiating and Transforming," 107–146, 110.

97. Cadbury Correspondence, April 25, 1866.

98. Cadbury Correspondence, April 25, 1866.

99. Jackson, *Negro Office-Holders*.

100. Cadbury Correspondence, April 25, 1866.

101. Cadbury Correspondence, April 25, 1866.

102. Elsa Barkley Brown further elaborates that in the wake of emancipation, Black Virginians developed their own political calendar and celebrated traditional US holidays as well as holidays celebrating important milestones in their own lived experience. White Southerners found these celebrations especially horrifying because they saw civic holidays and their traditions as "the historical possession of white Americans." Brown, "Negotiating and Transforming," 115.

103. Amy Murrell Taylor notes that white missionaries failed to acknowledge that "the invisible church" that had existed in slavery was "becoming visible." That this newly visible church often trumpeted antislavery themes was common. Taylor, *Embattled Freedom*, 183.

104. Engs, *Freedom's First Generation*, 71.

105. Taylor, *Embattled Freedom*, 191.

106. Cadbury, *Letters from Slabtown*, 87.

107. Cadbury Correspondence, April 19, 1866.

108. Taylor, *Embattled Freedom,* 190.

109. Chandra Manning notes finding a similar pattern in her research. According to Manning, "Religious services took place frequently, sometimes led by white missionaries with Black participation in both preaching and singing and sometimes conducted exclusively by freedpeople." Manning, *Troubled Refuge,* 117.

110. Cadbury, *Letters from Slabtown,* 90.

111. Lucy Chase, July 1, 1864. Chase Family Papers.

112. Cadbury Correspondence, March 26, 1866. Cadbury frequently commented on Sunday services. For examples see Cadbury Correspondence, March 22, 1866, and Cadbury, *Letters from Slabtown,* 30.

113. Thorpe, *Life in Virginia,* 49.

114. Willie Lee Rose noticed this democratic nature of church organization in her study of the South Carolina Sea Islands. Moreover, Rose explained, Black churches remained democratic institutions well after the end of the Civil War. Rose, *Rehearsal for Reconstruction,* 407.

115. Cadbury Correspondence, March 31, 1866.

116. As both Elsa Barkley Brown and Martha S. Jones have noted, Black churches were important political forums during the postwar period. Marked by a particular form of democratic speech, congregants—both male and female—were welcome to share their opinions with the group. M. Jones, *All Bound up Together* and Brown, "Negotiating and Transforming."

117. Cadbury Correspondence, April 1, 1866. It is unclear if "brother Cook" was Peter Cook, the Black teacher. Multiple men with the surname Cook appear on the 1865 census.

118. Cadbury, *Letters from Slabtown,* 64.

119. Cadbury Correspondence, April 15, 1866.

120. Cadbury Correspondence, April 22, 1866. Peter Dorsey was forty years old in 1865 and lived at "331 SlabTown." His occupation was not listed. Dorsey served as chairman of a "large mass meeting of the colored people of York and James City Counties" in December of 1866 and was clearly an influential leader. Roll 199, Letters Sent.

121. Cadbury Correspondence, April 25, 1866.

122. Manning, Troubled Refuge, 86.

123. Cadbury, *Letters from Slabtown,* 84. This "young preacher" may have been Baylor (sometimes Bailey or Bayley) Wyatt, a future pastor of Shiloh. In 1865, Wyatt appeared on the 1865 census living at Acretown and working as a carpenter. Already, Wyatt had made a name for himself as a leader in the community. It is impossible to know for certain if the person in question was Wyatt but given the fact that he later served as pastor of Shiloh, it is possible this was him.

124. Cadbury, *Letters from Slabtown,* 84.

125. Norton's political career is discussed more specifically in later chapters.

126. Roll 199, Letters Sent, August 9, 1866.

127. Cadbury, *Letters from Slabtown,* 61.

128. *Richard Hamilton v. Robert Francis,* Roll 202, *Proceedings of the Bureau Court Dec 1865–Jun 1867.*

129. Robert H. Power, Presiding Justice of York County to Lt. Massey, June 2, 1866, Roll 199, Letters Sent.

130. Robert H. Power, Presiding Justice of York County to Lt. Massey, June 2, 1866, Roll 199, Letters Sent.

131. Robert H. Power, Presiding Justice of York County to Lt. Massey, June 2, 1866, Roll 199, Letters Sent.

132. Massey to Armstrong, May 23, 1866. Roll 199, Letters Sent.

133. Engs, Freedom's First Generation, 70.

134. Engs, *Freedom's First Generation*, 70. The name Slabtown was commonly applied to settlements that appeared during the war because of the slab construction of the houses residents built for themselves. Engs does not specify if this "raid" was an officially sanctioned operation or an incident of white soldiers harassing the Black community. Regardless, by responding to the event with violence, Slabtown's residents rejected unwanted interference in their community.

135. Engs, Freedom's First Generation, 71.

136. Croxton Loomis to S. C. Armstrong, August 1, 1866. Roll 199, Letters Sent.

137. "United States vs. Croxton Loomis (col'd)," July 25, 1866, *Proceedings of the Freedmen's Court*.

138. Croxton Loomis to S. C. Armstrong, August 1, 1866. Roll 199, Letters Sent.

139. Croxton Loomis's petition is also mentioned in *Freedom's First Generation,* but Loomis is mistakenly identified as a white man. Records of the bureau court clearly indicate that he was Black, and that the two men who testified against him worked for the bureau, which is likely why Loomis identified them as "Massey's colored men." Engs, *Freedom's First Generation*, 98.

140. Armstrong to Massey, August 18, 1866. Roll 199, Letters Sent.

141. Newby-Alexander, *African American History,* 79.

Chapter 3: "We Can Take Care of Ourselves Now"

1. Massey to Brown, May 1, 1866. Quoted in Medford, "Transition from Slavery to Freedom in a Diversified Economy," (dissertation), 80.

2. Cary and Charles Redcross both appear on the 1860 census as free Black men living in York County and working as oystermen. Samuel Scott appears on the 1865 Freedmen's Bureau census, living at Darlington Farm while John Rich, also identified on this census, lived at Buck Point. Cary and Charles Redcross also appear on the 1850 census for York County in Mead Redcross's household, suggesting that they were brothers.

3. "Redcross, Cary & others to Major Genl J M Schofield, Comdg Disct No 5," Roll 200, Letters Received.

4. "Redcross, Cary & others to Major Genl J M Schofield, Comdg Disct No 5," Roll 200, Letters Received. It is unclear from the letter who forced the restrictive legislation through. In latter decades, conflicts would arise about oystering seasons because of concerns about preserving the reproductive capacity of oystering beds.

5. "Redcross, Cary & others to Major Genl J M Schofield, Comdg Disct No 5," Roll 200, Letters Received.

6. *The Friend,* July 23, 1864.

7. Saville, *Work of Reconstruction,* 4.

8. Mintz, *Moralists and Modernizers.* Institutions such as penitentiaries may not appear to fall under the category of "benevolent" by modern standards. However, the first penitentiary in the United States, Eastern State Penitentiary, resulted from the work of the Philadelphia Society for Alleviating the Miseries of Public Prisons. Related institutions evolved from the efforts of similar groups who saw their work as enabling social uplift.

9. Saville, *Work of Reconstruction,* 16.

10. Saville, *Work of Reconstruction,* 65–66.

11. Saville, *Work of Reconstruction,* 113.

12. In terms of differences of specific situations, along the South Carolina coast, for example, land

became available for public sale over the course of the war, so individual Northerners bought a large percentage of the land appropriated through a war tax instituted by the federal government. Thus, formerly enslaved people were encouraged to work for individual landowners. In other cases, such as at Yorktown, plantations remained under the jurisdiction of the federal government, and administrators appointed white overseers to direct the efforts at each farm. Saville, *Work of Reconstruction,* 32–65.

13. These patterns are visible in both Saville's and Rose's studies of the South Carolina Sea Islands, as well as Patricia Click's study of Roanoke Island, NC. White administrators understood that their efforts were part of a larger conversation about the best order for a free-labor society that existed beyond the boundaries of the individual settlements in which they labored.

14. Manning, *Troubled Refuge;* Taylor, *Embattled Freedom;* Click, *Time Full of Trials;* Rose, *Rehearsal for Reconstruction.* For conversations on the military importance of these various locations see: Brasher, *Peninsula Campaign;* Marvel, *Burnside.*

15. Medford, "Transition from Slavery to Freedom in a Diversified Economy," (dissertation), 45.

16. Medford, "Land and Labor," 572.

17. Medford, "Transition from Slavery to Freedom in a Diversified Economy," (dissertation), 8.

18. Medford, "Transition from Slavery to Freedom in a Diversified Economy," (dissertation), 8.

19. Medford, "Transition from Slavery to Freedom in a Diversified Economy," (dissertation), 32.

20. Richter and Allen, "Historical Overview of Africans," 663.

21. Medford, "Transition from Slavery to Freedom in a Diversified Economy," (dissertation), 12.

22. Medford, "Transition from Slavery to Freedom in a Diversified Economy," (dissertation), 37.

23. Medford, "Transition from Slavery to Freedom in a Diversified Economy," (dissertation), 32.

24. Medford, "Transition from Slavery to Freedom in a Diversified Economy," (dissertation), 32.

25. Wistar, *Autobiography,* 418. During the nineteenth century, oystering took multiple forms. Wistar's mention of "private beds" references the fact that waterways could be both public and private. Oystering actually required the planting of beds, and individuals could own certain beds. The Union army selling permits to oyster on private beds was consistent with their overall policy of wartime confiscation, allowing the army to profit from privately owned property. The key difference here, however, was that rather than paying people to labor on confiscated lands, the army simply sold permits to individuals who could then labor independently.

26. Wistar, *Autobiography,* 419.

27. Medford, "Land and Labor," 572 and J. E. Davis, "Oystering in Hampton Roads," 159.

28. J. E. Davis, "Oystering in Hampton Roads," 159.

29. Medford, "Land and Labor," 572.

30. Medford, "Land and Labor," 573.

31. Medford, "Land and Labor," 573. It bears noting that the petitioners described oystering as precarious financially because a series of particularly inclement winters had made conditions less profitable in the immediate postwar period.

32. Medford, "Land and Labor," 573.

33. Medford, "Land and Labor," 574. Medford also notes that in the latter decades of the nineteenth century as opportunities for oystering grew, white farm owners continually complained that oystering drew Black laborers away from agricultural work.

34. Fred. C. Newman v. Jackson Tolliver, Thomas Hughes, John Wilson, Joseph Dabney, Washington King, John Williams, John Banks, Joseph Smith, William Goodwin, Mingo Goodwin, Roll 202, *Proceedings of the Freedmen's Court Dec 1865–Jun 1867.*

35. *The Friend*, February 20, 1864.

36. "The Freedman's Relief Association," *The Friend*, February 27, 1864.

37. Manning, *Troubled Refuge*, 60.

38. Charles Wilder, Fort Monroe, December 30, 1864, in *The Wartime Genesis of Free Labor: The Upper South*, 2 (Cambridge, MA: Cambridge University Press, 1993), 12.

39. Newby-Alexander, *African American History*, 44.

40. Medford, "Transition from Slavery to Freedom in a Diversified Economy," (dissertation), 60.

41. Medford, "Transition from Slavery to Freedom in a Diversified Economy," (dissertation), 64–65.

42. Medford, "Transition from Slavery to Freedom in a Diversified Economy," (dissertation), 64.

43. Newby-Alexander, *African American History*, 58.

44. Newby-Alexander, *African American History*, 58.

45. This was likely Rodney Churchill who was eventually replaced with F. J. Massey after running afoul of bureau authorities for his accommodating practices towards the Black community. In December of 1865, Edward Darlington recommended to Major General Oliver Otis Howard, the bureau's leader, that Churchill be replaced because he had put himself "in a hostile attitude to the white inhabitants" and had further "rendered himself peculiarly obnoxious the whole tendency of his administration has been to widen and deepen the ill-feeling naturally existing to a certain extent between the white and colored people." E. C. Darlington to Maj. Gen. O. O. Howard, December 25, 1865. Oliver Otis Howard Papers, George J. Mitchell Department of Special Collections & Archives, Harthorne-Longfellow Library, Bowdoin University.

46. Assistant Superintendent of Negro Affairs at Yorktown to the Commander of the District of the Peninsula, April 21, 1865. In *The Wartime Genesis of Free Labor: The Upper South*, 237.

47. Morton, "Contrabands and Quakers," 425.

48. "Report of the Women's Aid Association of Friends," *Friends' Review*, May 28, 1864.

49. "Report of the Women's Aid Association of Friends," *Friends' Review*, May 28, 1864.

50. "Report of the Industrial Committee of Friends' Association of Philadelphia, for the Relief of Freedmen" *Friends' Review*, May 13, 1865.

51. 1850 York County Census. Of 112 Black men whose occupations were listed on the 1850 census, fifty were employed primarily as oystermen or fishermen.

52. Nancy Battey Letters, December 30, 1864.

53. Anthony Roberts v. Henry Billups, Henry Redcross, and John Roberts, *Proceedings of the Freedmen's Court*. Anthony Roberts appears on the 1865 Freedmen's Bureau census listed as age forty-six, living at Tinsley No. 1 and employed as an oysterman. The census also specified that he only had one arm. Henry Billups was listed as age thirty, living at Roberts Farm, which was owned by a Black man. Henry Redcross, age forty-nine, lived at Tinsley Farm and was also listed as an oysterman. Multiple John Roberts appear on the 1865 census, one residing at Tinsley Farm and the other at Tinsley No. 1. Both men are listed as farmers.

54. Davis, "Oystering in Hampton Roads," 158.

55. James N. Topping v. William Randall, *Proceedings of the Freedmen's Court*.

56. Charles L. Collins v. James Dabney, *Proceedings of the Freedmen's Court*.

57. Geo. W. Greenwood v. Frank Hobdy, *Proceedings of the Freedmen's Court*. Greenwood is identified as white in bureau court records.

58. Samuel Williams v. Abraham Spencer, *Proceedings of the Freedmen's Court*.

59. William Washington v. Horace Goodwin, *Proceedings of the Freedmen's Court*. It is unclear

what William Washington's trade was. A William Washington, age fifteen, appears in the 1865 census living at Sugar Hill. This Washington lived in the household of Jesse Washington, age thirty-five, who was listed as an oysterman. It is possible that this is the same William who appears in the bureau court records, and that he too became an oysterman, but there is not sufficient evidence to be certain.

60. Armstead Jones v. Watt Washington and Caesar Brooks, *Proceedings of the Freedmen's Court.*

61. Richard Hamilton v. William Charnic, *Proceedings of the Freedmen's Court.*

62. Matthew Taylor v. Abraham McKinney, *Proceedings of the Freedmen's Court.*

63. Thomas Jefferson v. Thomas Jones, *Proceedings of the Freedmen's Court.*

64. Griffin Beckett v. Saml Wooden, *Proceedings of the Freedmen's Court.*

65. Griffin Beckett v. Maxwell Crowfield, *Proceedings of the Freedmen's Court.*

66. D. M. Norton v. Harrison Williams, *Proceedings of the Freedmen's Court.*

67. Mary Francis Lockley v. Charles Coyler, *Proceedings of the Freedmen's Court.*

68. Mary Jane Graves s. Saml Croxton, *Proceedings of the Freedmen's Court.*

69. Martha Lane v. Edmund Garlick, *Proceedings of the Freedmen's Court.*

70. Louisa Kidd v. Peter Gillette, *Proceedings of the Freedmen's Court.*

71. Nancy Allen v. William Morris, *Proceedings of the Freedmen's Court.*

72. Adelaide Brisbee v. Danl Jackson, *Proceedings of the Freedmen's Court.*

73. William Allen v. John Banks, *Proceedings of the Freedmen's Court.*

74. Saville, *Work of Reconstruction,* 110.

75. Medford, "Transition from Slavery to Freedom in a Diversified Economy" (dissertation), 113.

76. Medford, "Land and Labor," 571.

77. Medford, "Land and Labor," 571.

78. June 1, 1867, Roll 202, Monthly Reports.

79. June 1, 1867, Roll 202, Monthly Reports.

80. McElya, *The Politics of Mourning,* 84.

81. McElya, *The Politics of Mourning,* 85.

82. Trowbridge, *The South,* 220.

83. Certainly, many Black communities on the Virginia Peninsula would have fit this description, including those surrounding Fort Monroe as well as Yorktown.

84. Trowbridge, *The South,* 220.

85. Trowbridge, *The South,* 220.

86. Trowbridge, *The South,* 222.

87. Trowbridge, *The South,* 221.

88. Trowbridge, *The South,* 221.

89. Trowbridge, *The South,* 221.

Chapter 4: "They Were Now Citizens"

1. Nieman, *To Set the Law,* 5.

2. Oakes, "Failure of a Vision," 70. Oakes notes that prior to the establishment of bureau courts, every Southern state except Louisiana barred Black testimony from civil courts, and in most cases Black Southerners were not allowed to bring suit against white Southerners for any reason. Bureau agents "saw this as the greatest single impediment to justice for the freedmen." Oakes, "Failure of a Vision," 68.

3. Hahn, *Nation Under Our Feet,* 148.

4. Nieman, *To Set the Law,* 11.

5. Hahn, *Nation Under Our Feet,* 127.

6. Hahn, *Nation Under Our Feet,* 128.

7. Hahn, *Nation Under Our Feet,* 128.

8. Rosen, *Terror in the Heart of Freedom,* 224.

9. While bureau courts experienced some degree of variability across the South, in September of 1865 Orlando Brown, directing bureau activity in Virginia, ordered that the community representatives had to be white. Nieman, *To Set the Law,* 22.

10. Jackson, *Negro Office-Holders,* 30.

11. Edmonie Norton testified in 1867 that she and Daniel married on January 2, 1860, in Philadelphia and that around February 1, 1866, Daniel left and went to Yorktown, VA. The 1866 year appears to be correct, according to Luther Porter Jackson's biography of Daniel Norton, but it is unclear if the specific date is accurate. Edmonie gave this testimony to obtain compensation from Daniel, who she mistakenly believed worked for the Freedmen's Bureau. Daniel Norton took issue with some of her account, particularly her claims that he was not supporting their child. According to Daniel, they had shared a child, but that child had passed away. Also according to Daniel, Edmonie left him on January 25, 1860, to go to Alexandria, VA, but because he was still a refugee from slavery he could not go with her. Daniel testified that in 1866 he sent Edmonie money to come to him, presumably in Yorktown. Roll 200, Letters Received.

12. May 1, 1866, Roll 202, Monthly Reports.

13. Magdol, *Right to the Land,* 113.

14. Massey to Armstrong, May 15, 1866. Roll 199, Letters Sent.

15. Hahn, *Nation Under Our Feet,* 177; Cimbala, *Under the Guardianship of the nation,* 208–9. As Paul Cimbala observes in reference to Black Georgians drilling and marching in armed displays of political unity, newly free people demonstrated their awareness that protection of their basic rights required community collaboration.

16. Massey to Armstrong, May 15, 1866. Roll 199, Letters Sent. Massey's consternation reflects James Oakes's point that bureau involvement in the South was complex. Most agents, Oakes observes, were dedicated to ensuring equal justice for Black Southerners and believed the bureau court was one of their most important responsibilities. Yet they also had to navigate a conflicted landscape in which their efforts were often questioned by a white public that was quickly gaining back political power through Andrew Johnson's conciliatory policies. Donald Nieman suggests that in the case of Virginia, Orlando Brown's order that elected court justices be white was a means of securing the "cooperation of prominent Virginia whites." Oakes, "Failure of a Vision," 67; Nieman, *To Set the Law,* 22.

17. Massey to Armstrong, May 15, 1866. Roll 199, Letters Sent.

18. Hahn, *Nation Under Our Feet,* 177; Saville, *Work of Reconstruction,* 150.

19. Other records testify to Norton's position of authority within the community and suggest that he held that authority through community agreement rather than force. In May of 1866, Sarah Cadbury mentioned in a letter home that John Carey, the Black pastor, and Daniel Norton stopped at the mission house to see "Mrs. H." This was likely Elizabeth Holway, who, along with her husband Edward, had been sent to oversee operations at the Warren Farm. May 2, 1866, Cadbury Correspondence.

20. Hahn, *Nation Under Our Feet,* 102. Moreover, as Chandra Manning points out, the meaning of citizenship, once granted, was not inevitable. Manning, *Troubled Refuge,* 285.

21. 1865 Census of Colored Population of York County.

22. Beverly Graves vs. Thomas Gay, *Proceedings of the Freedmen's Court.*

23. Beverly Graves vs. Thomas Gay, *Proceedings of the Freedmen's Court.*

24. According to the 1865 census, Miles Sewell was forty-two in 1865 and lived at 64 Slabtown with his two children, Carolina and Miles. Gallagher's store was one of two main stores in the Yorktown area according to Sarah Cadbury. Gallagher's Mill and Gallagher's store were likely both owned by Charles Gallagher, a white man from Delaware who owned considerable real estate and property in York County. According to the 1870 census, Gallagher was a "General Merchant," who owned $5,000 worth of real estate and $10,000 in his personal estate. Various members of his household were listed as having been born in both New York and California, suggesting that the family moved around before investing their resources in enterprises at Yorktown. The family may have been of Irish descent, as Ann Gallagher, age eighty-six, was listed as having been born in Ireland. 1870 census.

25. Miles Sewell vs. Louis Charles, *Proceedings of the Freedmen's Court.*

26. Benjamin Smith vs. Capt Frank B Mark, *Proceedings of the Freedmen's Court.*

27. Betty Larramore vs. Frank Hobdy, *Proceedings of the Freedmen's Court.*

28. Martha Turner vs. Elijah Turner, *Proceedings of the Freedmen's Court.*

29. Edward Smith vs. Harriet Smith, *Proceedings of the Freedmen's Court.*

30. Cimbala, *Under the Guardianship of the Nation,* 195–96.

31. Thomas Carey vs. Nancy Carey, *Proceedings of the Freedmen's Court.*

32. For example, National Park Service interpretation on the Yorktown National Battlefield identifies Slabtown's former location but does not note the larger community of which it was a part. Histories of York County sometimes comment on Slabtown's existence, but again fail to appreciate or demonstrate the larger landscape of freedom that existed after the Civil War. Conceptualizing Slabtown as a discrete location not only inaccurately reflects the past, but further serves to limit geographically the reach of Black history and Black residents in York County. It confines Black history to a single location within a larger landscape that is otherwise conceived of as white. For example, see Kale, *Yorktown, Virginia.*

33. 1865 census.

34. County deed books from this period record many of these transactions, often undertaken by white residents who were attempting to navigate a drastically altered economic landscape after the war.

35. John Taylor vs. Sally Green, *Proceedings of the Freedmen's Court.*

36. Massey reported in August of 1867 that it was the "universal desire of all classes of citizens" in York County that the county clerk, Bolivar Shield, be removed from office. Though "he took no active part in the rebellion" he had taken to "rebel boastings" and had recently been arrested for "disturbing the peace on a drunken frolic." August 8, 1867, Roll 200, Endorsements Sent and Received.

37. Joseph Price vs. Thomas Gibbons and Joseph Price vs. William Pryor, *Proceedings of the Freedmen's Court.*

38. 1865 census.

39. Jesse Mayo vs. William Wootten, *Proceedings of the Freedmen's Court.*

40. Griffin Becket vs. Daniel Stanley, *Proceedings of the Freedmen's Court.*

41. Robert Christian vs. Abram Stark and Robert Christian vs. Tillman Carter, *Proceedings of the Freedmen's Court.*

42. 1870 census.

43. In 1875, a Robert Christian purchased two lots in Slabtown from developers Wolf and Heyman for $104.40. Given that in the 1870 census, Robert Christian also owned real estate, this purchase was likely in addition to his other holdings. York County Deed Book 18.

44. "Freedmen's Stores in Virginia," *The Friend,* June 25, 1864.

45. *The Friend,* December 10, 1864.

46. "The Store Movement," *The Friend,* November 26, 1864.

47. "Freedmen's Stores," *The Friend,* November 19, 1864.

48. "Second Report of the Executive Board," *The Friend,* July 8, 1865.

49. *The Friend,* September 23, 1865.

50. Robert D. Ruffin, Case No. 4519, May 16, 1873, Southern Claims Commission.

51. Robert D. Ruffin, Case No. 4519, May 16, 1873, Southern Claims Commission.

52. 1870 census.

53. 1860 census.

54. Sarah Cadbury Correspondence, April 1, 1866. In later letters Cadbury returns to the topic of meeting the "colored Dr" at the store and confirms that the man she described initially as "a very pompous light man" was in fact Daniel Norton.

55. Sarah Cadburg Correspondence, April 19, 1866. Deed books indicate that in the postwar period Daniel and Robert Norton operated this store together. December 3, 1873, York County Deed Book 18.

56. 1865 census for Frank Cook states that he was thirty years old and lived at 113 Slabtown with his wife Harriett, age 27. John Ruff and John Taylor do not appear in this census. A John Taylor does appear in the census but is listed as living at Indianfield and employed as an oysterman, making it unlikely that this is the same Taylor involved in the case. Frank Cook vs. John Taylor, *Proceedings of the Freedmen's Court.*

57. 1865 census. Thomas Napper appears in the census, listed as living at Fort Yorktown with his wife Lucy and working as a carter.

58. Frank Cook vs. John Taylor, *Proceedings of the Freedmen's Court.*

59. Daniel Norton represented John Taylor as counsel in this case.

60. John Burnbridge vs. Robert Ruffin, *Proceedings of the Freedmen's Court.*

61. Thomas Brown vs. Robert Ruffin, *Proceedings of the Freedmen's Court.* Two Thomas Browns appear on the 1865 census. This was most likely Thomas Brown who lived at Stumptown with his wife Lucy, as this Thomas Brown was listed as a laborer on the census. The other Thomas Brown lived at 53 Slabtown with his wife Martha but was listed as an oysterman. It is difficult to know for certain which man this might have been though as many people worked multiple jobs while only one job was listed on the census.

62. Robert Ruffin vs. Robert Tibbs, *Proceedings of the Freedmen's Court.* In 1865 Robert Tibbs lived with his wife Eliza at Newtown, and the census listed Robert as a laborer. Richard Wilkinson also lived at Newtown with his wife Louisa and was likewise listed as a laborer. Clayborne Holmes does not appear on the 1865 census.

63. Clayborne Holmes vs. Robert Ruffin, *Proceedings of the Freedmen's Court.*

64. Edna Greene Medford notes that forestry was an important industry for nonagricultural Black laborers on the northern end of the lower peninsula. Numerous sawmills employed Black workers processing "large quantities of ship timber, railroad ties, and mine props" as well as cord wood for local markets. Greene, "Land and Labor."

65. Nathaniel Taylor vs. Henry Fergerson and R D Ruffin, *Proceedings of the Freedmen's Court.*

66. Frank Tazewell appears on the 1865 census at Newtown with his wife Codney and a seven-year-old child named James Bolden. Tazewell's occupation is listed as shoemaker. Census of the Colored Population of York County.

67. Daniel Cook vs. Frank Taswell, October 17, 1866, *Proceedings of the Freedmen's Court.*

68. Taswell's wife, identified in the court records as "Courtney" rather than "Codney" gave interesting information about the layout of Newtown in her testimony. She stated that she and her husband lived on Telegraph Street in Newtown, next door to Mat Harrod. Cook's boat, she explained, was at the wharf "back of Henry Diggs house about two miles from where they live."

69. Daniel Cook vs. Frank Taswell, December 12, 1866. *Proceedings of the Freedmen's Court.*

70. 1870 census. Daniel Cook appeared on the census with his wife Alice and two children, Rebecca and James.

71. David Jones vs. William Goodin & James Elliot, *Proceedings of the Freedmen's Court.*

72. David Jones vs. William Goodin & James Elliot, *Proceedings of the Freedmen's Court.* In the text of this case, Goodin repeatedly says he "loaned" a boat to Hughes. However, in a different case, Goodin brought Hughes to court for nonpayment of rent because he had in fact rented the boat to Hughes and Hughes had not yet paid for it. William Goodin vs. Wesley Hughes, *Proceedings of the Freedmen's Court.*

73. John Willis and Miles Sewell vs. I. Baker, *Proceedings of the Freedmen's Court.*

74. 1865 census. The census included a column "Does he support his family by his labor."

75. John Adams vs. John Carter, Proceedings of the Freedmen's Court.

76. Enos Washington vs. Gustavis Harris, *Proceedings of the Freedmen's Court.*

77. Enos Washington vs. Gustavis Harris, *Proceedings of the Freedmen's Court.*

78. "Fill Travers" was likely Philip Traverse, age sixty, who lived at Stumptown with Molly Traverse, age thirty-nine, in 1865. 1865 census.

79. E. J. Wynn vs. Fill Travers, *Proceedings of the Freedmen's Court.*

80. 1865 census. Buck Cook does not appear in the 1865 census.

81. Jackson Tolliver vs. Buck Cook, *Proceedings of the Freedmen's Court.*

82. Mira Ann Goldman vs. Robert Armstead, *Proceedings of the Freedmen's Court.* This sentence may at first appear extreme, but records suggest that Robert Armstead may have made a habit of larceny and the court's decision may have resulted from repeated offenses. Armstead appeared in court on multiple occasions for default of payment, and, in 1867 Massey made a passing reference to "Robert Armstead (col'd) larceny—found guilty, sent to Fort Monroe." Roll 199, Letters Sent.

83. Richard Jones vs. Martha Lane, *Proceedings of the Freedmen's Court.*

84. 1865 census.

85. Richard Jones vs. Martha Lane, *Proceedings of the Freedmen's Court.*

86. Cimbala, *Under the Guardianship of the nation,* 198.

87. Massey to Armstrong, February 22, 1867, Roll 199, Letters Sent.

88. Armstrong to Massey, December 14, 1866, Roll 200, Letters and Orders Received.

89. Massey to Mr. F. Lincoe, December 15, 1866, Roll 199, Letters Sent.

90. 1865 census. Milby lived at Buck Point with his wife Lina and another child, Cadelia. Cadelia was listed as only one year old, suggesting, perhaps, that she was born after Richard and Lina had escaped from slavery.

91. Massey to Mr. Blakey, Middlesex, Co. VA, Roll 199, Letters Sent.

92. 1865 census.

93. Massey to Armstrong, December 10, 1866, Roll 199, Letters Sent.

94. W. H. Sloan to S. C. Armstrong, January 18, 1868, Roll 200, Letters Received.

Chapter 5: "We Have a Right to the Land"

1. Peter Dorcy, identified in the 1865 Freedmen's Bureau census as "Dorsey" was forty years old and lived at 331 SlabTown. Sarah Cadbury also noted that Dorcy at times shared the pulpit with Thomas Napper in church services. Philip Tabb, identified as "Tabbs" in the 1865 census was thirty-four years old, worked as an oysterman, and lived at Buck Point with Mary Tabbs, age twenty, and George Tabbs, age one.

2. Peter Dorcy Chairman and Philip A Tabb Secretary to O. O. Howard, December 7, 1866. Roll 199, Letters sent. Mass meetings of Black Southerners were common during this period, especially when they needed to consider their futures relative to land ownership. Horace James, who headed the Freedmen's Bureau in North Carolina reported as early as January 1865 that Black residents routinely met to hold counsel with one another, and frequently validated rumors that land would be redistributed. Hahn, *Nation Under Our Feet,* 133.

3. Robert Engs notes that Rodney Churchill, who preceded F. J. Massey as head bureau agent in York County, incited the ire of local politicians by strongly protesting injustices against Black residents such as attempting to force them to abandon personal property and crops they had cultivated. Consequently, the bureau transferred Churchill to James City County. After serving there for two more months, Churchill was mustered out of service entirely. Engs, *Freedom's First Generation,* 85–6.

4. Samuel C. White to Col Brown Comm of the F Bureau, Roll 199, Letters Sent.

5. Taylor's *Embattled Freedom* and Manning's *Troubled Refuge* both conclude with the disbanding of refugee communities in 1865. Histories of the Freedmen's Bureau tend to be state specific, including Cimbala's *Under the Guardianship of the nation* and Nieman's *To Set the Law in Motion.*

6. Roll 199, Letters Sent, Genl B F Buster to Rodney Churchill, Assistant Supr Negro Affairs at Yorktown, May 20, 1864.

7. *The Friend,* December 10, 1864.

8. "Friends' Freedmen's Relief Association," *The Friend,* March 12, 1864.

9. "Friend's Freedmen's Relief Association," *The Friend,* February 20, 1864.

10. "The Executive Board of the Association of Friends of Philadelphia and its vicinity, for the relief of Coloured Freedmen," *The Friend,* February 20, 1864.

11. "Report of the Industrial Committee," *Friends' Review,* May 13, 1865.

12. Hahn, *Nation Under Our Feet,* 81.

13. Rose, *Rehearsal for Reconstruction,* 79.

14. Hahn, *Nation Under Our Feet,* 81.

15. Magdol, *A Right to the Land,* 156–60.

16. Manning, *Troubled Refuge,* 243.

17. Downs, 93.

18. Downs, 100.

19. Manning, *Troubled Refuge,* 247.

20. Manning, *Troubled Refuge,* 260.

21. Magdol, *A Right to the Land,* 160.

22. Morgan, *Emancipation in Virginia's Tobacco Belt,* 141.

23. "CIRCULAR," Roll 200, Letters and Orders Received, September 19, 1865.

24. Even before the war ended, Black South Carolinians had managed to purchase around two thousand acres of land cooperatively along the coast. Rose, *Rehearsal for Reconstruction,* 215.

25. Cimbala, *Under the Guardianship of the nation,* 174.

26. Hahn, *Nation Under Our Feet,* 132.

27. Morgan, *Emancipation in Virginia's Tobacco Belt,* 136.

28. Cimbala, *Under the Guardianship of the nation,* 166.

29. Morgan, *Emancipation in Virginia's Tobacco Belt,* 136–7.

30. Morgan, *Emancipation in Virginia's Tobacco Belt,* 137.

31. Hahn, *Nation Under Our Feet,* 154.

32. Hahn, *Nation Under Our Feet,* 136. Hahn argues that "the expectations of land ownership expressed almost universally held notions of just compensation for the travails of enslavement, of what was rightfully due those who tilled the soil, and of what could provide meaningful security in a postemancipation world."

33. Debates over land redistribution continued in Congress well into 1867, and rumors of future distributions persisted into the end of the century. Cimbala, *Under the Guardianship of the nation,* 189.

34. The specifics of each contract differed from tenant to tenant, even when negotiating with the same white landowner. Some people paid a proscribed rent, some gave the landowner a specified amount of produce—for example, "two barrels of shelled corn"—and others paid through a share of the crop—such as, "1/4 of all the crop produced on the land." Roll 203, Contracts, bills of lading, leases, records relating to court cases and other records, 1865–1868.

35. "Report of Farms rented & c in York County," Roll 201, Monthly Reports, Jul 1865–Mar 1866.

36. Rose, *Rehearsal for Reconstruction,* 225.

37. F. J. Massey to Dr Robs Powers, Senate Chamber, Richmond, Va, Fey 13th 1866, Roll 199, Letters Sent.

38. Circular 4, March 25, 1866, Roll 199, Letters Sent.

39. Circular 3, Feb 21, 1866, Roll 199, Letters Sent.

40. Massey to General, July 31, 1866, Roll 199, Letters Sent.

41. Circular I, Feby 7th, 1866, Roll 199, Letters Sent.

42. Paul Cimbala has observed similar resistance in residents of Sapelo Island in Georgia. He notes that formerly enslaved people refused to sign contracts without a community leader present and that even once they signed contracts bureau agents suspected some people sold their produce before the final division of crop. Additionally, Sapelo Island's Black residents continued to hunt deer, despite the bureau's restriction. Cimbala, *Under the Guardianship of the nation,* 183.

43. George Taylor (col[d]) vs. William and James Roberts (col[d]), Records of the Freedmen's Bureau Court. Records of contracts for York County are not organized by landowner, making it difficult to find specific contracts between specific people. It is unclear from the court transcript if Taylor paid a cash rent or rented on shares.

44. Sally Cook (col[d]) v. Major Fields (col[d]), Records of the Freedmen's Bureau Court.

45. Circular No. 17, Assistant Commissioner State of Va, Richmond, Va, May 7, 1866, Roll 199, Letters sent.

46. Hahn, *Nation Under Our Feet,* 156.

47. Hahn, *Nation Under Our Feet,* 153–56.

48. Morgan, *Emancipation in Virginia's Tobacco Belt,* 132.

49. Lucy Chase, July 1, 1864.

50. Chandra Manning illustrates this point poignantly in her discussion of the material realities of life at Fort Monroe. She explains, all refugee camps "were a mix of improvisation, sanctuary, and humanitarian crisis, but the exact ration of refuge to misery varied mightily from place to place, depending on the interplay of a number of concrete factors" such as geographical location and number of aid workers. Manning, *Troubled Refuge,* 37.

51. "Report of the Industrial Committee of Friends' Association of Philadelphia," *Friends' Review,* May 13, 1865.

52. C. B. Wilder to E. W. Coffin, Roll 200, Letters and Orders Received.

53. Cadbury, *Letters from Slabtown,* 87.

54. Cadbury Correspondence, April 19, 1866.

55. F. J. Massey to S. C. Armstrong, January 5, 1866, Roll 199, Letters Sent.

56. F. J. Massey to S. C. Armstrong, January 5, 1866, Roll 199, Letters Sent.

57. Massey to Hon Robt H Powers Presiding Justice York Co, June 26, 1866, Roll 199, Letters Sent. As Gregory Downs and others have chronicled, the initial shift back to civil authority in the Southern states that preceded Congressional Reconstruction instituted a period of near chaos in which violence against formerly enslaved people was endemic. Downs, *After Appomattox,* 81–87.

58. Engs, *Freedom's First Generation,* 67.

59. Engs, *Freedom's First Generation,* 84.

60. Slabtown 1866, Roll 202, Monthly Reports.

61. Samuel Thomas to Major General I. M. Schofield, November 28, 1866," Roll 199, Letters Sent.

62. Thorpe, *Life in Virginia,* 57.

63. Thorpe, *Life in Virginia,* 57.

64. 1865 Census of Colored Population of York County, March 11, 1865.

65. 1865 Census of Colored Population of York County, March 11, 1865.

66. Thorpe, *Life in Virginia,* 57.

67. M. D. Warren to Gel Armstrong, October 19, 1866, Roll 200, Letters and Orders Received.

68. In early 1866, residents of Warren's farm actually made their contracts with Massey, not Warren. Contracts varied by person, but generally renters agreed to pay Massey three-fourths to one barrel of shelled corn per acre they rented at the end of the year. Renters may have made their contracts with Massey because Warren had not yet claimed his land at the beginning of the year, or because Massey negotiated in Warren's stead. Regardless, between the lines of Warren's assertion was also a further implication: He did not want to make a fixed amount of profit from his land, but rather wanted to have enough control over production to ensure he could maximize his profit. Roll 203, Contracts, Bills of Lading, Leases, Records Relating to Courts Cases and Other Records, 1865–1868.

69. "The Freed-People in Virginia," *Friends' Review,* November 24, 1866.

70. March 28, 1866, Roll 199, Letters Sent.

71. March 28, 1866, Roll 199, Letters Sent.

72. 1865 Census of Colored Population of York County, March 11, 1865. Wyatt is alternately identified as "Bayley," Bailey," and "Bailor" in different records of the period.

73. Rose, *Rehearsal for Reconstruction,* 354.

74. Engs, *Freedom's First Generation,* 82.

75. 1866, Roll 202, Monthly Reports.

76. Harper, *The End of Days,* 27.

77. "Bailor Wyatt and Stafford G. Cooke," Roll 203, Contracts, Bills of Lading, Leases, Records Relating to Courts Cases and Other Records, 1865–1868.

78. "A Freedman's Speech: Bayley Wyat's Speech," *Friends' Review,* January 5, 1867, and *The Friend,* December 29, 1866.

79. "A Freedman's Speech: Bayley Wyat's Speech," *Friends' Review,* January 5, 1867, and *The Friend,* December 29, 1866. I have corrected the spelling in these quotations because in the copy of the speech that *The Friend* circulated, they employed a dialect clearly intended to mimic a racist speech pattern.

80. *The Friend,* December 29, 1866; *Friends' Review,* January 5, 1867.

81. Taylor, *Embattled Freedom,* 183.

82. O. O. Howard to Major General J. M. Schofield, August 22, 1866, Roll 199, Letters Sent.

83. "A Meeting of the 'Freedmen' in York Co.," September 5, 1866, Roll 199, Letters Sent.

84. Massey to Armstrong, September 8, 1866, Roll 199, Letters Sent.

85. Massey to Armstrong, September 8, 1866, Roll 199, Letters Sent.

86. Massey to Armstrong, September 9, 1866, Roll 199, Letters Sent.

87. Hahn, *Nation Under Our Feet,* 221.

88. Hahn, *Nation Under Our Feet,* 225.

89. Massey to Armstrong, December 1, 1866, Roll 199, Letters Sent.

90. Circular No. 10, August 22, 1866, Roll 199, Letters Sent.

91. Circular No 21, November 23, 1866, Roll 199, Letters Sent.

92. According to the April 1866 register of individuals receiving rations, less than three hundred people were still receiving rations in York County in the months prior to Howard's order. Roll 202, Registers of persons receiving ration tickets, vol 1–2, Feb 1865–Apr 1866.

93. Massey to Armstrong, September 1, 1866, Roll 199, Letters Sent.

94. "Extracts from the Superintendent," *The Friend,* December 22, 1866.

95. December 1, 1866, Roll 202, Monthly Reports.

96. February 15, 1867, Roll 200, Letters and Orders Received.

97. Massey to Armstrong, May 15, 1866, Roll 199, Letters Sent.

98. February 1, 1867, Roll 202, Monthly Reports.

99. Massey to Armstrong, November 6, 1866, Roll 199, Letters Sent.

100. February 19, 1867, Roll 199, Letters Sent.

101. Massey's letters frequently mention that the unavailability of transportation provided a constant impediment to people's relocation. As Greg Downs explains, these problems typified the life of bureau agents. In an effort to demobilize and scale down the cost of the war effort, the Union army sold off most of their horses in 1865. This limited access to transportation for agents as well as people wishing to relocate. Downs, *After Appomattox,* 92.

102. March 1, 1867, Roll 202, Monthly Reports.

103. March 1, 1867, Roll 202, Monthly Reports.

104. March 1, 1867, Roll 202, Monthly Reports.

105. Massey to Armstrong, May 1, 1867, Roll 202, Monthly Reports.

106. Massey to O. Brown, May 1, 1867, Roll 202, Monthly Reports.

107. Engs, *Freedom's First Generation,* 94.

Chapter 6: Landscapes of Freedom, Landscapes of Memory

1. In the decades after the Civil War, residents began referring to Slabtown as Uniontown. It is unclear when exactly this transition took place, but deed books began using Uniontown and Slabtown interchangeably in the late nineteenth century. According to a former resident, in the twentieth

century there was a sign on the entrance road next to the national cemetery designating the town "Uniontown."

2. Much like white teachers after the Civil War described York County as a desolate place, white visitors to Yorktown in the postwar period would frequently refer to it as a "forlorn" place, unkept and lacking modern development. In this they dismissed the Black residents' industry and community, framing Yorktown as a place stuck in the past.

3. "A Southern Woman Writes of Yorktown," *Richmond Dispatch,* July 13, 1902.

4. York County's Black population was 2,607 in 1860, 4,627 in 1864, and 4,691 in 1870. The only county on the Virginia Peninsula with a larger Black population was Elizabeth City County, numbering 5,417. Elizabeth City County included cities like Norfolk and Hampton. Medford, "The Transition from Slavery."

5. Roll 201, Monthly Reports, July 1865–Mar 1866.

6. Massey to Armstrong, Jany 3d, 1867, Roll 199, Letters Sent. Bureau records were not consistent in the terms they used to identify settlements or landholdings. Especially in the case of Slabtown and Newtown, bureau agents switched from referring to the communities by name or by the name of the white landowner with no apparent consistency.

7. Lob Wolf's naturalization record, dated March 11, 1868, identified him as formerly of German nationality having immigrated to the United States in 1865. Daniel Heyman's naturalization record, dated May 20, 1869, identified him as formerly of French nationality and specified that Lob Wolf was his witness to naturalization. An 1886 New York City directory listed Lob Wolf as working in the lumber industry, a trade he would continue to pursue in York County, VA. Details about Wolf and Heyman remain murky, as various records suggests that they did not both reside in York County throughout the tenure of their business dealings. How they wound up in York County in the first place is unclear, but they were already in the area during the Freedmen's Bureau's tenure, as they appear in records of the Freedmen's Bureau Court. They seem to have engaged in numerous business ventures, including the timber industry, and it is possible that their choice to purchase Powers's land, given the presence of Slabtown, was something of an instance of land speculation. With the community present, it was likely clear to Wolf and Heyman that residents would desire to retain the land, and that they would gain the finances necessary to eventually buy parcels.

8. The name "Slabtown" was common among wartime refugee communities. Another community, also called "Slabtown" took root farther down the peninsula near Fort Monroe.

9. Deed Book 18, 280. Wolf and Heyman paid $4,020 for the entire farm. Powers had inherited this particular property upon his father's death prior to the Civil War. It appears he may have mortgaged it after the war to pay other outstanding debts, and by 1869 had defaulted on those payments. Consequently, his creditors initiated a suit against him to have the property sold at public auction, a fate that befell numerous white landowners in York County in the immediate postwar years.

10. Deed Book 18, 280.

11. Deed Book 18, December 12, 1870, Robert Christian and Robert Sheild. Robert Christian did not appear on the 1865 Freedmen's Bureau census of Black York County residents, but he does appear on the 1870 census living in Nelson Township—where Slabtown was located—and owning $105 in real estate.

12. Using landholdings as collateral for loans in the form of deeds of trust were also common in the postwar era.

13. Deed Book 22, 355.

14. Massey to Armstrong, Jan 3, 1867, Roll 199, Letters Sent and Received.

15. As Robert Christian's case indicates though, this does not necessarily mean actual purchases of land increased in 1873. Rather, residents recorded a series of purchases with the county clerk's office at this time.

16. John W. Thomas purchased lot no. 20, consisting of 3.5 acres for $105; Celia Fields purchased lot no. 22, consisting of 2 acres for $60; Washington Fields purchased lot nos. 30, 31, 37, and 38, consisting of 8 acres for $270; Louisa Coffin purchased lot no. 39 consisting of 2 acres for $60; and William Washington purchased lot no. 10 consisting of 2 and 1/16 acres for $78. Deed Book 18.

17. Celia Field is perhaps the only person who may have been living at Slabtown in 1865. The bureau's records noted a Celia Smith living in the household of John Smith, along with William Fields at 167 Slabtown. It is possible that bureau agents misidentified the marriage relationships within the household, or perhaps Celia married William Fields after the fact.

18. Further details about the building identified as the "Freedmen's Seminary" are not available, as sources cited throughout this project do not reference it.

19. Deed Book 18, 572.

20. Deed Book 18, 553, April 15, 1875. Daniel and Sadie sold a second piece of land containing four acres at the same time to William Thomas. This lot was part of a parcel of land called the "Goodwin Tract." "Widow Goodwin's" land is identified on the quartermaster map to the south of Slabtown. An eleven-year-old William Thomas appears on the 1865 Freedmen's Bureau map living at Indian Field in the household of Matthew Thomas who bureau agents listed as "very industrious."

21. Deed Book 18, 583. Schively is identified as the superintendent of the national cemetery in a register of superintendents. "Superintendents of National Cemeteries," Department of Commerce and Labor, Bureau of the Census. Official Register of the United States, Containing a List of the Officers and Employees in the Civil, Military, and Naval Service. Digitized books (77 volumes). Oregon State Library, Salem, Oregon. It is interesting to note that Shively paid Wolf and Heyman $200 for lot no. 1, which consisted of 2.61 acres. Lot no. 2, which Norton sold to Lewis the same year, consisted of only 1.5 acres.

22. "Inventory of Farms in York County, Va upon which are collected rents, &c," Roll 203, Bills of Lading, Leases, Records Relating to Court Cases, and Other Records 1865–68.

23. Deed Book 17, October 6, 1866.

24. The 1870 census recorded Washington and Catharine Fields as having a personal estate valued at $250. As Fields did not purchase the lots in Slabtown until 1873, this figure likely represents the property mentioned here. 1870 census.

25. Deed Book 17, November 26, 1866.

26. Deed Book 19, William Taylor Homestead Deed.

27. Deed Book 17, December 8, 1866. Armistead Taylor appears on the 1870 census listed as a farmer owning $250 worth of real estate, suggesting that perhaps he owned another tract of land or had expanded his holdings by that date.

28. Deed Book 17, December 8, 1866.

29. Deed Book 18, 536.

30. That the 1870 census for York County recorded Fields's occupation as "farmer" while the 1865 Freedmen's Bureau census listed him as a "carpenter," suggests that Fields purchased this land for his own farming purposes rather than as rental property.

31. Deed Book 17, March 14, 1868.

32. S G Cooke to Massey, July 16, 1866, Roll 200, Letters Received, Feb 1865–Feb 1867.

33. "Circular 2," February 16, 1866, Roll 199, Letters Sent.

34. Roll 202, *Proceedings of the Freedmen's Court.*

35. Cooke to Massey, February 21, 1867, Roll 200, Letters and Orders Received.

36. Cooke named: Thomas Brown, Peter Brown, Isaac Jones, Armond Morris, Levi Washington, Abram William, Robert Brown, Ceasar Brooks, Alfred Beale, Miles Cary, Mat Harwood, Robert Hughes, George Johnson, George Lousen, Humphrey Ross, and Samuel Vernon.

37. Cooke, February 23, 1867, Roll 199, Letters Sent.

38. Massey to Cooke, February 25, 1867, Roll 199, Letters Sent.

39. Cooke to Armstrong, March 19, 1867, Roll 200, Letters Received.

40. Cooke also took his case to Oliver Otis Howard, the head of the Freedmen's Bureau and made sure to note that bureau agents had compelled him to rent his land to Black residents against his will. Cooke to Maj. Genl. Howard, January 21, 1867, Roll 199, Letters Sent.

41. Reel 34, York County Minute Book. London Cooke appears on the 1880 and 1890 censuses for York County living in Grafton and working as an oysterman and farmer.

42. Reel 34, York County Minute Book.

43. Engs notes that Black inhabitants of York and Elizabeth City Counties knew that they significantly outnumbered white residents and proceeded in their political efforts accordingly. Engs, *Freedom's First Generation,* 103.

44. Deed Book 17, February 25, 1867.

45. Deed Book 18, April 22, 1873.

46. Deed Book 18, 377.

47. Deed Book 17, 61.

48. Deed Book 18, 534.

49. 1870 census. The census identified individuals as "black" as well as "mulatto." However, for the purposes of these statistics, I have categorized both groups as Black community members.

50. May 28, 1862. *Potter Journal.*

51. May 23, 1862. *Oneida Sachem.*

52. "Yorktown and Surroundings," *Southbridge Journal,* May 23, 1862.

53. "Our Army Correspondence, May 13, 1862," *Farmer's Cabinet,* May 22, 1862.

54. "Our Army Correspondence," *Altoona Tribune,* May 15, 1862.

55. May 22, 1862. *Concord Independent Democrat.*

56. May 17, 1852. *Columbia Democrat.*

57. "From the Seat of War," *Cambridge Chronicle,* May 17, 1862.

58. May 7, 1862. *Geneva Courier.*

59. "The Fourth," *The Cavalier,* July 2, 1862.

60. "Sketches," *The Cavalier,* March 17, 1863.

61. Lucy Chase, May 19, 1864.

62. Cadbury Correspondence, March 23, 1866.

63. Cadbury Correspondence, March 23, 1866.

64. Lucy Chase, May 19, 1864.

65. Cadbury, *Letters from Slabtown,* 97.

66. Cadbury, *Letters from Slabtown,* 102.

67. A. P. Smith, "To the President of the United States," *Douglass' Monthly,* October 1862.

68. J. T. W., Company G, 3rd USCT, "For the Christian Recorder," *The Christian Recorder,* September 10, 1864.

69. Steere, Shrines of the Honored Dead, 1.

70. Faust, *This Republic of Suffering*, xviii.

71. Steere, *Shrines of the Honored Dead*, 9.

72. Steere, *Shrines of the Honored Dead*, 14.

73. Steere, *Shrines of the Honored Dead*, 16. Originally, only Union soldiers who had died during the Civil War were eligible for burial in national cemeteries. However, the Grand Army of the Republic—a national organization for Union veterans—opposed this policy which was reversed in the early 1870s to include anyone who had served in the United States armed forces.

74. Massey to Col W L James, Office Asst Supt Bureau, Chief Quartermaster, Dept of Va. Roll 199, Letters Sent.

75. Deed Book 17.

76. Ignatio, Jr. "No. 2," *The Cavalier*, March 24, 1863.

77. "Removal of Soldiers' Bodies," *The Cavalier*, April 14, 1863.

78. "Yorktown and Surroundings," *Southbridge Journal*, May 23, 1862.

79. "The Yorktown Monument," *The Cavalier*, March 3, 1863.

80. Smith, *Old Yorktown and Its History*, 10.

81. A. H. Ackley to Depot Officer, Subject: Cornwallis Monument, June 18, 1920. National Archives and Records Administration, Yorktown National Cemetery, Letters Sent.

82. F. J. Massey to Col W L James, Chief Quartermaster, Roll 199, Letters Sent. Massey also noted that in addition to the soldiers buried in the national cemetery, he estimated that "not less than from fifteen to twenty thousand graves of soldiers" were "scattered throughout the entire county." Describing a situation that would plague the national cemetery administrators after the Civil War, he continued "It will be impossible to identify the bodies as there are no head boards to the graves."

83. Two primary factors contributed to lack of identification of Civil War soldiers. First, neither army had a system for identifying soldiers before they died in battle—no equivalent to modern-day dog tags existed. Second, many soldiers were buried first on the field where they fell and later disinterred, so if their peers who had buried them initially had marked their graves, it was unlikely those markers remained legible by the time of their disinterment for burial in a national cemetery. Many Civil War Era national cemeteries, including Yorktown and Fredericksburg, actually contain graves filled with any number of soldiers. Though the federal government wanted to lay US soldiers to rest in a designated place, they were hard-pressed to do so in a way that could acknowledge the individuality of a soldier. As Faust notes, the reality of anonymous death in the Civil War was extremely difficult for Victorian Americans to process as it interrupted the traditional grieving process. Donald C. Pfanz, *Where Valor Proudly Sleeps*.

84. Faust, This Republic of Suffering, 236.

85. Neff, *Honoring the Civil War Dead*, 1.

86. Neff, *Honoring the Civil War Dead*, 1.

87. Zipf, "Marking Union Victory," 27.

88. Zipf, "Marking Union Victory," 27.

89. Goldberger, *Repatriating Yorktown*, 88.

90. Zipf, "Marking Union Victory," 30.

91. Zipf, "Marking Union Victory," 32.

92. Zipf, "Marking Union Victory," 37.

93. Zipf, "Marking Union Victory," 37.

94. Zipf, "Marking Union Victory," 39.

95. "Circular to all Superintendents," July 22, 1905, Records of Yorktown National Cemetery Superintendent, Letters Received, Records of Colonial National Historical Park, Yorktown, VA.

96. Records of Colonial National Historical Park, Letters Received, October 27, 1909.

97. Records of Colonial National Historical Park, Letters Sent, January 24, 1910.

98. October 30, 1912, Letters Sent, National Cemetery Superintendent Records, Colonial National Historical Park, Yorktown, VA.

99. Steere, *Shrines of the Honored Dead,* 2.

100. June 21, 1904, Letters Sent, National Cemetery Superintendent Records, Colonial National Historical Park, Yorktown, VA.

101. Letters Sent February 21, 1905, Letters Sent, National Cemetery Superintendent Records, Colonial National Historical Park, Yorktown, VA.

102. Letters Sent, February 13, 1905, Letters Sent, National Cemetery Superintendent Records, Colonial National Historical Park, Yorktown, VA.

103. Letters Sent February 21, 1905, Letters Sent, National Cemetery Superintendent Records, Colonial National Historical Park, Yorktown, VA.

104. "General Assembly of Virginia," *Daily Dispatch,* April 7, 1882.

105. For an analysis of this celebration, see Goldberger, "Repatriating Yorktown."

106. "The Corner-Stone of the Monument to Commemorate the Surrender of Cornwallis Laid," *Daily Dispatch,* October 19, 1881.

107. US Department of the Interior, Yorktown Custom House, National Register of Historic Places and National Historic Landmarks Program, 1999.

Chapter 7: "We Build Our Memorial in Our Lives"

1. "House of Delegates," *Virginian-Pilot,* March 26, 1870.

2. Hahn, *Nation Under Our Feet,* 367.

3. This was nowhere more true than in Virginia where in 1867 military district commander John Schofield had delayed ratification of a Republican-produced state constitution that prohibited anyone who had voluntarily supported the Confederacy from political office.

4. Hahn, *Nation Under Our Feet,* 370–74.

5. Hahn, *Nation Under Our Feet,* 370.

6. Dailey, *Before Jim Crow,* 8.

7. Hahn, *Nation Under Our Feet,* 385.

8. "A Pretty Quarrel as it Stands," *Virginian-Pilot,* May 15, 1868. Thomas Bayne escaped from slavery in North Carolina in 1846 and relocated to the city of Norfolk, VA. According to Luther Porter Jackson, Bayne was active in the Underground Railroad in Norfolk and in 1855 escaped again from slavery in Norfolk, traveling to New Bedford, MA, where he practiced dentistry. Like Daniel Norton, Bayne returned to the peninsula at the close of the Civil War where he became "the most spectacular, the most radical, and one of the most hated of [Black politicians]." Jackson, *Negro Office-Holders.*

9. "The Issue to be Settled," *Virginian-Pilot,* May 12, 1868.

10. "A Debate in the Convention with a Fact as its Commentary," *Virginian-Pilot,* February 12, 1868. Both Daniel Norton and Thomas Bayne were delegates to Virginia's constitutional convention, 1867–68. Virginia did not have the opportunity to send representatives to Congress until 1870, so it is unclear why conversations about Norton's candidacy began so early. The topic returned to

newspapers in 1869, suggesting that Norton expected to run for office once Virginia's seats in Congress were reinstated.

11. "The Canvass," *Virginian-Pilot*, November 1, 1874.

12. "Sauce for the Goose is Sauce for the Gander," *Virginian-Pilot*, October 29, 1870.

13. "Sauce for the Goose is Sauce for the Gander," *Virginian-Pilot*, October 29, 1870.

14. "Negroes Ruled Out," *Virginian-Pilot*, November 2, 1870.

15. "Election Returns," *Virginian-Pilot*, December 28, 1870. In her history of the Virginia Peninsula during and after the Civil War, Cassandra Newby-Alexander asserts that the 1869 election of Governor Gilbert Walker "heralded the takeover of the Conservatives, an antiblack party composed of old-line Democrats, former Whigs, and Liberal Republicans." While the Conservatives did dominate state-level offices until the rise of the Readjuster movement, the Nortons's continued political success indicated that at the local level the situation was not so one-sided. Newby-Alexander, *African American History*, 92.

16. "Radical Convention at Oxford Hall- Hon. Jas. H. Platt Renominated," *Virginian-Pilot*, June 26, 1872.

17. *Virginian-Pilot*, June 26, 1872. It is unclear if this article was written by a correspondent for *The Virginian-Pilot* or by an attendee from the convention who wished to disseminate news of Norton's candidacy. While white Democrats certainly had an interest in highlighting and celebrating the increasing divisions in the Republican Party, the Nortons' and their supporters did utilize this paper as a means to share party news and especially alert the peninsula community to the party's political events.

18. Clark, *Defining Moments*, 31.

19. Clark, *Defining Moments*, 32–33.

20. "The Republican Convention-Harmonious Proceedings," *Virginian-Pilot*, September 20, 1872.

21. "Letter from Dr. Norton," *Virginian-Pilot*, September 30, 1872.

22. "Lee or Norton—White or Colored?" *Virginian-Pilot*, September 23, 1872. Again, the source of this commentary is suspect because *The Virginian-Pilot* was a Democratic newspaper. However, such charges that the Republican Party did allow Black candidates their share of political offices was increasingly common in the 1870s. Hahn, *Nation Under Our Feet*, 372.

23. "The Triangular Fight," October 3, 1872.

24. Despite these concerns, *The Virginian-Pilot* was also more than willing to continue to point out the hypocrisy of the Radical Republicans in their treatment of Daniel Norton. In October, the paper reprinted an article from *The New York Times* that referred to Norton as a Black man "of more vanity than brains, who seems determined to give trouble to the party, has determined, encouraged by a few enemies of Mr. Platt, to measure strength against him." Reflecting on this treatment of Norton, *The Virginian-Pilot* wondered, "May it not happen that [Norton], who is well educated . . . rebel against the subjugation of his race to the carpet bag element?" Clearly, the Radicals were limited in their views of Black voters because they stated, "Here we see what a fate threatens the colored man who dares maintain that he and his race have rights which white Radicals 'are bound to respect.'" "What a Representative Colored Man Gets as his Reward," *Virginian-Pilot*, October 5, 1872.

25. Celebrations often doubled as political rallies during this time and both Black participants and white observers understood them as such. As William Blair notes that celebrations of freedom especially resembled political rallies and had political implications that could be read by contemporary observers. Blair, *Cities of the Dead*, 24.

26. "Norton vs. Platt," *Virginian-Pilot*, July 11, 1874.

27. L. E. Fisher, President and Richard Brooks, Secretary, "Headquarters of Norton Campaign Club," *Virginian-Pilot,* August 19, 1874.

28. L. E. Fisher, letter to the editor, *Virginian-Pilot,* August 18, 1874.

29. *Virginian-Pilot,* September 27, 1874.

30. "Custom House Ring Defeated," September 27, 1874.

31. "Platt and Norton," *Virginian-Pilot,* September 22, 1874.

32. Hahn, Nation Under Our Feet, 266.

33. "Flanked," *Virginian-Pilot,* September 25, 1874.

34. "Norton Meeting in Princess Anne," *Virginian-Pilot,* October 15, 1874; "Norton Meeting," *Virginian-Pilot,* October 14, 1874, "ATTENTION, NORTON CAMPAIGN CLUB," *Virginian-Pilot,* October 8, 1874, "ANOTHER RALLY!" *Virginian-Pilot,* October 30, 1874, "MEETING AT GETTY'S STATION," *Virginian-Pilot,* October 16, 1874.

35. "Norton Represented," *Virginian-Pilot,* October 22, 1874. Interestingly, Frederick Norton does to appear to have been a legal brother to Robert and Daniel Norton. In 1869 and 1870, articles appeared noting that Frederick S. Norton, previously known as "Frederick Smith" had assumed the name of "Norton" while running for political office. It appears that he may have changed his name to align himself more readily with the Norton brothers. *Virginian Pilot,* March 21, 1870, and June 22, 1869. Frederick S. Norton successfully served in Virginian's House of Delegates from 1869–1871.

36. Here too Platt refused to split time with the Norton representative, as *The Virginian-Pilot* reported in a separate article. October 24, 1874.

37. L. E. Fisher was the Norton Campaign Club president and Richard Brooks was the secretary.

38. "Flanked Again!" *Virginian-Pilot,* October 13, 1874.

39. "The Canvass," *Virginian-Pilot,* November 1, 1874.

40. "The Yorktown Riot!—Letter from Robert Norton," *Virginian-Pilot,* November 3, 1874. As Steven Hahn notes, being "ku kluxed" became a "general signifier for" violence perpetrated by "any vigilante band operating in disguise." Hahn, *Nation Under Our Feet,* 267.

41. In election returns published on November 5, 1874, Norton appeared as a delegate only in Williamsburg, York County, and Warwick County. For the remainder of the counties in the district, only Goode and Platt appeared as candidates. "Election Returns: The Second Congressional District," *Virginian-Pilot,* November 5, 1874.

42. "Norton and his Votes," *Virginian-Pilot,* November 6, 1874.

43. "Let the People Speak," *Virginian-Pilot,* November 10, 1874.

44. "Papers in the Matter of James H. Platt Jr., vs. John Goode, Jr. Second Congressional District of Virginia," January 27, 1876, https://www.google.com/books/edition/House_Documents/8WloAAA AcAAJ?hl=en&gbpv=1&bsq=norton.

45. Turner, *Soul Liberty,* 116.

46. Hahn, *Nation Under Our Feet,* 373–74.

47. Turner, *Soul Liberty,* 120.

48. Hahn, *Nation Under Our Feet,* 401.

49. Turner, *Soul Liberty,* 122.

50. Dailey, *Before Jim Crow,* 3.

51. "The Negro as a Factor in Politics," *Virginian-Pilot,* July 29, 1880.

52. "Revolutions Never Go Backward," *Virginian-Pilot,* August 26, 1880.

53. "A Colored Readjuster Family," June 2, 1881.

54. "Yorktown—How Dezendorf Held the Port," *Virginian-Pilot,* August 5, 1882.

55. *Virginian-Pilot,* May 19, 1887.

56. "Helpful but Dangerous," *Virginian-Pilot,* September 14, 1887.

57. "A Political Straw," *Virginian-Pilot,* November 1, 1887.

58. Hahn, Nation Under Our Feet, 408.

59. For examples see, "Memorial Day," *Virginian-Pilot,* May 28, 1876, and "National Memorial Day," *Virginian-Pilot,* May 31, 1879.

60. Blair, *Cities of the Dead,* 135.

61. Kachun, *Festivals of Freedom,* 4.

62. Kachun, *Festivals of Freedom,* 6.

63. Litwicki, *American's Public Holidays,* 3.

64. Blair, *Cities of the Dead,* 138.

65. Kachun, *Festivals of Freedom,* 6.

66. "Memorial—The Nation Honors its Dead," *Virginian-Pilot,* May 31, 1881.

67. "Memorial—The Nation Honors its Dead," *Virginian-Pilot,* May 31, 1881.

68. Turner, *Soul Liberty,* 131.

69. Litwicki, *American's Public Holidays,* 46.

70. Clark, *Defining Moments,* 11.

71. From *The Virginian-Pilot:* "Federal Decoration Day," May 30, 1891; "National Decoration Day," May 31, 1896; "Decoration Day," June 1, 1897; "Two Decoration Day Bands," May 28, 1899; "Federal Memorial and Decoration Day," May 24, 1896.

72. Letters Sent June 7, 1902, Letters Sent, National Cemetery Superintendent Records, Colonial National Historical Park, Yorktown, VA.

73. Letters Sent June 7, 1902, Letters Sent, National Cemetery Superintendent Records, Colonial National Historical Park, Yorktown, VA.

74. Shiloh changed locations during the administration of Reverend Baylor Wyatt in the 1890s. "History of the Shiloh Baptist Church," Shiloh Baptist Church website, http://o3bd6a2.netsolhost .com/wpshiloh2015/about-shiloh/history/. It is unclear if this was the same Baylor Wyatt who gave a speech imploring white Northerners to assist the Black community at Yorktown in resisting the Freedmen's Bureau's efforts for removal.

75. COLO Letters Sent May 31, 1906.

76. "Decoration Day," *Virginian-Pilot,* May 31, 1900.

77. "Decoration Day Observances," *Virginian-Pilot,* May 29, 1902.

78. "Memorial Day," *Virginian-Pilot,* May 15, 1902.

79. Bederman, *Manliness and Civilization,* 4.

80. Bederman, *Manliness and Civilization,* 25.

81. "Favors Purchase Wharf for Jamestown," *Virginian-Pilot,* April 6, 1906.

82. Domby, *The False Cause,* 59–60.

83. Letters Sent, May 30, 1914, Letters Sent, National Cemetery Superintendent Records, Colonial National Historical Park, Yorktown, VA.

84. Letters Sent, May 31, 1915, Letters Sent, National Cemetery Superintendent Records, Colonial National Historical Park, Yorktown, VA.

85. A. H. Ackley to Q. M. General, National Archives and Records Administration, Yorktown National Cemetery, letters sent May 31, 1919.

86. Ackley's reference to "where the colored soldiers were interred" seems to suggest a level of segregation in Yorktown's national cemetery. It is unclear if this was by design. Yorktown's national

cemetery was never large, and in the last decades before it closed for internments, superintendents made the decision to bury veterans on top of the graves of unidentified soldiers. This practice may have inadvertently produced an apparent Black section because so many of the postwar burials were veterans of the United States Colored Troops. If it was an intentional effort to segregate the cemetery, superintendents did not comment on that when they reported on new burials.

87. Litwicki, *American's Public Holidays,* 4.

88. Clark, *Defining Moments,* 33.

89. "Decoration Day to be Observed," *Virginian-Pilot,* May 31, 1915.

90. "Norfolk Honors Decoration Day," *Virginian-Pilot,* May 31, 1917. As Patricia Clark and others have noted, the participation of school children and civic organizations was a key feature of Memorial Day celebrations during the postwar era.

91. "Virginia Negroes in the Legislature," *Richmond Planet,* May 29, 1920.

92. Clark, *Defining Moments,* 194.

93. "Are we united?" *New Journal and Guide,* June 3, 1922.

94. "When the Colored Spanish American War veterans went to war," *New Journal and Guide,* April 19, 1924.

95. "Annual Memorial Day Services Carried Out Thruout the City," *New Journal and Guide,* June 5, 1926.

96. As Michael Kammen asserts, a useable past is necessary for the maintenance of a national identity. Kammen, *Mystic Chords of Memory,* 6.

97. "Memorial Day," *New Journal and Guide,* May 29, 1926.

98. "Klan Ceremonial Plans Announced," *Virginian-Pilot,* May 26, 1926.

99. "Norfolkians Honor War Dead with Impressive Ceremonies Here," *New Journal and Guide,* June 6, 1931.

100. "Colorful Parade Is Feature of the Day's Observance," *New Journal and Guide,* June 3, 1933.

Conclusion

1. J. C. Harrington to Mrs. Zola Miller Donahoe, May 31, 1946. "Cemetery Sites, Yorktown, National Cemetery," Letters Sent, National Cemetery Superintendent Records, Colonial National Historical Park, Yorktown, VA.

2. During the 1940s various superintendents reported the same information to the GAR. The cemetery was in good condition, but no ceremonies were held. In 1945 Superintendent Harrington explained, "As you know, the Yorktown National Cemetery is an inactive one." "Misc. Papers," Letters Sent, National Cemetery Superintendent Records, Colonial National Historical Park, Yorktown, VA.

3. "This class of material is of first importance because the story of the siege is at present our most capital story and the one about which we should be able to speak with authority." B. Floyd Flickinger to Superintendent Robinson, July 26, 1932, B. Floyd Flickinger Papers.

4. The National Park Service uses the term "interpretation" to describe the act of communicating the significance of a site to the public. In the eyes of the NPS, "interpretation" can mean public programs such as tours as well as signage, park literature, museum displays, etc.

5. Horace Albright was the chief architect of the incorporation of historical sites into the National Park Service. This included places such as Yorktown and Jamestown as well as Civil War battlefields that had previously been under the jurisdiction of the War Department. Albright vacated his position as director of the NPS when he secured the incorporation of these initial historical parks. Albright, *Origina of National Park Service Historic Sites.*

6. John Bodnar notes that the 1930s initiated a process in which the government "attempted to increase its influence over many aspects of American society and culture," and the national Park Service's historical program was one aspect of this effort. Through these programs government leaders sought to "consolidate their own authority and reinforce loyalty and calm anxiety about the future by memorializing the history of nation building, a story which implied that change in the past had been purposeful and positive." Bodnar, *Remaking America,* 169. Additionally, Gary Gerstle details how race played a "constitutive role in shaping the American nation" during the early twentieth century. A "racialized tradition" established during World War I "remained an important strain in 1930s politics and culture." Gerstle, *American Crucible,* 83, 162.

7. Riley, *History of the Development of Colonial National,* 1. The shift to "National Historical Park" status indicates that the park was authorized by Congress after its initial preservation by presidential proclamation.

8. As Marguerite Shaffer has detailed, World War I "marked a pivotal moment for the promotion and status of the national parks." The war and its aftermath "intensified the discourse of patriotism and loyalty in the United States." Initially, park service development focused on the western "natural parks" where administrators believed they could promote the idea of the United States as "nature's nation" and could "inscribe the nation in 'the nature of things.'" Shaffer, *See America First,* 100–1.

9. Gilkeson, *Anthropologists and the Rediscovery,* 4.

10. As Fitzhugh Brundage has argued, public ceremonies like pageants are "powerfully didactic performances that act out group identity and put historical consciousness into words." Such performances are "central to historical memory because . . . they provide a framework within which individual and collective memories acquire broader meaning." Moreover, "by participating in commemorative events, people 'learn what to remember.'" Brundage, *Where These Memories Grow,* 8–9.

11. Official Program of the Yorktown Sesquicentennial.

12. Official Program of the Yorktown Sesquicentennial.

13. As one of the nation's first colleges, William & Mary always maintained a central place in the mythology of colonial America depicted at Williamsburg and Yorktown. During Colonial Historical Park's early years, park staff maintained a close relationship with the college and its history department.

14. *Official Program of the Yorktown Sesquicentennial.* Inviting Tyler to speak at the dedication ceremony was a choice loaded with political implications. As William & Mary's Department of History acknowledges today, Tyler was not only a Confederate apologist, but maintained that slavery had in fact "civilized" enslaved people and that the reunited nation remained beholden to "Northern" interests. "Lyon Gardiner Tyler," https://scrc-kb.libraries.wm.edu/lyon-gardiner-tyler-1853-1935.

15. Official Program of the Yorktown Sesquicentennial.

16. Rothman, *Devil's Bargains,* 77.

17. Official Program of the Yorktown Sesquicentennial.

18. Shaffer, *See America First,* 195.

19. It is worth noting that during this period, National Parks were expressly *not* for Black Americans. At a parks conference in 1922, an administrator had explained, "One of the objections to colored people is that if they come in large groups they will be conspicuous, and will not only be objected to by other visitors, but will cause trouble among the hotel and camp help, and it will be impossible to serve them. Individual cases can be handled, although even this is awkward, but organized parties could not be taken care of . . . While we cannot openly discriminate against them, they should be told that the parks have no facilities for taking care of them." Shaffer, *See America First,* 126.

20. Bodnar, Remaking America, 173.

21. Again, this was a strategy employed throughout the national Park Service. As Hal Rothman notes, the NPS placed a high value on explaining, or interpreting, the meaning of its sites. In the 1920s the "agency invested heavily in creating an educational division to interpret" the western scenic parks. Rothman, *Devil's Bargains,* 153.

22. Flickinger's concern reflected the reality of development of national parks in the East by this time. Just five years earlier, Acadia National Park in Maine had been the only national park in the East. In May of 1926, Congress authorized three more parks: Great Smoky Mountains National Park, Shenandoah National Park, and Mammoth Cave National Park. Meringolo, *Museums, Monuments, and National Parks,* 84. Creation of all of these parks would also require displacement of local residents.

23. B. Floyd Flickinger to Mr. Wm. M. Robinson, August 30, 1931, B. Floyd Flickinger Papers.

24. Shaffer, *See America First,* 178.

25. Shaffer, *See America First,* 194.

26. Arthur Demaray was an NPS administrator in the Washington, DC, office, he would become the assistant director of the agency in 1933.

27. William M. Robinson, Jr., Superintendent to B. Floyd Flickinger, assistant park historian, August 15, 1931, B. Floyd Flickinger Papers.

28. B. Floyd Flickinger to Mr. Wm. M. Robinson, August 30, 1931, B. Floyd Flickinger Papers.

29. Announcement of Lectures, Summer Season, 1932, B. Floyd Flickinger Papers.

30. Other memorial groups in Yorktown at this time, specifically the Association for the Preservation of Virginia's Antiquities Yorktown Branch, likewise focused many of their efforts on establishing an exclusionary heritage for white Virginia gentry. Among their prime concerns in their earliest days was saving colonial deed books—allowing them to preserve the names of the "first families of Virginia" and their early economic dominance—installing a plaque honoring the man who saved those records during the Civil War, and locating and marking the site of a Confederate cemetery.

31. Shaffer, *See America First,* 4.

32. Robert D. Meade to Flickinger, December 29, 1934, B. Floyd Flickinger Papers.

33. Bruggeman, *Here, George Washington Was Born.* That the NPS even considered this site worthy of inclusion is noteworthy because, as Bruggeman notes, George Washington spent only the first few years of his life there. Moreover, little of the home Washington would have known as an infant remained—his original family home having burned down. However, such a focus on the Wakefield Plantation suggested that even as a small child, the landscape of Virginia had influenced Washington and contributed to the man he would later become. Such a construction reinforced the view that through contact with the physical landscape, Americans could learn to be better citizens.

34. Clarke Venable, historical technician to Verne E. Chatelain, chief historian, June 4, 1934, B. Floyd Flickinger Papers. It worth noting that the "more important" Civil War battlefields, especially in Virginia, were in contested locations in the center of the state—places such as Fredericksburg, Richmond, and Petersburg. None of these locations witnessed long-term Union occupation during the war, and consequently lacked the history of refugee communities. Their importance stemmed specifically from the nature of the military combat that occurred in those locations.

35. Bodnar, *Remaking America,* 175.

36. Malcom Gardner, historical technician, to Mr. Flickinger "Re: Mr. Venable's June 4 Report," June 9, 1934, B. Floyd Flickinger Papers. It bears noting here that all three battlefields Gardner listed were located in parts of Virginia that remained largely under Confederate control through most of

the war. Consequently, they did not have the same history of refugee communities as battlefields along the Virginia Peninsula.

37. Joseph C. Robert, Historical Technician, Memorandum to Mr. Flickinger, June 9, 1934, B. Floyd Flickinger Papers.

38. Arno B. Cammerer to B. Floyd Flickinger, November 11, 1933, B. Floyd Flickinger Papers.

39. Unnamed speech, Guidebooks and Presentations, B. Floyd Flickinger Papers.

40. Unnamed speech, Guidebooks and Presentations, B. Floyd Flickinger Papers. As Marita Sturken has noted, "Forgetting is a necessary component in the construction of memory." Flickinger and his coworkers' assertions reflect a perspective common among people who actively construct public memories. "A desire for narrative closure," Sturken explains, forces upon historical events the limits of narrative form and enables forgetting." Sturken, *Tangled Memories*, 7–8.

41. B. Floyd Flickinger, Confidential Memorandum, July 8, 1936. "Cemetery Sites, Yorktown, National Cemetery," Records of Colonial National Historical Park.

42. F. H. Payne, The Assistant Secretary of War to The Honorable Secretary of the Interior, January 7, 1933, Miscellaneous Papers, Records of Colonial National Historical Park, Yorktown, VA.

43. B. Floyd Flickinger, Superintendent to The Director, National Park Service, June 16, 1936, COLO archives.

44. The National Park Service uses the term "acting" to designate individuals who are operating in a role but have not been permanently appointed to that position. In the early years of the Colonial National Historical Park, it is clear that leadership roles shifted with relative frequency, as reflected in B. Floyd Flickinger's fairly quick rise to his role as the park superintendent.

45. Bingham Duncan, Acting Park Historian, Memorandum to Superintendent Flickinger, August 12, 1936, "Cemetery Sites, Yorktown, National Cemetery," Records of Colonial National Historical Park.

46. A. Wilhelm, Res. Landscape Arch., Williamsburg, VA Memorandum to Mr. Flickinger, August 3, 1936. "Cemetery Sites, Yorktown, National Cemetery," Records of Colonial National Historical Park.

47. Elbert Cox, Superintendent, Memorandum to the Director, April 6, 1940. "Cemetery Sites, Yorktown, National Cemetery," Records of Colonial National Historical Park.

48. The national cemetery superintendent's home was not replaced, suggesting that at some point the NPS did allocate funds for its upkeep. Most likely they determined it was necessary for safety reasons when it became clear they would not have the option to remove it. By this era national cemeteries within the NPS did not have separate superintendents living on site.

49. Arno B. Cammerer, Memorandum for the Superintendent of Colonial National Historical Park, April 30, 1940. "Cemetery Sites, Yorktown, National Cemetery," COLO Archives. Cammerer did have his way to some extent as the headstones in the national Cemetery that had originally been upright were removed and replaced with headstones that lay flat on the ground. By this time, Shiloh Church had relocated to a building directly across the street from the national cemetery's entrance.

50. In 1944 Thomas M. Pitkin, acting superintendent, again advised the director of the NPS of the situation with the national cemetery, noting that "at the present time the cemetery does not have a place in the interpretive guided tour of the park" and that "there are no figures of outstanding importance buried in the cemetery." Thomas M. Pitkin, Memorandum to the Director, November 28, 1944. "Cemetery Sites, Yorktown, National Cemetery," COLO Archives.

51. Bingham Duncan and C. L. Coston to Mr. Flickinger, June 12, 1934, B. Floyd Flickinger Papers.

52. December 3, 1935, "Abstracts" Slabtown N. Records of Colonial National Historical Park.

53. Memorandum, Dec. 21, 1964, Land Acquisition Program, Records of Colonial National Historical Park.

54. Goldberger, "Repatriating Yorktown," 198. The ten-year period between 1956 and 1966 represented a banner decade in National Park Service development as the federal government made special funds available through the "Mission 66" program which was initiated to "properly rehabilitate, develop, interpret, and maintain every park in the system." Expansion of park boundaries and an emphasis on military history marked this period. Martha Temkin, "Freeze-Frame, September 17, 1862: A Preservation Battle at Antietam National Battlefield Park," in Paul Shackel, *Myth, Memory, and the Making of the American Landscape* (Gainesville: University Press of Florida, 2001), 126.

55. Memorandum, Dec. 21, 1964, Land Acquisition Program, Records of Colonial National Historical Park.

56. Displacement, particularly of underrepresented groups such as Black Americans at Manassas National Battlefield, poor white residents in Shenandoah National Park, and countless Native Americans, is not uncommon in the history of the national Park Service. Katrina Powell, *The Anguish of Displacement: The Politics of Literacy in the Letters of Mountain Families in Shenandoah National Park* (University of Virginia Press, 2007); Rothman, *Devil's Bargains;* and Erika K. Martin Seibert, "The Third Battle of Manassas: Power, Identity, and the Forgotten African-American Past," in Shackel, *Myth, Memory, and the Making of the American Landscape.*

57. Interview with Floyd Hill, 2015, Records of Colonial National Historical Park.

BIBLIOGRAPHY

Newspapers

Altoona (PA) Tribune

Cambridge (MA) Chronicle

The Cavalier (Williamsburg, VA)

The Christian Recorder (Philadelphia)

Columbia (PA) Democrat

Concord (NH) Independent Democrat

Daily Dispatch (Richmond, VA)

Daily Press (Newport News, VA)

Douglass' Monthly (Rochester, NY)

Farmer's Cabinet (Amherst, NH)

The Friend (Philadelphia, PA)

The Friend's Review (Philadelphia, PA)

Geneva (NY) Courier

Geneva (NY) Gazette

Lockport (NY) Daily Journal Courier

New Journal and Guide (Norfolk, VA)

Oneida Sachem (Oneida, NY)

Orleans (VT) Independent Standard

Potter Journal (Coudersport, PA)

Richmond (VA) Dispatch

Southbridge (MA) Journal

The Virginian-Pilot (Norfolk, VA)

Waltham (MA) Sentinel

Waterbury (CT) American

Yates County Chronicle

Primary Sources

1850 Census Free Population and 1850 Slave Schedule, York County, VA.

1850 Slave Schedule, York County, VA.

1860 Census, York County, VA.

1870 Census, York County, VA.

Albright, Horace. *Origins of National Park Service Administration of Historic Sites.* Eastern National Parks & Monument Association, 1971.

Department of Commerce and Labor, United States Bureau of the Census. *Official Register of the United States, Containing a List of the Officers and Employees in the Civil, Military, and Naval Service.* Digitized books (77 volumes). Oregon State Library, Salem.

Erikson, Mark St. John. "Lost Black Township Lives on in Memory," *Daily Press.*

Hawkins, Van. *The Historic Triangle: An Illustrated History.* Donning, 1980.

"History of Shiloh Baptist Church," Shiloh Baptist Church, Yorktown, VA http://03bd6a2.netsolhost .com/wpshiloh2015/about-shiloh/history/.

Lucy Chase Correspondence. Chase Family Papers. Alexander Street, 2009.

Official Program of the Yorktown Sesquicentennial. Lewis Printing, 1931.

O'Hara, Lucy Hudgins. *Yorktown, as I Remember.* McClure Printing, 1981.

Reid, Whitelaw. *After the War: A Tour of the Southern States,* May 1, 1865, to May 1, 1866. Sampson Low, Son, & Marston, 1866.

Riley, Edward M. *The History of the Development of Colonial National Monument.* National Park Service, 1936.

"Slabtown Genesis," Compiled by Jordan Smiley and Ryan Brookens, Records of the Interpretive Branch, Colonial National Historical Park. Yorktown, VA.

Smith, Sydney. *Old Yorktown and Its History.* Richmond Press, 1920.

Trowbridge, John. *The South: A Tour of its Battlefields and Ruined Cities.* L. Stebbins, 1866.

"War Memorial Monument," https://www.yorkcounty.gov/1478/War-Memorial-Monument.

Wistar, Isaac J. *Autobiography of Isaac Jones Wistar, 1827–1905.* Wistar Institute of Anatomy and Biology, 1937.

York County History: Essays and Memories. York County Historical Committee.

"Virginia, Freedmen's Bureau Field Office Records, 1205 – 1212" Sub Assistant Commissioner, Yorktown, VA, NARA microfilm publication M1212. College Park, MD: National Archives and Records Administration, n.d."

Roll 199, Letters Sent, vol. 1–2, Jan 1866–May 1868; Aug–Dec 1868.

Roll 200, Endorsements Sent and Received, vol. 1–3, May 1865–Dec 1868.

Roll 200, Letters and Orders Received, Feb 1865–Feb 1867.

Roll 200, Letters Received, Mar 1867–Dec 1868.

Roll 201, Letters and Orders Received, Mar 1867–Dec 1868.

Roll 201, Monthly Reports, Jul 1865–Mar 1866.

Roll 202, General Orders, Special Orders, Circulars, & Circular Letters Received, 1867–1868.

Roll 202, Monthly Reports, Apr 1866–Dec 1868.

Roll 202, Proceedings of the Freedmen's Court, Dec 1865–Jun 1867.

Roll 202, Registers of Persons Receiving Ration Tickets, vol. 1–2, Feb 1865–Apr 1866.

Roll 203, Census Returns of the Black Population of York County, Mar 1865.

Roll 203, Contracts, Bills of Lading, Leases, Records Relating to Courts Cases and Other Records, 1865–1868.

Roll 203, Misc. Registers, 1865.

Roll 203, Register of Infirm and Destitute Freedmen.

York County Microfilm, Library of Virginia

Deed Book 16, 1854–1866, Reel 67.

Deed Book 17, 1867–1871, Reel 67.

Deed Book 18, 1871–1876, Reel 68.

Deed Book 19, 1876–1882, Reel 68.

Deed Book 20, 1882–1886, Reel 69.

Deed Book 21, 1886–1890, Reel 69.
Deed Book 22, 1890–1894, Reel 70.
Minute Book, 1870–1875, Reel 61.
Plat Book, 1868–1951, Reel 74.

Records of Colonial National Historical Park, Yorktown, VA

"Cemetery Sites, Yorktown, National Cemetery." Records of the Interpretive Division.
General Orders No. 12–July 17, 1863. Records of the Interpretive Division.
Miscellaneous Papers. Records of the Interpretive Division.
Yorktown National Cemetery Superintendent Correspondence, Letters Sent.
Yorktown National Cemetery Superintendent Correspondence, Letters Received.

Records of Yorktown National Cemetery, National Records and Archives Administration Philadelphia. Record group 13.10.4 Miscellaneous documents of the House of Representatives for the First Session of the Forty-Fourth Congress

"Papers in the Matter of James H. Platt, Jr. vs. John Goode, Jr., Second Congressional District of Virginia," January 27, 1876.

Earl G. Swem Special Collections Research Center, William & Mary, Williamsburg, VA

Association for the Preservation of Virginia Antiquities, Yorktown Branch Records.
Flickinger, B. Floyd, Papers 1927–1950.
Margaret Newbold Thorpe, *Life in Virginia by a Yankee Teacher.*

George J. Mitchell Department of Special Collections & Archives, Harthorne-Longfellow Library, Bowdoin College

Oliver Otis Howard Papers, 1833–1908.

Southern Claims Commission

Testimony of Mary Ashby.
Testimony of J. Lemuel Bowden Estate.
Testimony of Robert Ruffin.
Testimony of Thomas Clark.
Testimony of William Scott.

Haverford College Quaker and Special Collections. Haverford, PA

Sarah Cadbury, *Letters from Slabtown.* Sarah Cadbury Papers.
Correspondence, 1866. Sarah Cadbury Papers.
Letters of Nancy S. Battey (1837–1865), Yorktown and elsewhere, to brother Thomas J. Battey and father Smith Battey, 1864–1865, 1866.

Secondary Sources

Bederman, Gail. *Manliness and Civilization: A Cultural History of Gender and Race in the United States, 1880–1917.* University of Chicago Press, 1995.
Bentley, George R. *A History of the Freedmen's Bureau.* University of Pennsylvania Press, 1955.

Berlin, Ira. "Who Freed the Slaves? Emancipation and Its Meaning." In *Union and Emancipation: Essays on Politics and Race in the Civil War Era.* Edited by David Blight and Brooks Simpson. Kent State University Press, 1997.

Berlin, Ira, and Barbara J. Fields, Thavolia Glymph, Joseph P. Reidy, and Leslie S. Rowland, eds. *Freedom: A Documentary History of Emancipation, 1861–1867. Series 1, volume 1. The Destruction of Slavery.* Cambridge University Press, 1985.

Berlin, Ira, and Steven F. Miller, Joseph P. Reidy, and Leslie S. Rowland, eds. Freedom: A Documentary History of Emancipation, 1861–1867. Series 1, volume 2, The Wartime Genesis of Free Labor: The Upper South. Cambridge University Press, 1993.

Blair, William. *Cities of the Dead: Contesting the Memory of the Civil War in the South, 1865–1914.* University of North Carolina Press, 2004.

Blight, David W. *Race and Reunion: The Civil War in American Memory.* Belknap Press of Harvard University Press, 2001.

Bodnar, John. *Remaking America; Public Memory, Commemoration, and Patriotism in the Twentieth Century.* Princeton University Press, 1992.

Bragdon, Kathleen, Bradley M. McDonald, and Kenneth E. Struck, "'Cast Down Your Bucket Where You Are:' An Ethnohistorical Study of the African-American Community on the Lands of the Yorktown Naval Weapons Station, 1865–1918." Atlantic Division, Naval Facilities Engineering Command, Norfolk, VA, 1992.

Brasher, Glenn David. *The Peninsula Campaign and the Necessity of Emancipation: African Americans and the Fight for Freedom.* University of North Carolina Press, 2012.

Brown, E. B. "Negotiating and Transforming the Public Sphere: African American Political Life in the Transition from Slavery to Freedom." *Public Culture* 7, no. 1 (1994): 107–46. https://doi.org /10.1215/08992363-7-1-107.

Bruggeman, Seth. *Here, George Washington Was Born.* University of Georgia Press, 2008.

Brundage, Fitzhugh. *Where These Memories Grow: History, Memory, and Southern Identity.* University of North Carolina Press, 2000.

Butchart, Ronald E. *Schooling the Freed People: Teaching, Learning and the Struggle for Black Freedom, 1861–1876.* University of North Carolina Press, 2010.

Cimbala, Paul. *Under the Guardianship of the nation: The Freedmen's Bureau and the Reconstruction of Georgia.* University of Georgia Press, 2003.

Clark, Kathleen Ann. *Defining Moments: African American Commemoration & Political Culture in the South, 1863–1913.* University of North Carolina Press, 2005.

Click, Patricia. *Time Full of Trials: The Roanoke Island Freedmen's Colony.* University of North Carolina Press, 2001.

Dailey, Jane. *Before Jim Crow: The Politics of Race in Postemancipation Virginia.* University of North Carolina Press, 2000.

Davis, J. E. "Oystering in Hampton Roads." *Southern Workman,* March 1903.

Davis, William Watts Hart. *History of the 104th Pennsylvania Regiment from August 22nd, 1861 to September 30th, 1864.* Philadelphia: Jas. B. Rodgers, 1866.

Deetz, Kelley. "Slabtown: Yorktown's African American Community 1863–1970." Undergraduate honors thesis, College of William and Mary, 2002.

Depew, Diane. "'They Had Bidden a Final Farewell to Slavery": The African-American Civil War Experience at Yorktown, Virginia.'" Copy provided by the author.

Domby, Adam. *The False Cause: Fraud, Fabrication, and White Supremacy in Confederate Memory.* University of Virginia Press, 2020.

Downs, Gregory P. *After Appomattox: Military Occupation and the Ends of War.* Harvard University Press, 2015.

Downs, Gregory P. *Declarations of Dependence: The Long Reconstruction of Popular Politics in the South, 1861–1908.* University of North Carolina Press, 2011.

Downs, Jim. *Sick from Freedom: African-American Illness and Suffering During the Civil War and Reconstruction.* Oxford University Press, 2012.

Dubbs, Carol Kettenburg. *Defend This Old Town: Williamsburg During the Civil War.* Louisiana State University Press, 2002.

Du Bois, W. E. B. *Black Reconstruction: An Essay Toward a History of the Part Which Black Folk Played in the Attempt to Reconstruct Democracy in America, 1860–1880.* Harcourt, Brace, 1935.

Engs, Robert F. *Freedom's First Generation: Black Hampton, Virginia, 1861–1890.* University of Pennsylvania Press, 1979.

Fahs, Alice, and Joan Waugh, eds. *The Memory of the Civil War in American Culture.* University of North Carolina Press, 2004.

Faust, Drew Gilpin. *This Republic of Suffering: Death and the American Civil War.* Penguin Random House, 2009.

Foner, Eric. *The Fiery Trial: Abraham Lincoln and American Slavery.* W.W. Norton, 2010.

Gerstle, Gary. *American Crucible: Race and Nation in the Twentieth Century.* Princeton University Press, 2001.

Gilkeson, John S. *Anthropologists and the Rediscovery of America, 1886–1965.* Cambridge University Press, 2010.

Goldberger, Sarah. "Challenging the Interest and Reverence of all Patriotic Americas: Preservation and the Yorktown National Battlefield." In *Destination Dixie: Tourism and Southern History,* edited by Karen Cox. University of Florida Press, 2012.

Goldberger, Sarah. *Repatriating Yorktown: The Politics of Revolutionary Memory and Reunion.* unpublished dissertation. University of Chicago, 2010.

Hahn, Steven. *A Nation Under Our Feet: Black Political Struggles in the Rural South from Slavery to the Great Migration.* Harvard University Press, 2005.

Harper, Matthew. *The End of Days: African American Religion and Politics in the Age of Emancipation.* University of North Carolina Press, 2016.

Harris, Travis. "Lost Tribe of Magruder: The Untold Story of the Navy's Dispossession of a Black Community." Unpublished dissertation, 2019.

Kachun, Mitch. *Festivals of Freedom: Memory and Meaning in African American Emancipation Celebrations, 1808–1915.* University of Massachusetts Press, 2003.

Kale, Wilford. *Yorktown, Virginia: A Brief History.* Arcadia, 2018.

Kammen, Michael. *Mystic Chords of Memory: The Transformation of Tradition in American Culture.* Alfred A. Knopf, 1991.

Jackson, Luther Porter. *Negro Office-Holders in Virginia, 1865–1895.* Guide Quality Press, 1945.

Janney, Caroline E. *Burying the Dead but not the Past: Ladies' Memorial Associations & the Lost Cause.* University of North Carolina Press, 2008.

Janney, Caroline E. *Remembering the Civil War: Reunion and the Limits of Reconciliation.* University of North Carolina Press, 2013.

Jones, Jacqueline. *Soldiers of Light and Love: Northern Teachers and Georgia Blacks, 1865–1873.* University of Georgia Press, 1980.

Jones, Martha S. *All Bound up Together: The Woman Question in African American Public Culture, 1830–1900.* University of North Carolina Press, 2007.

Litwicki, Ellen M. *American's Public Holidays, 1865–1920.* Smithsonian Institution Press, 2000.

Magdol, Edward. *A Right to the Land: Essays on the Freedmen's Community.* Greenwood, 1997.

Mahoney, Shannon. "Community Building After Emancipation: An Anthropological Study of Charles' Corner, Virginia, 1862–1922." Unpublished dissertation, 2013.

Manning, Chandra. *Troubled Refuge: Struggling for Freedom in the Civil War.* Alfred Knopf, 2016.

Marvel, William. *Burnside.* University of North Carolina Press, 2000.

Masur, Kate. *An Example for All the Land: Emancipation and the Struggle over Equality in Washington, D.C.* University of North Carolina Press, 2010.

Masur, Kate. "'A Rare Phenomenon of Philological Vegetation': The Word 'Contraband' and the Meanings of Emancipation in the United States." *Journal of American History* 93, no. 4 (2007): 1050–84.

McElya, Micki. *The Politics of Mourning: Death and Honor in Arlington National Cemetery.* University of Harvard Press, 2016.

McPherson, James. "Who Freed the Slaves?" in *Drawn with the Sword: Reflections on the American Civil War.* Oxford University Press, 1996.

Medford, Edna Greene. "Land and Labor: The Quest for Black Economic Independence on Virginia's Lower Peninsula, 1865–1880." *Virginia Magazine of History and Biography* (October 1992).

Medford, Edna Greene. "The Transition from Slavery to Freedom in a Diversified Economy: Virginia's Lower Peninsula, 1860–1900." Dissertation, University of Maryland, 1987.

Meringolo, Denise M. *Museums, Monuments, and National Parks: Towards a New Genealogy of Public History.* University of Boston Press, 2012.

Mills, Cynthia J., and Pamela H. Simpson. *Monuments to the Lost Cause: Women, Art, and the Landscapes of Southern Memory.* University of Tennessee Press, 2003.

Mintz, Steven. *Moralists and Modernizers: American's Pre-Civil War Reformers.* Johns Hopkins University Press, 1995.

Morgan, Lynda J. *Emancipation in Virginia's Tobacco Belt, 1850–1870.* University of Georgia Press, 1992.

Morton, Richard L. "Contrabands and Quakers in the Virginia Peninsula, 1862–1869." *Virginia Magazine of History and Biography* (October 1953).

Morton, Richard L., and Margaret Newbold Thorpe, "Life in Virginia." *Virginia Magazine of History and Biography* (April 1956).

Nash, Eugene. *A History of the Forty-Fourth Regiment New York Volunteer Infantry in the Civil War, 1861–1865.* Morningside Book Shop, 1988.

Neff, John R. *Honoring the Civil War Dead: Commemoration and the Problem of Reconciliation.* University of Kansas Press, 2005.

Newby-Alexander, Cassandra L. *An African American History of the Civil War in Hampton Roads.* History Press, 2010.

Nieman, Donald G. *The Day of the Jubilee: The Civil War Experience of Black Southerners.* Garland, 1994.

Nieman, Donald G. *To Set the Law in Motion: The Freedmen's Bureau and the Legal Rights of Blacks, 1865–1868.* KTO Press, 1979.

Oakes, James. "A Failure of a Vision: The Collapse of the Freedmen's Bureau Courts." *Civil War History* (March 1979).

Oakes, James. *Freedom National: The Destruction of Slavery in the United States, 1861–1865.* W. W. Norton and Company, 2012.

Pfanz, Donald C. *Where Valor Proudly Sleeps: A History of Fredericksburg National Cemetery, 1866–1933.* Southern Illinois University Press, 2018.

Powell, Katrina M. *The Anguish of Displacement: The Politics of Literacy in the Letters of Mountain Families in Shenandoah National Park.* University of Virginia Press, 2007.

Powell, Katrina M. "Answer at Once": Letters of Mountain Families in Shenandoah National Park, 1934–1938. University of Virginia Press, 2009.

Pruitt, Hillis Earl. "No Longer Lost at Sea: Black Community Building in the Virginia Tidewater, 1865 to the post-1954 era." Unpublished dissertation, College of William and Mary, 2013.

Reidy, Joseph P. *Illusions of Emancipation: The Pursuit of Freedom and Equality in the Twilight of Slavery.* University of North Carolina Press, 2019.

Richter, Julie, and Jody L. Allen. "Historical Overview of Africans and African Americans in Yorktown, at the Moore House, and on Battlefield Property, 1635–1867." Yorktown: Colonial National Historical Park, 2012.

Rose, Willie Lee. *Rehearsal for Reconstruction: The Port Royal Experiment.* Vintage Books, 1964.

Rosen, Hannah. *Terror in the Heart of Freedom: Citizenship, Sexual Violence, and the Meaning of Race in the Postemancipation South.* University of North Carolina Press, 2009.

Rothman, Hal. *Devil's Bargains: Tourism in the Twentieth-Century American West.* University of Kansas Press, 1998.

Saville, Julie. *The Work of Reconstruction: From Slave to Wage Laborer in South Carolina.* Cambridge University Press, 1994.

Sawyer, Roy T. *America's Wetland: An Environmental and Cultural History of Tidewater Virginia and North Carolina.* University of Virginia Press, 2010.

Sears, Stephen W. *To the Gates of Richmond: The Peninsula Campaign.* Tickner & Fields, 1992.

Shackel, Paul A. *Memory in Black and White: Race, Commemoration, and the Post-Bellum Landscape.* AltaMira, 2003.

Shaffer, Marguerite. *See America First: Tourism and National Identity, 1880–1940.* Smithsonian Institution Press, 2001.

Stanley, Amy Dru. *From Bondage to Contract: Wage Labor, Marriage, and the Market in the Age of Slave Emancipation.* Cambridge University Press, 1998.

Steere, Edward. *Shrines of the Honored Dead: A Study of the National Cemetery System.* US Army Military History, 1954.

Sturken, Marita. *Tangled Memories: The Vietnam War, the AIDS Epidemic, and the Politics of Remembering.* University of California Press, 1997.

Swint, Henry Lee. *The Northern Teacher in the South, 1862–1870.* Vanderbilt University Press, 1941.

Taylor, Amy Murrell. *Embattled Freedom: Journeys Through the Civil War's Slave Refugee Camps.* University of North Carolina Press, 2018.

Torkelson, Jacob. "Where Shall We Go?": Race, Displacement, and Preservation at Slabtown and Yorktown Battlefield." Master's thesis, University of Pennsylvania, 2019.

Turner, Nicole. *Soul Liberty: The Evolution of Black Religious Politics in Postemancipation Virginia.* University of North Carolina Press, 2020.

US Department of the Interior, Yorktown Custom House, National Register of Historic Places and National Historic Landmarks Program, 1999.

Williams, David. *I Freed Myself: African American Self-Emancipation in the Civil War Era.* Cambridge University Press, 2014.

Williams, Heather Andrea. *Self-Taught: African American Education in Slavery and Freedom.* University of North Carolina Press, 2005.

Zipf, Catherine W. "Marking Union Victory in the South: The Construction of the national Cemetery System." In *Monuments to the Lost Cause: Women, Art, and the Landscapes of Southern Memory,* edited by Cynthia Mills and Pamela H. Simpson, 27–45. University of Tennessee Press, 2003.

INDEX

Page numbers in italics refer to illustrations.